AN ATLAS OF INDUSTRIAL PROTEST IN BRITAIN
1750–1990

ANDREW CHARLESWORTH
DAVID GILBERT
ADRIAN RANDALL
HUMPHREY SOUTHALL
CHRIS WRIGLEY

with contributions from
Jim Phillips
Gillian Rose
Richard Sheldon
David Walsh

cartography by
Ed Oliver

First published in Great Britain 1996 by
MACMILLAN PRESS LTD
Houndmills, Basingstoke, Hampshire RG21 6XS
and London
Companies and representatives
throughout the world

A catalogue record for this book is available
from the British Library.

ISBN 0–333–56599–1 hardcover
ISBN 0–333–64074–8 paperback

 First published in the United States of America 1996 by
ST. MARTIN'S PRESS, INC.,
Scholarly and Reference Division,
175 Fifth Avenue,
New York, N.Y. 10010

ISBN 0–312–15889–0

Library of Congress Cataloging-in-Publication Data applied for.

10   9   8   7   6   5   4   3   2   1
05   04   03   02   01   00   99   98   97   96

Printed in Malaysia

Contributors

Main Authors

Andrew Charlesworth is Reader in Human Geography at Cheltenham and Gloucester College of Higher Education. Before taking up that position he taught at the University of Liverpool. He was principal co-investigator with Adrian Randall on the ESRC project 'Social Protest and Community Change in the West of England 1750–1850'. He edited the *Atlas of Rural Protest in Britain* and has written extensively on social protest in Britain between 1500 and 1900. More recently he has begun to publish on the landscapes of Nazi death camps.

David Gilbert is a lecturer in Geography at Royal Holloway, University of London. He is the author of *Class, Community and Collective Action. Social change in two British coalfields, 1850–1926* and a number of articles exploring the relationships between industrial protest, social geography and identity among British miners. He has also written more generally on industrial conflict. He is currently working with Humphrey Southall on an account of the geography of economic distress in pre-1914 Britain.

Adrian Randall is currently Head of the School of Social Sciences and Senior Lecturer in the Department of Economic and Social History at the University of Birmingham. He was principal co-investigator with Andrew Charlesworth on the above-named ESRC research project. He is author of *Before the Luddites* and has published extensively on labour protest in the woollen textile industry in eighteenth- and early nineteenth-century England.

Humphrey Southall is a lecturer in Geography at Queen Mary and Westfield College, University of London. He has published extensively on both pre-1914 British labour markets and the development of the early trade union movement, is co-author with David Gilbert of *Nineteenth Century Trade Union Records: an introduction and select guide*, and with Noel Whiteside of *Wages and Welfare: Unemployment and the industrial labour movement, 1794–1950*.

Chris Wrigley is Professor of Modern British History at Nottingham University. His extensive output includes books on *David Lloyd George and the British Labour Movement*, *Arthur Henderson*, *Lloyd George and the Challenge of Labour* and *Lloyd George*. He has edited a three volume *History of British Industrial Relations*.

Other contributors

Jim Phillips has just completed his Ph.D. thesis at the University of Edinburgh where he now teaches in the Department of History. The subject of the thesis was 'The Labour Government and the docks 1945–51: international and industrial tension'. A forthcoming piece based on this work will appear in C. J. Wrigley (ed.) *The History of British Industrial Relations* volume III.

Gillian Rose is a lecturer in the Department of Geography at the University of Edinburgh, having previously been a research student and lecturer at Queen Mary and Westfield College. She has written extensively on the political and cultural history of the East End, and is the author of *Feminism and Geography*.

Richard Sheldon is currently a Ph.D. student in the Department of Economic and Social History at the University of Birmingham. He was research assistant on the ESRC research project on 'Social protest and community change in the West of England 1750–1850' and will be one of the co-authors of essays derived from that project in a forthcoming book on popular protest, markets and market culture in eighteenth century Britain and Ireland.

David Walsh has taught at the University of Salford and held a Research Fellowship at the Institute of Historical Research, University of London. He was the senior research assistant on the above named ESRC project and will also be one of the co-authors of the essays referred to above. His publications to date are based on his University of Salford Ph.D. thesis on working class political integration and the Conservative Party in the Northwest of England 1800–1870, which he is now preparing for publication.

Cartography and design

Ed Oliver is the departmental cartographer in the department of Geography, Queen Mary and Westfield College, University of London. He completed the Oxford Polytechnic Diploma in Cartography course and has specialised in producing maps and diagrams for academic books and journals.

Contents

Preface

The origins of this book can be found in the *Atlas of Industrializing Britain 1780–1914*. Jack Langton invited Andrew Charlesworth and Humphrey Southall to contribute a section on trade unions and social protest to that project. After the successful publication of Charlesworth's *Atlas of Rural Protest in Britain*, they felt that a companion volume on industrial protest was justified. Adrian Randall, David Gilbert and Chris Wrigley were subsequently invited onto the team. Each member of the team has been responsible for a particular period, and Jim Phillips, Gillian Rose, Richard Sheldon and David Walsh were invited to contribute their expertise to particular case studies. The maps and text were produced in the Geography Department at Queen Mary and Westfield College by Ed Oliver, the departmental cartographer. Without Ed's contribution in terms of design, layout and cartographic skill the book in its present form would have been impossible. Adrian Randall edited the texts of the contributions, and the other authors thank him for taking on this invidious task. Some of the maps were originally drafted by Sandra Mather, Head of the Graphics Unit at the Department of Geography, University of Liverpool. We must thank Vanessa Graham, our editor at Macmillan's, for her patience and encouragement. Lastly, the Nuffield Foundation helped support David Gilbert as a research fellow at Queen Mary and Westfield College in 1989–91, and thereby made possible the systematic analysis of the strike registers compiled by the Board of Trade and later the Ministry of Labour; Carol Bryce and Pat Furniss assisted in this work.

Introduction

This *Atlas* can be read as a series of self-contained accounts of episodes of industrial protest. However, it also provides a new and distinctive account of industrial protest in Britain from the industrial revolution onwards. It is distinctive because it is an *Atlas* and as such adds geography to narrative. Strikes and other industrial protests are often treated as single events, but are revealed here as combinations of different events taking place in a range of settings. A geography of industrial protest highlights a number of important themes. Regional differences in industrial and political culture point to the importance of links between industrial conflict and broader social and economic changes which were themselves geographically diverse. Accounts of the conduct of disputes within specific localities bring out the significance of alternative modes of protest — the picket line, the rally, the march — and the use of places as symbolic spaces. A theme running through many of the studies is that of community: how the nature of local power structures influenced the course of disputes; how the changing nature of communities was reflected in patterns of industrial conflict; and how communal resources helped sustain resistance against employers or the state.

Although much of this *Atlas* is concerned with strikes, our definition of 'industrial protest' is catholic, embracing events both more public, such as the Hunger Marches, and more private, such as machine breaking. The border between industrial and political protest is not easily drawn, although in general we have restricted ourselves to protest with an economic focus, or where the participants defined themselves by occupation. Our selection of case studies necessarily balances two sets of considerations: first, how important was a dispute or incident to the development of industrial relations or the wider history of a period; second, what contribution could a geographical approach make to our understanding, and whether suitable sources were available for mapping. This last point means that while the narratives provided here may draw extensively on existing accounts, the maps often required substantial new archival research.

The *Atlas* embraces several scales over both time and space. The individual case studies generally deal with short periods, sometimes only a few days or weeks, but address a wide range of spatial scales, from individual streets through localities and counties to the national scale and beyond; a recurrent theme is the garnering of support from abroad by both workers and employers. These case studies are grouped into four periods, each the subject of an introductory essay exploring the effects of economic and social change on protest and the interaction between industrial and political events. From 1850 on, each period is also the subject of a statistical overview which maps the incidence of *all* disputes and seeks to identify regional differences in militancy, following a consistent methodology. Writing each of these three components of the *Atlas* posed its particular challenges, which varied with the period.

First, our selection of case studies may appear uneven. In the early part of the *Atlas* the textile workers of different localities in England figure largely, in the middle the engineers and in the final part the miners. This reflects both the importance of their industries in the various stages of development of an expanding capitalist economy and the historiography of labour and social protest. But one cannot help musing about certain key groups of workers who are absent. For example, why were oil refinery workers not the shock troops of the post-1945 period, when the economy became so dependent on oil? The oil tanker drivers in the 'winter of discontent' in 1978/79 demonstrated the extent of that dependency. It is clear that the electrical workers, the controllers of the power stations, were successfully muted by the government's care and attention through the 1980's. Gender is similarly often subsumed within this study. We have been able to include a piece on the matchgirls' strike but women textile workers, women who worked in the coalmines in the nineteenth century and unemployed women are not distinguished from their male colleagues in protests that involved both men and women. We did try to include in the last section of the *Atlas* the NHS 'days of action' but failed because of the lack of spatially representable information, hence in the post-1939 era we are left with miners, lorry drivers, car and dock workers, all groups among whom women are under-represented.

Second, the statistical overviews are intended to place our case studies in the broader context of developing industrial relations. However, over our long time span the sources which record individual dispute and the channels which collated reports from across the country changed immensely. In our first century, we must rely mainly on necessarily irregular reports. From the 1850's onwards we can draw on the systematic records of individual national trade unions, themselves growing bureaucracies, and from the 1880's on central government records and in particular on the strike registers of the Board of Trade Labour Department. The details of these sources and the special problems they pose are discussed in the appropriate introductory essays. What we would wish to emphasise here is firstly that the availability of systematic data for later periods may seem to make patterns of protest in earlier periods appear more ephemeral, troubled islands in large quiescent seas. Conversely the use of systematic data presented as maps plotting strike rates for whole regions can easily conceal the often localised nature of disputes revealed in the case studies for the later periods. Geographers have long been familiar with the dangers of the ecological fallacy, of correlations which hold for statistical aggregates but not for the underlying entities with which we are concerned — one of the best known examples is that ethnic minorities and reports of crime are both typically concentrated into the poorer areas of cities, but this is no evidence of the criminality of 'immigrants'. Students of industrial relations must learn the same lesson when interpreting our maps of regional rates: they say little of events or processes in particular towns or factories.

In earlier periods we are dependent upon sources of evidence — official and private papers, newspapers, legal records, fragmentary trade union records — all of which pose their own particular problems when reconstructing the geography of industrial protests. For example, Wells has pointed out that many eighteenth century justices of the peace, among the main agents for reporting disorder to central government, refrained from so doing because such reports would have amounted to an admission that they had lost control of the situation in their localities. In extreme crises such as 1811–1812 or 1826, or in years when disorder was endemic, small demonstrations and minor incidents of protest were similarly neither reported to higher authorities nor found their way into newspaper accounts simply because the local authorities were overwhelmed by the volume of such incidents. Can we say with certainty that all such events in that extreme crisis of the twentieth century, the 1926

General Strike, or the spatially extensive and long drawn out battle of attrition which was the 1984/85 coal strike, were recorded? The answer must be 'no'. Conspiracies of silence or selective use of information have been part of the culture of newspapers since they were first printed. The suppression of reports of industrial disorder in the eighteenth century and the prominence given to reports of miners returning to work during the 1984/85 strike are two sides of the same coin.

We must beware of biases in how the information was gathered. For example, Dobson has attempted a systematic survey of industrial disputes for the period 1700–1850. When all the individual disputes are mapped, London stands out as *the* centre of industrial protest within Britain. However, Dobson relies entirely on London-based newspapers in a period when newspaper circulations were predominantly local, and it is almost certain that the map is revealing not the geography of late eighteenth- and early nineteenth-century disputes but the limitations of the source materials. Certainly, if we contrast Dobson's map with patterns of food rioting over the same period, we find that industrial workers in areas outside London were just as disputatious as those of the metropolis when it came to their daily bread, and it is hard to accept that they would have been largely quiescent over their working conditions and wage rates. Given these problems, this *Atlas* makes no attempt to provide a statistical overview for the pre-1850 period.

Third, we have sought to balance the selectivity of the case studies and the narrow perspective of the statistical overviews by the introductions to sections. Each author was asked to consider a number of themes which we believe run through the *Atlas*: industrialisation, de-industrialisation and the structure of employment; the legal context of industrial protest; the relationship between industrial protest and political protest; the geographic scale of protest, especially the relationship between locality and nation; and the cultural character of protest and the use of symbolic spaces. Here the challenge was one of compression. A detailed account of changes in the structure of the economy and in systems of employment would bring in most aspects of the economic and social history of the long and turbulent period which we cover, as manufacturing replaced agriculture as the dominant employer of male labour and was in turn eclipsed by the service sector.

Similarly, the legal context was both highly complex and saw great changes. The *Atlas* is obviously no substitute for a historical text on labour law but as historians and geographers, rather than lawyers, we would emphasise that the history of legislation provides only a partial and often misleading view of the relationship between industrial protest and the state. In the early years, local magistrates either chose not to impose the draconian penalties available to them or lacked the coercive power to do so. In other places and periods, the state impeded industrial protest without too much concern for the legal niceties. The difficulties encountered by the Agricultural Labourers in the 1870s provide one example, police restrictions on the movement of flying pickets during the 1984/85 miners' strike another.

Our remaining themes all connect, in different ways, to our special concern with the local and the spatial, and above all with community. This is perhaps least obviously true of the relationship between industrial and political protest, but again and again in our case studies we observe what starts as a dispute between worker and employer broadening into a community-based political protest. Langton has convincingly argued that the Industrial Revolution made the localities of Britain increasingly distinct, and this was because the dynamic of industrial capitalism created ever finer spatial divisions of labour, localised mineral resources and rural products plus economies of scale promoting regional specialisations into particular niche markets within an increasingly global economy — generically the mill town and the pit village, specifically the Staffordshire Potteries, the shipyard communities of Tyneside and so on. The economic fortunes of such communities were indistinguishable from those of the dominant industry, while local politics and the magistracy were often controlled by a dominant group of employers.

As the power of these local oligarchies declined, the central state became more and more deeply involved in the economy, and hence in the labour market, in industrial relations, and often in the management of particular industries. At times workers sought to achieve their aims through legislation controlling working conditions, hours of work or minimum wages, and this led to organised workers seeking power through the ballot box. The 'revolt of the field' of 1872 and the dockers' strike of 1888 were clearly industrial not political in origin, but were key events in the evolution of a labour movement which sought to achieve its end through electoral politics — and we suggest that the engineers' defeat in 1898 was equally important, through its demonstration of the limitations of a purely industrial strategy.

At other times, the state viewed industrial protests as attacks on the established order. In the resulting struggles, from the quasi-insurrectionary aspects of Luddism through the General Strikes of 1842 and 1926 and the rise of the May Day demonstrations at the end of the nineteenth century it has not been possible to neatly categorise workers' aims as economic or political. In the twentieth century the state intervened in wage bargaining to control inflation and, through taxation and welfare

benefits, directly influenced the spending power of those in work. This culminated in the 'winter of discontent' of the late 1970s, when the failure of the Labour Government and the rank and file trade unionists to resolve tensions over wages and public expenditure cuts led to a wave of strikes. The subsequent election of the Conservatives in 1979 saw a decisive shift in the political climate of Britain, and a government notionally committed to reduced intervention in industrial matters. In practice, however, the 1984/85 miners strike, a single-industry dispute concerned with plant closures, was fought between the miners and the cabinet: Margaret Thatcher, the Conservative Prime Minister, and Arthur Scargill, the NUM leader, were as one concerning the wider significance of the strike.

Because most industrial protest arose out of economically-specialised communities, we have a clear contrast with the subject matter of the earlier *Atlas of Rural Protest*. Agricultural protest lends itself more readily to cartographic analysis because it sprang from an economic and social base which was itself spatially extensive. To its credit, since that atlas's publication more rural social historians have included maps in their works, but labour historians seem reluctant to think about the geography of their subject matter and a map of a particular strike or set of protests is a rarity. In our case studies, four broad geographical approaches can be discerned:

One approach charts the geographical diffusion of a wave of protest, using a similar methodology to much of the *Atlas of Rural Protest*. In the late eighteenth and early nineteenth centuries, we can map and date incidents using police or newspaper reports. However, most such labour disputes developed within particular localities and were shaped by their social relations and cultures, limiting the geographical scale of our analysis. For example, in the woollen textile industry, grievances about particular types of textile machinery were specific to particular trades. There was thus a problem in getting concerted action between, for example, the woollen areas of the West Riding of Yorkshire and Wiltshire. The disputes over machinery within woollen trade thus had different rhythms, so Wiltshire's Luddism occurred ten years before that in West Yorkshire. By contrast in the eighteenth century grievances over food, its price, supply and quality, were issues ubiquitous to all industrial workers and hence there was a national geography of food rioting.

This localisation of labour protest often meant that an intense solidarity *within* communities was balanced by a lack of solidarity *between* localities. Sometimes local loyalties were linked through a broader conception of the common interest of labour, exemplified by attempts at General Strike, such as that of 1842. However, while its geography was truly national only certain groups of workers were at the heart of the strike. Over time national disputes emerged as labour sought to override the constraints of locality through trade union organisation. The miners' disputes of the 1920s, 1930s and 1980s show that these attempts were not always successful, and in general the localised solidarity of mining communities can be contrasted with more broadly-based solidarity of artisan trades such as the engineers.

The second geographical approach explores the degree of involvement of different localities in either a single dispute or in all disputes over a period. The lack of suitable sources for early periods has already been noted, but a more general caveat is necessary. Such maps are only possible for relatively formal modes of protest and most obviously for strikes: if we can say whether or not an individual is on strike and we know either the total membership of their union or the total workforce of their industry we can calculate the percentage involved in a dispute, and given a suitable reporting framework we can map it. It is easy to conclude from the resulting patterns that large areas of the country, especially the rural south, knew little of industrial protest. However, the quiescence of particular communities must be seen in the context of the complex reality of industrial and social relations out of which industrial protest arose.

Two aspects should be considered: first, what Brewer and Styles label, with reference to eighteenth-century protest, a 'negotiative process'; and second, the use of repressive measures against direct collective action when negotiation broke down. Litigation, mobbing of employers, threatening letters and arson were amongst the methods used by workers to pressurise their employers as part of a 'negotiative process'. Direct collective action, be it the destruction of machinery or a strike, was most often employed when other tactics had failed. Hobsbawm's classic phrase 'collective bargaining by riot' fits such a model but less dramatic 'rough' methods often sufficed, partly because they carried with them an implied threat of insurrection. The chances are that these less prominent acts will not have been recorded.

Similarly, workers might hold back on certain issues to promote their case over other grievances, as, for example, the textile workers of the West Country in 1756–57. Again, the warning to us should be clear. Blanks on the maps cannot be read as an absence of class conflict. The work of scholars such as James Scott reveals a whole repertoire of 'weapons of the weak' that could be deployed in localities and periods that our maps of strikes and lock-outs might suggest were quiescent. Often those weapons permitted only limited resistance to employers' activities but even such hesitant and barely visible resistance must not be confused with the conflict-free, consensual industrial relations that have been the proclaimed goal of Conservative administrations since 1979. The 'revolt of the field' of 1872 may have been a quite exceptional episode in the history of relations between farm labourers and their employers, but the speed with which the movement spread across the country was only possible because of the long-standing frustrations which it tapped, and the reports of the union's organisers as they travelled from village to village provide a fascinating insight into the myriad petty tyrannies of parson and squire which had kept the workers 'quiescent' but scarcely content.

The use of the state's repressive machinery was another major factor in shaping the geography of protests, and its efficacy varied through time. For the General Strike of 1842, Mather has pointed out how the newly-integrated railway network was used to mobilise troops to particular trouble spots and hence contain the spread of the strike more effectively than in any other previous industrial political crisis, so what Foster has argued was the first genuinely national struggle by workers also became the first where the state could orchestrate its repressive agencies across the nation efficiently and effectively. In the Harworth dispute of 1936/7 we find close parallels with the miners' strike of 1984/85 through the use of outside police to control pickets and so break the strike

The third type of geography, often the most local, concerns the symbolic use of space within particular modes of protest. Industrial action has rarely been simply inaction: strikers simply sitting at home rather than going to work. Whether the issue was broadly political or narrowly economic, both sides of a dispute wished to demonstrate their strength and commit-ment both to intimidate the other side and maintain their own solidarity. We

consequently observe a wide range of modes of protest, each with its associated venue. As we argue in each of the sectional introductions, in these modes of protest we can observe both changes and continuities. We have been very careful not to impose certain judgements about traditional and modern modes of protest, the political or a-political nature of workers' actions. When miners in the 1984/85 strike attacked NCB property we would not want to draw the conclusion that their actions should be viewed as atavistic. Similarly the strike by Gloucestershire weavers in 1756–57 is not to be seen as the actions of a group of workers ahead of their time, as more progressive than fellow workers in other trades.

One interesting example of continuity which the *Atlas* brings out is the long-distance march, travelling between towns and regions to symbolise the inter-dependence of localities. The well-known marches of the unemployed in the 1930s did not spring from a cultural vacuum. The tactic of marching to raise support to supply the marchers with money and victuals, to remind employers and local elites of their responsibilities to those worse off in the social order has a long history. The 'pilgrimage' of agricultural labourers to northern industrial towns in the 1870s to raise funds during the 1874 lock-out can be placed within this tradition. In 1842 one of the precursors to the General Strike was bands of workers moving into the country-side and to the wealthy residential districts demanding money and beer. This is in turn can be linked back to 'doleing day' customs in which villagers sought similar 'gifts' from their wealthy neighbours. When there are large gaps in the historical record, we should be aware of the imperfection of that record and the rich cultural fund that is reproduced and transformed genera-tionally that workers can draw on.

Communities of working people have

long memories but so do employers and especially the state. The word 'Luddite' is firmly established as a pejorative to be used whenever an issue of new innovations and working practices arises. The crisis of machine-breaking in Lancashire, Yorkshire and Cheshire in 1826 cast a long shadow in the nineteenth century. If coalmining communities preserved their history of resistant struggles against coalowners and the state, so too did their opponents. It can be argued that the 1984/85 coal strike was fought out so bitterly and so tenaciously by the second Thatcher administration not just because of the miners' part in the downfall of the Heath Government in 1974 but also because of the perceived threat from such a vigorously resistant set of workers over a long historical span. This undoubtedly added weight to Mrs. Thatcher's conviction that the defeat of the miners was a prerequisite if the cultural parameters of working class life in Great Britain were to be transformed and workers' collectivistic sentiments dismantled.

Our final geographical perspective concerns relations between levels in a hierarchy, and especially between locality and nation. This opposition is not necessarily between community-based protesters and the central state, although again the 1984/85 miners' strike provides a already mythic example of such a struggle. Centre-local relations also exist within the state, local magistrates or town councils not necessarily being at one with Westminster. Within our case studies, there are interesting example of such relations within trade unions, as in the 1871 Nine Hours movement which began in the North East without the initial support of a London-based union executive, and between formal union structures and unofficial labour movements, as with our studies of miners and dockers in the 1940s.

However, these examples of conflict within the state or within the labour movement reinforce the continuing importance of community as a basis for loyalty often overriding commitment to employer or class. The theme of 'community', a word and a concept denigrated in the Thatcher years but now once more in vogue, runs like a thread through the volume. In the period before national trade unions workers had to draw on the solidarity of their local community, a solidarity based on the workplace, the chapel, the factory, the pub and localised kinship networks, in order to organise effectively against their employers. Yet the importance of community support from neighbours and workmates has persisted to the present day. This can be clearly seen in the matchgirls' strike in the East End of London in the 1880s, on Clydeside in the 1920s and Harworth in the 1930s. One aspect of community support has always been practical assistance to strikers, in money or in kind, from those with money still coming in. Our case studies reveal another aspect: collective action by a community, extending beyond those in dispute with their employer, frequently added a wider political dimension and sought to harness public opinion. In 1889, East Enders marched through the City of London to Hyde Park in support of the dockers. In 1936, it was the town of Jarrow which metaphorically marched to London, not the Tyneside shipbuilders. In 1984/85, it was the wives of the striking miners who sent the message that colliery closures were an attack on whole communities; they thereby transcended women's traditional role of 'making ends meet' during a dispute to take on a pro-active and political role.

Industrial action cannot be divorced from the political culture of a locality. In 1842 one of the great strongholds of Chartist activity and the centre of the General Strike was northwest England. The history of the strike shows that the decision whether or not to strike and the reasons for striking were argued out at the foci of street level politics — in pubs, at factory gates, on street corners — as well as in the usual arenas of political debate and persuasion — the Chartist mass meetings. Nearly 150 years later in 1989 the strike ballots of the Association of University Teachers, which were never revealed publicly, reportedly showed much higher percentages for strike action in the north as opposed to the south with the highest 'for' votes being in areas like the northwest of England. In such localities university staff felt their disenchantment with Conservative policy on higher education more keenly precisely because they were embedded in local political cultures that were resistant to the wider sweep of the Thatcherite Revolution.

The defeat of the miners in 1984/85 was wrongly seen by some as marking the end of community, of working class collective action rooted in the social life of particular villages and towns. Often these same observers and politicians were pleased to see the demolition of society, both as a concept and as a collectivistic defence against rampant individualism. In recent times, national organisational bases — trade unions, parties and other social movements — have seemed to many on the left to make local communities irrelevant. However, the persistence over 250 years of localities both as symbolic foci and as sources of practical support for industrial collective action demonstrates the resilience of 'community' and is clear proof that in industrial protest geography still matters.

Section A: 1750–1850

by Adrian Randall and Andrew Charlesworth

Industrial protest: 1750–1850

The century from 1750–1850 witnessed major changes in the economy, society and politics of Britain, changes associated with what is usually termed the 'Industrial Revolution'. While some recent economic historians have argued that the Industrial Revolution was little more than a process of gradual economic growth, contemporaries had no doubt that they were experiencing major change. The burgeoning expansion of the new industrial towns, the application of new technologies and new forms of labour organisation, the mounting social and political discontent, all tokened to them the advent of a new age. It was not one of which they all approved. Many labour groups found their trades and their ways of work coming under mounting pressure.

Yet the Industrial Revolution also created or developed new sectors of the labour market. Thus while the skilled elite of wool combers in the worsted industry saw mechanised combing engines displace them, the powered water frame which displaced the domestic spinners in turn gave rise to a new and increasingly powerful labour elite, the mule spinners. Where new technology led, new labour organisation modes followed. The rise of the factory system may certainly be ascribed principally to the need for a centralised source of power to drive new machines. But once established from need, the advantages to the employer of concentrating and hence controlling labour under one roof proved attractive even where no technological need existed. Thus weaving sheds or factories pre-dated the power loom

by decades while in Northampton the application of the model of factory subdivision of labour established a provincial boot and shoe industry very different to the craft-based industry found in London and one which increasingly undercut the Metropolitan trade. Labour groups in the Industrial Revolution had to adapt and adjust to a changing economy and a changing social and political environment. Their methods of safeguarding or enhancing their position were to change too.

The period of the early Industrial Revolution has been seen by many historians as marking the origin of British trade unionism for, from the 1790s, the characteristic form of eighteenth-century protest, the riot based around the crowd, has been seen as giving way to more 'orderly' forms of protest with formal organisations of labour appearing increasingly frequently in the historical record. The Webbs' pioneering study of trade unionism very much emphasised this view. Their definition of trade unions, widely accepted by subsequent historians, as 'continuous associations of wage earners' laid great emphasis on formal and overt organisation, upon regular meetings and orderly negotiations. This has resulted in a bias towards the study of Metropolitan artisan trades whose historically more accessible combinations most clearly approximate to this model and conversely to the neglect of the more fragmentary and apparently transient protests and combinations which were typical of many other trades across the country in the eighteenth and early nineteenth centuries. The Webbs in fact excluded such 'ephemeral combinations against their social superiors' from their remit. While Turner and Rule have both criticised this approach as narrow and distorting of our understanding of eighteenth–century combinations, others such as Dobson have continued to emphasise the 'level of organisation' and labour groups' need for 'a permanent base for continuous association'.

Historians, wedded to such a nineteenth-century view of 'orthodox' trade union structures, have sought to impose a model of 'orthodoxy' on the form and character of eighteenth– and early nineteenth–century labour protests and to view the development of industrial protest as a linear one. Thus Musson, echoing the Webbs, views the riots and violence of many pre-industrial disputes with distaste, seeing them as indicative of a lack of order and organisation. 'The development of peaceful constitutional collective bargaining in place of crude violence was part of the process from primitive barbarism to a more civilised society.' (Musson, 1972, p. 15). Even Hobsbawm's pioneering study of violence in eighteenth-century industrial disputes classed this form of conflict as 'collective bargaining by riot', a form of protest found where 'organised unions hardly as yet existed'. Stevenson claims to have discovered a 'modernisation of protest' taking place in the early nineteenth century. He believes that riots gradually gave way to other types of protest such as strike action more suited to an industrial environment. Underpinning all these views is the assumption that the industrial organisational forms and methods of the nineteenth century were the clear product of 'progress' from the more violent and 'riotous' methodologies of pre-industrial labour groups.

This 'progressive' and linear reading of the pattern of labour protest and develop-ment in the Industrial Revolution does, however, give rise to problems. Firstly, while overt and formal organisation in the years before 1824 was practicable for some labour groups, above all for the highly skilled and craft conscious artisans of the West End of London, it was not the only form of labour association since it was by no means appropriate for all labour groups or labour contexts. We must be careful not to impose an essentially nineteenth-century matrix of the trade union, itself a product as much of the assiduous propagandist skills of such men as Applegarth and Allen, upon an environment which in the previous century was very different. The attitudes towards market forces, bargaining strategies and social relations of the mid-Victorian labour elite were not those of the early Industrial Revolution. Indeed, they were in many respects quite alien to the context of pre-industrial manufacture.

In the eighteenth century, combinations and labour protest arose as much from a community context as from a craft context. They were a product of a society where 'life' and 'work' were much less segregated than in the nineteenth century. Attitudes were forged as much in the market place and public house as in the work place since a large section of those engaged in manufacture worked in their own homes under the putting out system, in the docks, on ships or in the mines, not in workshops or proto factories. This social context informed attitudes to work, to labour autonomy and to society as a whole. This relationship of labour groups to their wider community can be clearly seen in the case of the Gloucestershire weavers in their disputes in 1756–66 (see below, pp. 7–11).

Recognition of this community context of much industrial protest in the eighteenth century should alert us to the fact that such communities were not only the location for industrial conflict but also for a wide array of other social protests. The eighteenth century witnessed a far higher level of popular protest than did the nineteenth, involving, among other things, hostility to new turnpikes, to new taxes, to innovations in the workplace and above all to perceived exploitation in the market place. Indeed, food riots accounted for perhaps as many as one in four of all disturbances in this very riotous century. These protests were, according to E. P. Thompson, 'a highly complex form of direct popular action, disciplined and with clear objectives', and were characterised by a legitimising notion which Thompson calls 'the moral economy of the crowd'(Thompson, 1971, pp. 78–9). Drawing upon the concept of paternalism, statute and common law and customary practice, the crowd could assert their 'rights' to protection from overbearing capitalists and middlemen who sought to further their own financial interests at the expense of the poor. The experience of successful popular protest within a community often reinforced a 'rebellious traditional culture' in which actions in one area of life informed and sustained actions elsewhere. They likewise made the authorities very much more sensitive to the ways in which they handled potentially disruptive issues. Indeed, the magistracy often demonstrated a considerable capacity at conflict management. Food riots, industrial riots and other protests in the eighteenth century thus often reveal a complex theatre in which the various elements played out their allotted roles.

A characteristic of industrial protests in the eighteenth century was the frequent involvement of the authorities as peace-makers and arbitrators. We need to ask why the justices believed it necessary to interfere in this way, and what they sought to achieve. One answer may be found in the self-imposed absence of an effective police force and in the gentry's fear of 'a standing army in the midst of peace', the old bugbear of those who feared an over-powerful executive. Magistrates therefore often found themselves confronted with difficult problems of social control without the immediate means of law enforcement. By intervening in a placatory manner, they might hope to control the situation without loss of order or of face. The need to be seen by central government to be able to control these situations without recourse to the army also curtailed their options.

There is also, however, an ideological element to be decoded. While the crowd appealed to the 'moral economy', a belief that they were entitled to protection of their legitimate interests from over-powerful predators, many of the gentry likewise shared in some significant respects the crowd's ideal of a regulated and controlled economy. This was not simply a matter of custom. It was also underpinned in both food marketing and industrial relations by the law. The strength of the crowd thus depended not only upon numerical weight. On some issues they could appeal to statute or to common law, as for example that relating to apprenticeship or the operation of food markets. Whilst much of this legislation dated back to the sixteenth century, Parliament was not averse to adding regulatory functions. Thus in 1756 Parliament empowered the bench in Gloucestershire to rate weavers' wages, a power given to the magistrates in Spital-fields in 1773 and to their counterparts in Manchester as late as 1803 in the Cotton Arbitration Act.

This belief in paternal intervention was, however, under threat even in the eighteenth century. The new political economy of Adam Smith, with its emphasis upon free markets and free trade, undermined the intellectual fabric of old paternal philosophy while manufacturers pushed ever-more vigorously for their interests to be freed from ancient restraints. The crucial break may be seen as coming not with the

Industrial but with the French Revolution. The loss of confidence in the English landed ranks in the face of the militant advance of *The Rights of Man* fractured the old approach. After 1793 protest increasingly was equated with treason and sedition. The old script of the theatre of popular protest was abandoned. Protest which before had been as at most a source of alarm was now seen as threatening the security of the state. The Combination Acts of 1799–1800 can be seen as symbols of the change. While historians have queried their effectiveness as a instrument of oppression, in many respects they may be seen more as a symbolic abdication by the State from its role as neutral arbitrator in industrial conflict.

Hedged about by old and antiquated restrictive statutes which reflected the industry's age-old importance as the country's principal staple, the woollen industry proved the test case for the survival of the regulatory system. The relatively new and unregulated cotton industry had shown the way forward and entrepreneurs wished to apply the technologies and organisational forms of the new to the old. Parliament held two major enquiries into the woollen industry in 1803 and 1806. In 1809 the old regulatory legislation was swept away to be followed in quick time by the Elizabethan apprenticeship statutes. Indeed, the battle over the Apprenticeship Campaign can be legitimately seen as the last great stand of the pre-industrial crafts. Thereafter the State and its local agencies stood far nearer to the interests of capital, the old arbitrator role fading. The Luddite disturbances, which occurred very much at the point of this transition, showed this clearly (see below, pp. 32–46).

The new industrial, political and legal climate which followed the wars against France changed the context for industrial protest. The rapid advance of machinery and of the factory system forced labour to develop new forms of organisation and tactics. The older informality which had permitted trades to maintain a form of semi-continuous organisation was replaced by more formal and more confrontational modes of action. In the van of this were the cotton spinners, the archetype of the new labour force. Work in the factory may have involved a loss of autonomy and acceptance of a harsh and onerous work regime. But the factory also permitted the spinners to associate easily and to develop a powerful and aggressive trade union consciousness. Their ability to organise and to regulate recruitment to the trade placed them at times in advantageous bargaining positions with the cotton lords. It was the spinners who pioneered the rolling strike and gave the lead to both federal and general trade union organisation. Their strikes were frequently aggressive ones, in marked contrast to those of the cotton weavers who, like weavers around the country in the years before and after 1815, were forced into defensive action, seeking to uphold wages rather than to raise them. This reflected the growing pressures of surplus weaving numbers which placed increasing pressure upon living standards. The weavers continued to hope for regulation and intervention by the State to protect their trade. It was not forthcoming. Meanwhile, the artisan unions, which in the War years had sought to extend their recruitment base and, as had the London tailors, to associate with the 'dishonourable' trade, shrank back increasingly into exclusivity.

The repeal of the Combination Acts in 1824 marked a significant changing point in labour protest. Its immediate result, coupled with a major trade boom, was a rapid increase in aggressive strike action. The partial reimposition of controls the following year stopped short of outlawing combinations once more. Thereafter, combinations could maintain a legal existence, if one subject to formidable constraints. If Joseph Hume was wrong in his assumption that legalising trade unions would cause their demise, he was perhaps proved partly correct in that they increasingly looked to legal methods of conducting disputes rather than to more direct action. In this, the State can be seen as again establishing the context within which industrial protest developed.

The change in industrial protests from riot to strike which has been noted by historians should nonetheless not blinker us to the many continuities. The industrial conflicts among the miners of the North East in 1844 bore many of the characteristics of the disputes in that coal field in the mid-eighteenth century. The miners of the Forest of Dean likewise continued to terrorise the authorities at times well into the nineteenth century. Mining communities were able to resist change longest since their isolation from the growing pressure of the forces of social control was most marked. We must also note the interconnectedness of industrial protests and other grievances. This was particularly noticeable in the industrial conflicts in the later 1820s and early 1830s, a period of industrial conflict still under-researched.

The years following 1824 saw increased efforts to link labour groups nationally. Many modes of industrial protest crop up all over the country in the 1820s: the rolling strike, the secret society, the swearing of illegal oaths. How these linkages were created has only recently been researched and they did not come to full fruition until the 1850. We should, however, note that workers in the early Industrial Revolution were not as 'isolated' as some historians suggest. There was in fact a considerable interchange of both information and men right through the eighteenth century and beyond. The tramping system was firmly established among the artisan trades from before 1700. Silk weavers moved between Spitalfields and Coventry whenever trade fluctuated. Communications intercepted during the Wiltshire Outrages in 1802 indicate the tip of a continuing iceberg of cross-county and -country inter-trade correspondence. The leader of the Gloucestershire weavers tramped over one thousand miles on union business between May and November 1838 and miners in the 1840s were able to forge the makings of a genuinely national union. The 'New Model Unions' of the 1850s were building upon already well developed foundations.

Finally we must note that, from the 1790s, labour organisation began to play an increasing role in the diffusion of radical ideas. The artisans were in the forefront of the radical movement in the 1790s and it was in part fears that the London and provincial trades were instrumental in propagating Jacobinism that led to the passage of the Combination Acts in 1799. The Luddite disturbances of 1811–12 revealed, for the government, some alarming connections between industrial protest and radical, even revolutionary, politics. Historians have continued to debate how far, in Thompson's phrase, 'Luddism was a quasi-insurrectionary movement, which continually trembled on the edge of ulterior revolutionary objectives' but there is no doubt that the disturbances did allow radicals to gain support since the failure of government to uphold the old 'rights' of the trades concerned was bitterly felt (Thompson, 1968, p. 604).

The post-war depression with its unemployment and wage cuts witnessed growing labour conflict and the accession to the radical ranks of many previously apolitical labour groups, most notably the outworkers. The field at Peterloo bore eloquent witness to this. Repression and economic upturn after 1819 drew off some of the radical support but the repeal of the Combination Acts in 1824 was followed by increased interest by labour groups in politics. In the late 1820s and early 1830s it was to cooperation and Owenite socialism that many turned but from 1838 labour groups across the country were swept up in the Chartist movement. From 1838 to 1842 unions frequently marched to Chartist meetings under their own banners, adopted the Charter and provided general support. In particular, the Chartists' main weapon, the General Strike, relied upon organised labour to provide its core. Significantly it was the trades, not the Chartist leaders, who endorsed the call for a political strike in 1842, turning a series of local and regional disputes and lock outs into the first General Strike (see below, pp. 51–8). The strike's defeat, and the severity of the strikers' treatment, marked the beginning of a retreat from radical politics by organised labour which was to last until the end of the century.

Sources and further reading

On combinations and labour protests in the eighteenth century: E. J. Hobsbawm, *Labouring Men: Studies in the History of Labour* (London, 1968); A. E. Musson, *British Trade Unions, 1800–1875* (London, 1972); R. Dobson, *Masters and Journeymen: a Prehistory of Industrial Relations, 1717–1800* (Beckenham, 1980); and J. Rule, *The Experience of Labour in Eighteenth–Century Industry* (Beckenham, 1981). The study of popular protest in the eighteenth century has been massively influenced by E. P. Thompson, 'The moral economy of the English crowd in the eighteenth century' in *Past and Present*, 50, 1971. See also J. Stevenson, *Popular Disturbances in England, 1700–1870* (London, 1979). For labour's response to the introduction of machinery and to the removal of regulatory legislation, see A. J. Randall, *Before the Luddites: Custom, Community and Machinery in the English Woollen Industry 1776–1809* (Cambridge, 1991), and I. Prothero, *Artisans and Politics in Early Nineteenth-Century London* (London, 1979) which has the best account of the Apprenticeship Campaign of 1811. On the growing links between radical politics and labour unrest in the years from 1793 to 1815, see E. P. Thompson, *The Making of the English Working Class* (Harmondsworth, 1968). For the growing industrial conflict in the nineteenth-century cotton industry, see H. A. Turner, *Trade Union Growth, Structure and Policy; a Comparative Study of the Cotton Unions* (London, 1962); D. Bythell, *The Handloom Weavers* (Cambridge, 1969); and J. Foster, *Class Struggle and the Industrial Revolution* (London, 1974). G. D. H. Cole, *Attempts at General Union: a Study in British Trade Union History, 1818–1834* (London, 1953), remains one of the few volumes to attempt to trace the development of the growing links between combinations in this period on a national basis. The best source on the links between the Chartist movement and industrial labour is D. K. G. Thompson, *The Chartists: Popular Politics in the Industrial Revolution* (London, 1984).

1. Strikes and popular protest in Gloucestershire, 1756–66

While recent social historians have done much to place eighteenth-century popular protest within a wider context of social, political and economic relations, the study of eighteenth-century industrial protest remains too frequently confined within a narrow definition of 'orthodox' trade union organisation and behaviour which excludes more disorderly forms of protest, violence to property and riot. This, and an assumption that trade unionism was the preserve only of shop-based artisan crafts, has deflected attention from the far more numerous ranks of outworkers and miners whose experience of combination, if more episodic, was clearly extensive. While artisan combinations may have been firmly based in the workshop, however, the basis of combination for outworkers and miners lay within their community and within a powerful sense of collective community solidarity displayed whenever threatened either as producers by their employers or as consumers by those who provided their bread. The disturbances in 1756/7 and 1766 in the woollen manufacturing districts of Gloucestershire indicate how the community provided both a springboard for action and a value system which over–spanned both industrial and consumer protest.

The eighteenth-century woollen industry in Gloucestershire employed upwards of 60,000 workers, the greatest number of whom were weavers, working in their homes in the towns and villages along the scarp slopes of the Cotswolds. These woollen–producing communities frequently proved very difficult to manage, a fact not helped by the shortage of magistrates there, for the Gloucestershire bench was more reluctant than neighbouring Wiltshire to enrol practising clothiers as justices. In both 1756 and 1766 the area witnessed two protracted periods of conflict and protest, the former concerning the issue of weavers' wages, the latter the cost of food.

Tension had been growing in the Gloucestershire woollen industry for some time before 1755 as some clothiers sought to combat the effects of depressed trade by reviving old abuses such as truck, payment in promissory notes, the use of illegal warping bars and the

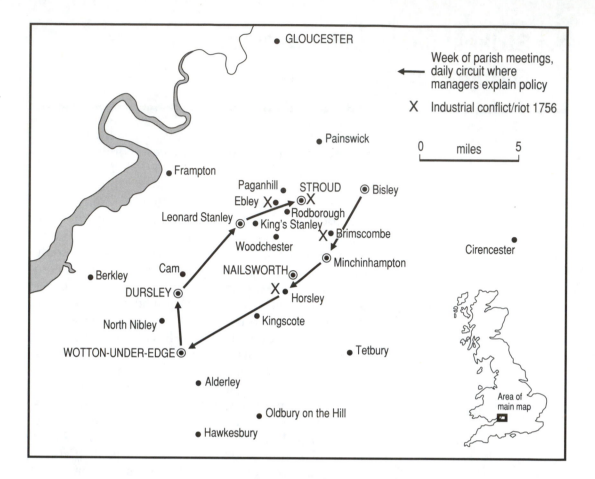

Figure 1.1
The Gloucestershire weavers'
strike of 1756.
The weavers' strike of 1756 was
remarkable for its orderliness
and unity. The basic unit of
organisation, the parish
committee, sent delegates to a
county-wide association which
coordinated the strike.
*Source: Gloucester Journal; A State
of the Case and a Narrative of Facts
relating to the late Commotions and
Risings of the Weavers in the
County of Gloucester (1757).*

employment of non–apprenticed labour. However, it
was the decision of a few clothiers to cut wage rates in
1755 which precipitated conflict. Recognising that, though
few, these clothiers would put pressure on all employers
to cut wages, the Gloucestershire weavers responded
collectively. In a short period, a county-wide association
was constituted, built upon parochial societies which
sent two delegates to form a central committee. After
holding discussions with sympathetic magistrates, they
decided to petition Parliament to enact new legislation
enabling the bench to arbitrate and fix piece rates for
weaving on an annual basis, a device established
previously in an act of 1727 but which had proved
incapable of enforcement. The association levied
subscriptions and explained their policy to the weavers
en masse in a series of daily meetings on a circuit around
the county. The petition was presented to Parliament
and delegates gave evidence before a select committee.
On the basis of this and some careful lobbying, the
weavers were rewarded with an Act passed in May 1756

empowering the bench to fix piece rates for weaving annually at the Michaelmas sessions.

The clothiers had ignored the weavers' petitions but they were outraged to find that the bench intended to take the new Act seriously. They responded with a two-pronged attack: a propaganda barrage emphasising the impossibility of establishing rates for all types of cloth and the impolitic consequences of interfering with trade in this way; and pressure on their weavers to sign documents accepting the old rates. The bench, under this pressure, vacillated and adjourned the Michaelmas sessions without fixing a rate. The weavers were clearly angry but their discipline held. They decided upon a strike. Across the country shuttles stood idle. There were some disturbances when clothiers tried to brow beat a resumption of weaving and some returned to work. But the strike remained remarkably solid and peaceful. It lasted for some six weeks. It was ended when some Stroud clothiers, anxious to see the strike over, agreed a new rate and this was ratified by a reconvened bench. The weavers could with good reason see this as a famous victory. Their employers, however, could see no reason why they should obey the new rate and many continued to refuse to grant them. There were further disturbances but again the weavers' union held strong and brought successful prosecutions against two of the most eminent clothiers. This decided the clothiers that the law must be repealed. Secretly they organised and lobbied and in 1757 secured their aim. Some violence was meted out to those weavers who gave evidence on the clothiers' behalf to Parliament and some clothiers' cloths were destroyed. But the weavers for the most part accepted their defeat with dignity.

Interesting parallels emerge when comparing the industrial actions of the weavers in 1756 with the actions of the food rioters in the county ten years later. These food riots were very extensive, emanating throughout from the woollen towns and villages. Large crowds rose in protest at rapidly accelerating prices and diminishing supplies of bread and grain. Spreading out from the markets in the towns where they seized food stocks and sold them at the 'just price', the crowds, highly organised and surprisingly disciplined, marched around the district, visiting neighbouring markets, mills, shops and warehouses to uncover hoarded food stocks and to set the price. The rioters had a strong sense of community participation. All were pressed, willing or not, into service

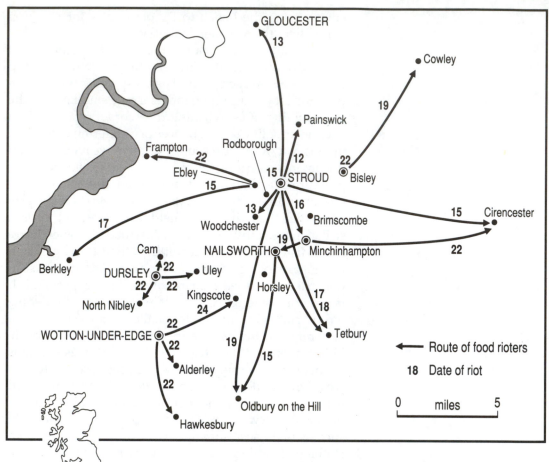

Figure 1.2
Food riots in Gloucestershire,
September 1766.
A characteristic of the food riots
in Gloucestershire in 1766 was
their orderliness and the way in
which groups of 'regulators'
toured the county, setting the
price at markets and searching
out caches of grain, flour and
cheese.
Source: A. J. Randall, 'The
Gloucestershire food riots of
1766', *Midland History*, X, 1985.

in the work of 'regulating'. Distances traversed and
numbers involved were often considerable. In the largest
demonstration over a thousand people assembled at
Minchinhampton and marched twelve miles to
Cirencester, the largest corn market in the county. Some
then continued on as far as Ampney, Fairford and
Lechlade, some twenty-five miles from Minchinhampton,
at each market attempting to set the price. Though damage
was often meted out to property, particularly to mills
where substances for adulterating flour was discovered,
the crowds were generally well-behaved by their own
lights, despite claims to the contrary by their outraged
victims. An offer to bring grain to market at a fixed price
would often satisfy them.

Both protests shared similar aspects. Certainly the
participants in both had a common core of weavers. In
both we can see the strong sense of a community mobilised
to defend its interests against the actions of unscrupulous
capitalists who used their power over work or food
stocks to maximise their profits at the expense of the

workers. In both, too, actions were aimed not only at these men but also at the magistrates. The weavers struck work not only to compel the clothiers to see sense but also to coerce the magistrates to do their duty as laid down by the new Act. Likewise, the food rioters in 1766 frequently claimed that 'all the gentlemen' were on their side. They certainly expected the bench to uphold the laws against forestallers and regrators and to establish market custom and practice as before. A common value system, based upon order, stability and regulation underpinned the actions of both 1756 and 1766. Likewise, in both cases weavers and food rioters received sympathetic help and support from many ratepayers who felt little love for either the clothiers or the corn dealers.

The protesting crowd of Gloucestershire drew upon a tradition of protest and an organisation inherent in their community. Protests in turn reinforced the willingness and ability of the woollen workers to protest in future. It was for this reason that the clothiers, having beaten off their weavers in 1757, did not subsequently feel it prudent to lower wages and why the old marketing practices and gentry concern to monitor markets was enhanced in the years after 1766. Though both strike and food riots were eventually defeated, the victors could not afford another such triumph. Thus protest proved a successful technique for safeguarding the customs and rights of the woollen workers, whether as producers or consumers.

Sources and further reading
A. J. Randall, 'The industrial moral economy of the Gloucestershire weavers in the eighteenth century' in J. Rule, ed., *British Trade Unionism, 1750–1850: the Formative Years* (Harlow, 1988). A. J. Randall, 'The Gloucestershire food riots of 1766', *Midland History*, X, 1985. E. P. Thompson, 'The moral economy of the English crowd in the eighteenth century', *Past and Present*, 50, 1971.

2. The London sailors' strike of 1768

by Richard Sheldon

In May 1768 the Port of London, capital and commercial centre of the British Empire, was brought to a complete standstill by the actions of merchant sailors who went on strike for higher wages. The strike took place at a time of widespread social and political disorder. This year was also an election year in which many popular grievances came together under the banner of 'Wilkes and Liberty'. Whereas the political contests of this year are now well researched, the industrial conflicts, in particular those involving maritime workers, have been comparatively neglected. This is unfortunate since these actions were a part of one of the most important industrial strikes of the eighteenth century. Indeed, labour history has, to date, paid relatively scant attention to sailors and other labourers engaged in the maritime commerce that was so crucial to eighteenth century economic expansion.

At mid-century there were around 100,000 men employed as shipboard labourers in the British merchant service. Aside from agricultural labourers, this was a work force matched in strength only by the colliers and the textile workers. The 'British tars' of this period were of course far from being just that. They were remarkable for their national and racial heterogeneity. 'Nay,' complained one observer of events in 1768; 'some of these Englishmen were the immediate sons of Jamaica, or African blacks by Asiatic Mulatoes, or Muscovites born in the distant provinces of Siberia'. Many sailors at this time would have experienced at first hand the growing social divisions and political challenges to British rule on the urban seaboard of colonial North America.

As collective workers, the sailors show many of the qualities of a proletariat: hired as units of labour — 'hands' — to perform specified tasks in return for a cash wage, owning or controlling no means of production. But the propensity to act as a body was always limited by the nature of seafaring employment — work was performed in isolated communities under strict discipline — and also by the hazardous nature of the work which called for a high degree of co-operative cohesion. Thus the sailors` strikes that took place in the eighteenth century tended to occur in port under circumstances which forced under-employed men together. Noteworthy instances of such occurrences took place in 1762 (Liverpool), 1768, and 1775 (Liverpool again). The first took place during the war-time boom; the second in the trough of the post-war depression; the third was a spectacular confrontation between merchants and men, which at its high point saw cannon dragged ashore and used to fire upon the exchange building in Liverpool.

The years following the end of the Seven Years War in 1763 were marked by a number of serious difficulties involved in the transition to a peace-time economy. Mass demobilisations from army and navy — more than 150,000 men — resulted in high levels of unemployment. This situation was exacerbated by a series of unusually harsh winters and deficient harvests, which in turn led to rapid increases in the prices of basic foodstuffs and the setting-in of a trend towards general price inflation. In the winter of 1767/68 severe frosts were experienced and for a time the navigation of the Thames was blocked by ice. This winter witnessed the outbreak of a host of smaller disputes, often over the issue of remuneration, in the various trades of London and the provinces. Tailors, glass-grinders, coal-heavers, canal diggers, Thames bargemen, sawyers, lawn clippers ('a female combination'), weavers, carpenters, joiners and others all took some form of direct action as a general spirit of contestation swept the land from Port Glasgow/Greenock in the north to Southampton in the south. In London a strike amongst the men employed in the unloading of coastal-collier ships from the Northern coalfields (called coal-heavers) brought severe disruption to the London trades and gave rise to widespread fears of insurrection on the River.

Strike action by sailors was first taken in the North-East. Here they closed the ports of Newcastle, North Shields and Sunderland by unrigging ships that were prepared to sail and by holding large scale demonstrations on land. With the weapons of surprise and strength of numbers on their side, the seamen were able to win speedy concessions from their employers. Later in May there is an account of an unsuccessful move for strike action by the mariners of Bristol.

The first stage of the strike in London began on 1st May when well-organised parties of around 40 men each toured the vessels at anchor that were prepared for outbound voyages, demanding to see the ships' articles in order to ascertain the current rates of pay. These ships

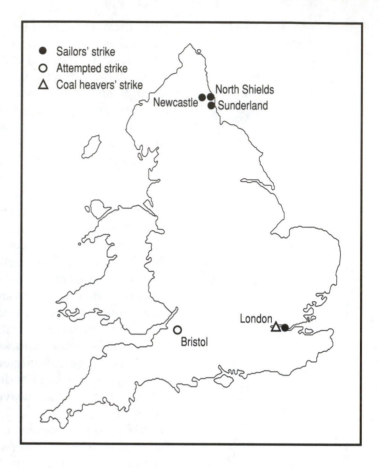

Figure 2.1
Sailors' strike of 1768.
The map is based on the author's
'Going on Strike in 1768'
University of London unpub-
lished M.A. dissertation, 1991.

were then disabled from setting sail by the removal of their rigging. Other parties visited the city homes of merchants and ship-owners to inform them of their actions and to lay demands.

The central issue animating the actions of the strikers was that of pay. A rate of 40s per month was demanded for the northern and Eastern routes and 35s for the western trade. Other grievances were complained of, especially the practice of turning off sailors in foreign ports without a contract for the return voyage. When the sailors' committees drew up a petition to Parliament, which was presented on their behalf by one Captain Fall (with the seeming support of a handful of patrician parliamentarians), claim was also made for the incorporation of the merchant service and for the parliamentary regulation of pay and conditions of service.

The immediate reaction of the merchant and ship-owning community was a refusal to countenance any of the sailors' demands and to seek counsel from the government for martial assistance in suppressing the strike. Urgent representations were made through the Southwark sessions, and by the deputy governor of the Hudsons' Bay Company, as to the calamitous prospect that a continuing strike posed. Armed cutters were ordered to patrol the Pool of London. However, decisive action was put off. It was complained that legal confusions would arise due to the River coming under the various legal jurisdictions of the bordering counties. Nobody seems to have been prepared to take the decisive action to tackle the strikers, despite the offer of merchants to recruit and fund a mercenary force to take on the sailors. The most pressing reason not to force the issue appeared to lie in the voiced concern of provoking 'a general riot on the river'.

Faced with recalcitrant employers, the sailors staged impressive public demonstrations of their unity and purpose. At the same time, constant vigilance was kept on outward bound vessels and Dutch and other foreign ships off Deptford were visited by parties of sailors and unrigged. On May 7th sailors gathered in large numbers ('many thousands' according to the press) in St Georges Fields and marched on St James Palace to deliver a petition to the King. On May 11th (the day after soldiers had fired upon and killed eleven by-standers at the demonstration in support of John Wilkes in St Georges Fields) the largest of the sailors' marches took place, contemporary estimates of numbers range from 5 to 15,000. Proceedings were orderly and disciplined. The men marched in formation, led and interspersed by flags, and marshalled by ringleaders carrying boatswains' whistles. Addressed by a leader in Stepney Fields, those sailors who had come armed with large sticks were persuaded to leave them behind. This demonstration was bound for Parliament where another petition was to be delivered. At Westminster the sailors were addressed by Captain Fall and others from atop a coach. They were assured that, although no immediate action could be taken, their demands were receiving urgent consideration. On this, the sailors retired, apparently satisfied.

Other actions by the sailors in between the two mass parades took a more unruly form. One morning at 4am, the sailors, acting in concert with striking coal heavers, had landed at Millbank and Westminster and forced all labourers they encountered to leave work, touring the wharfs and alehouses. All carts carrying flour, wood and coals were detained and West Country barges were

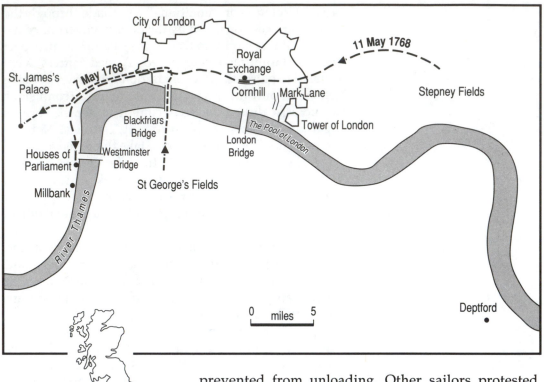

Figure 2.2
The London sailors' strike 1768.
For source see figure 2.1.

prevented from unloading. Other sailors protested outside the City's Royal Exchange, on one occasion forcibly occupying it. Men paraded the commercial coffee houses carrying banners bearing the unambiguous message, 'More Wages'.

The sailors' presence was encountered in a similar fashion by the corn merchants of Mark Lane. Bills were printed and posted around the City stating the sailors' case. A report in the Shelburne papers illustrates the determination of a hardened core of the sailors to employ acts of outright rebellion in support of their claims. One is quoted as having threatened that: 'there is ships and great guns at hand which we will use as occasion shall require in order to redress ourselves'.

Although no action was subsequently taken by Parliament for the regulation of the merchant service, deals on pay were thrashed out for many sailors during meetings between a joint committee of sailors and merchants at the King's Arms tavern in Cornhill, the details of which remain sketchy. Large companies such as the Hudson's Bay Company did agree to pay the stipulated rates, as did others dealing in perishable commodities who were concerned to see traffic moving again. The sailors returned to their ships after the 12th May and ships began to sail shortly thereafter. The strike involving the coal-heavers had been under way before the commencement of the sailors' strike and was to run on into the summer. Disputes flared between these workers and the sailors of the coastal colliers who had begun to undertake the work of the coal-heavers themselves. This conflict occasioned much violence and bloodshed. These antagonisms were based on long held mutual antipathies and suspicions as to sharp practice in the coal trade and can be seen as separate from the strike of the deep sea sailors.

Sources and further reading
A fully referenced study of the strike and the sources used in this account can be found in the author's 'Going on Strike in 1768' University of London unpublished M.A. dissertation, 1991. On the 18th century seafaring world see, for example, P. Linebaugh, *The London Hanged* (Harmondsworth, 1993); M. Rediker, *Between the Devil and the Deep Blue Sea* (Cambridge, 1987); N. A. M. Rodger, *The Wooden World* (London, 1986); C. Howell and R. Twomey eds., *Jack Tar in History* (New Brunswick, 1991).

3. Protests over cotton machinery in Lancashire, 1768–79

Figure 3.1
Disturbances over cotton machinery Lancashire 1768. The maps are based on A. G. Rose 'Early Cotton Riots in Lancashire 1769–1779' *Trans. Lancs. & Ches. Antiq. Soc. 73/74* (1963–64); A. P. Wadsworth and J. de la Mann,*The Cotton Trade and Industrial Lancashire* (Manchester, 1931); J. L. and B. Hammond, *The Skilled Labourer* (London, 1919).

Some of the most notorious attacks on machinery in the Lancashire cotton textile trade took place in 1768, which coincided with the relocation from Lancashire to Nottinghamshire of two of the trade's most heroic innovators, James Hargreaves and Richard Arkwright. There is little extant evidence of these events but local historians of the nineteenth century were quite clear that Hargreaves' homestead had been attacked in the spring of 1768 and the jenny and looms destroyed. This was clearly an organised and pre-planned attack involving not only the craftsmen of Blackburn but also weavers from the Blackburn hinterland who assembled in the town and marched in a body to Stanhill, Hargreaves' village. The crowd then proceeded to destroy Peel's mill and machinery, including jennies, at nearby Brookside.

More widespread attacks followed in February and March 1769 in the same region and in June in the Bolton

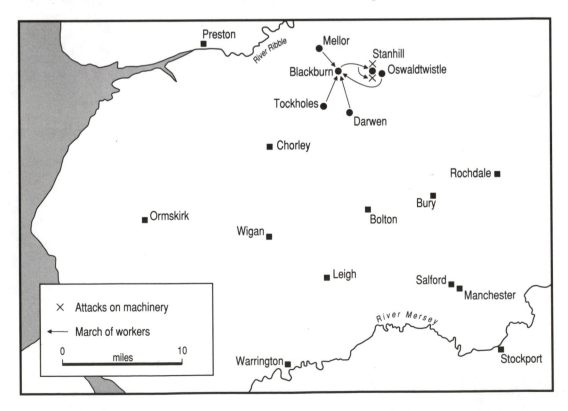

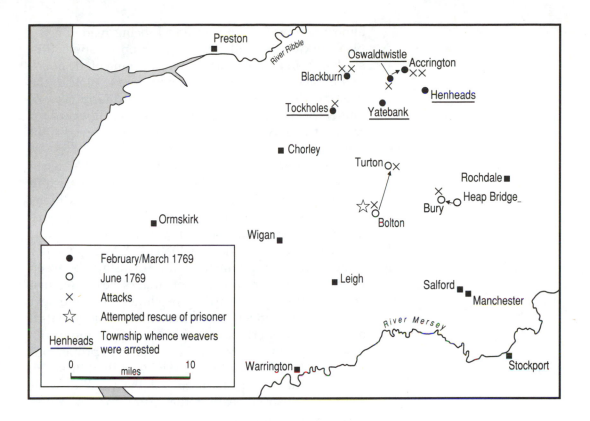

Figure 3.2
Disturbances over cotton
machinery Lancashire 1769.

Area of
main map

area. In the first attacks, only houses and furniture were destroyed or damaged, a typical form of collective bargaining by riot in the eighteenth century. In the summer, however, the 'mob arose, burnt what machines they could discover, and carried about their fragments *in triumph*' (author's emphasis) (quoted in Rose 1963/64, p. 67).

The real test of strength occurred in 1779 and this time clearly involved Arkwright. Arkwright's textile business was now firmly established in Nottinghamshire but he also owned a major mill at Birkacre near Chorley in Lancashire. In both counties he found himself best with major protests.

In 1779 the Nottinghamshire framework knitters petitioned Parliament for a bill to regulate their trade. This was opposed by the master hosiers of Nottingham and the bill was thrown out in early June, as had another bill to regulate wages in the industry the previous year. News of their defeat immediately led the framework knitters in Nottingham to commence violent protest against the leading opponent of the bill, Samuel Need, a powerful master hosier and joint owner of Arkwright's cotton mill and other master hosiers. Riots continued for almost two weeks with an attack being made on the Need-Arkwright mill, the destruction of some fifty stocking frames at Arnold and the burning of the house of a master hosier. Though troops were deployed, the master hosiers came to an agreement with the framework knitters on a scale of wages that was to be observed for the next twenty years. Those arrested received light sentences.

This success for militancy and the apparent leniency of the authorities may well have influenced Lancashire cotton workers when, later that year, trade conditions there worsened. Unemployment sharpened anxieties about the increasing use of new larger jennies, new carding engines and the new 'patent' Arkwright water frames. On 27 September in the townships between Bolton and Wigan, a series of attacks began against spinning, roving and carding machines. Over the next few weeks such attacks swept across the whole of central and south eastern Lancashire. By 2 October the disturbances had spread to the Bolton area proper and 2,000 had marched on to Arkwright's mill at Birkacre. The first attack was repulsed but the workers went round the district beating the drum and collecting firearms and ammunition. In a second attack, colliers and others joined the textile workers. The attackers, some 3 to 4,000 strong, succeeded in destroying all the machinery and a good part of the mill.

During the first weeks of rioting when the workers appeared to command whole districts, the authorities made concessions. The Wigan magistrates, for example, without military assistance, had promised to suspend the use of all cotton machines worked by water or horses and to lay the spinners' grievances before Parliament. The available troops were posted to the key centres of the industry to protect capital investment from destruction. Manchester and Stockport, for example, only had disturbances on their outskirts. Eventually even smaller centres received troops in response to the threat of attack, as at Halsall near Ormskirk. When force arrived, the concessions stopped and arrests began. But in that first week of October the workers had the upper hand and the attacks on machinery were carried southward as far as Golborne, westward through Worsley to the villages to the south of Manchester and Stockport and northward by 11 October to the Blackburn area. The rioters claimed that their design was to destroy all works and engines at Manchester, Stockport and Macclesfield, make their way

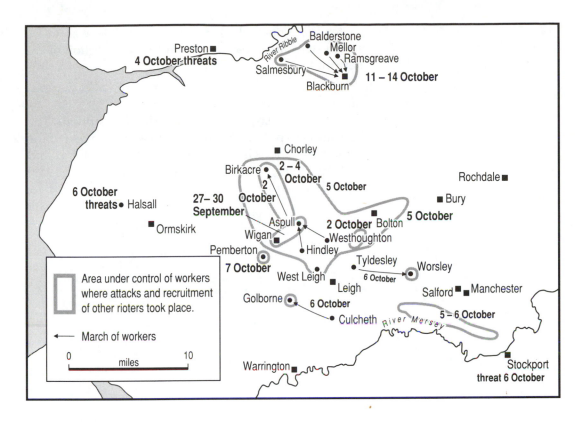

Figure 3.3
Disturbances over cotton
machinery Lancashire 1779.

Area of
main map

to Cromford and then on to destroy all the engines throughout England. Arkwright certainly figured large in the crowd's demonology. For example, the town of Preston was alarmed because it had his patent machines. The threatened march on Cromford, taken seriously by Arkwright and the Derbyshire authorities, reflected the spinners' view that, first, his firm was the centre of diffusion of the new machinery and that, secondly, his and Hargreaves' flight to Nottinghamshire in 1768 had only temporarily ended their troubles. This time accounts could be finally settled with Arkwright.

Parliament, petitioned at the end of the disturbances, gave strong support to the new 'patent' machines. The national interest came first. Since mechanisation was deemed the key to English supremacy in the international cotton trade, the hand spinners must adapt to new conditions. Yet this strident political economy, backed up by a continued and expanded military presence in the disturbed towns, was ameliorated in two ways. The petition of Arkwright and his partners for compensation for the damage caused by the rioters at Birkacre was rejected. Similarly, those convicted for the earlier Nottingham incidents, were given relatively light sentences. Nonetheless, the spinners' fate was to be sealed that same year by Crompton's perfection of his new mule.

Sources and further reading

For sources see sources referred to in map captions. The best study to put the protests in the wider context of the evolving relations in the cotton industry is still J. L. and B. Hammond, *The Skilled Labourer* (London, 1919) especially chapter 4.

4. Protests against machinery in the west of England woollen industry, 1776–1802

The woollen cloth industry in the West of England counties of Gloucestershire, Somerset and Wiltshire in the eighteenth century presents one of the best examples of the 'putting out' system, the form of large-scale manufacture most prevalent in the age before the factory. Dominated by large capitalists called 'gentlemen clothiers', production of cloth was sub-divided among specialised groups of skilled workers who were paid on a piece-work basis and worked either in their own homes or in small workshops. The gentlemen clothier bought the raw wool, sorted it and then had it carded and scribbled by adult male scribblers who were usually employed directly by him in his own shops. From this point on, however, while the gentlemen clothier retained ownership of the wool, it was put out to be spun, woven, fulled and dressed by spinners and weavers who worked in their own cottages and to fullers and cloth dressers or shearmen who worked for small craft masters in their workshops. While fullers and shearmen tended to be concentrated in or near the larger manufacturing towns, spinning and weaving was put out long distances. Indeed, the demand for spun yarn meant that some clothiers put out wool over a 20 or 40 mile radius. While many spinners were the wives of textile workers, the trade provided a very important by-employment for the wives of agricultural and general labourers across the region.

Such specialisation brought many advantages for the clothiers. It reduced the need for heavy fixed capital investment and meant that in depressions it was the workers who, owning their own tools of production, bore much of the cost. The sub-division of labour also enabled the West of England to produce cloths whose quality was unrivalled. However, clothiers found that it was impossible to regulate the speed of production when so much took place outside their immediate authority. Indeed, the woollen workers were notorious for their worship of 'St. Monday' and for working least when food was cheap. Equally, specialism gave rise to a strong sense of craft-consciousness and the male trades of scribbling, weaving and finishing were quick to react vigorously when any employer sought to undermine

Figure 4.1
Anti-machinery riots in Wiltshire and Somerset 1776–1823: spinning jennies, scribbling and carding engines and flying shuttles. The very considerable delay in introducing the spinning jenny, scribbling engine and flying shuttle into Wiltshire and Somerset reflected the very great hostility of the woollen workers to machines they believed threatened their livelihoods.

At Malmesbury, however, the flying shuttle was established in 1792 without overt conflict.

Source: A. J. Randall, *Before the Luddites* (Cambridge, 1991).

Area of
main map

piece rates, apprenticeship or custom. The woollen workers in Wiltshire were particularly jealous of their 'privileges' and independence and were prepared to use violent means to protect their interests as the extensive riots in 1726–7 and 1738 showed. These circumstances meant that, with the Industrial Revolution and the advent of machinery, the region was to experience major and protracted conflict.

The introduction of machinery into Wiltshire and Somerset proved to be particularly problematic, with riots, attacks on property, threatening letters and industrial conflict greeting almost every new piece of labour-saving innovation. Spinning jennies, scribbling and carding engines, flying shuttle looms, gig mills and shearing frames all provoked angry pre-emptive responses from the woollen workers and did much to delay the mechanisation of the industry. Clothiers were only too aware of the dangers they ran. Thus, for example, the first attempt to establish the spinning jenny in the region took place in 1776 in Shepton Mallet, a town which was declining as a textile centre. The clothiers were anxious to reduce animosity and agreed with the woollen workers that jennies would first be tested in public in the workhouse to ascertain its effects. While there was clearly scepticism, the Shepton Mallet weavers were prepared to give the machine a chance. The same, however, was not true for their colleagues in the neighbouring main woollen towns of Frome, Warminster and Westbury and on the night of 10 July 'a riotous mob' assembled, marched into Shepton Mallet, cleverly avoided dragoons who had been placed in the town in readiness for trouble, and smashed all the machines. They were attacking the house of one of the more prominent clothiers behind the experiment when dragoons arrived, the Riot Act was read and the troops opened fire. One man was killed and six wounded. The riot galvanised the clothiers of the region into a public campaign to convert their workers into acceptance of the jenny but to no avail. Petitions to Parliament seeking to have the machine abolished failed but hostility was not assuaged. An attempt to introduce the machine to Frome in June 1781 provoked extensive disturbances and it was not until the late 1780s that it was taken up in numbers in the main woollen-making districts.

Scribbling engines and carding engines which displaced the scribblers likewise encountered violent hostility. The first to be set up was in May 1791 in

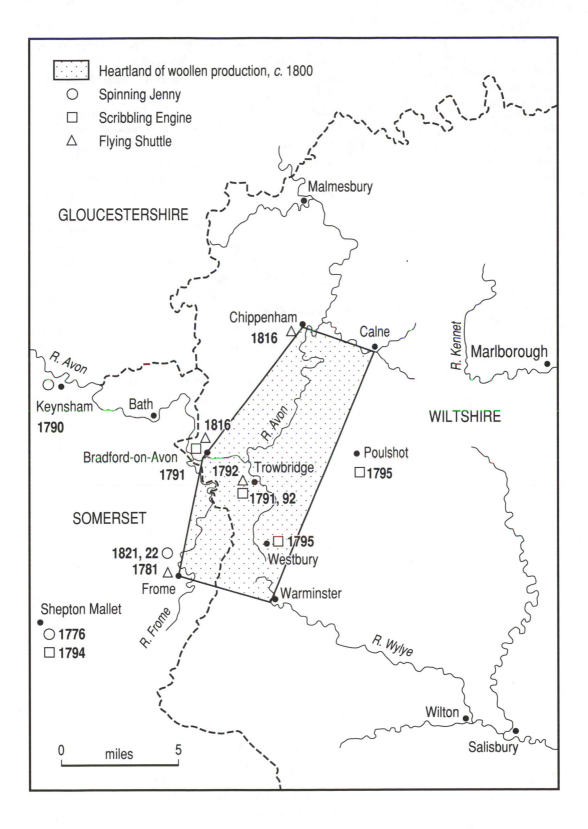

Legend:

- Heartland of woollen production, *c.* 1800
- ○ Spinning Jenny
- □ Scribbling Engine
- △ Flying Shuttle

GLOUCESTERSHIRE

Malmesbury

Chippenham
1816 △

Calne

R. Kennet

Marlborough

R. Avon

○ Keynsham
1790

Bath

WILTSHIRE

1816
△

Bradford-on-Avon
1791 □

1792 △
□ Trowbridge
1791, 92

Poulshot
□ **1795**

SOMERSET

1821, 22 ○
1781 △
Frome

□ **1795**
Westbury

Warminster

Shepton Mallet
○ **1776**
□ **1794**

R. Frome

R. Wylye

Wilton

Salisbury

0   miles   5

Figure 4.2
The introduction of finishing machinery into Wiltshire.
The earliest introductions at Horningsham (1767), Malmesbury (1792) and Twerton (1797) took place well away from the main woollen-manufacturing centres and fear of the shearmen's reprisals.
Source: A. J. Randall, *Before the Luddites* (Cambridge, 1991).

Bradford on Avon where a prominent clothier, Joseph Phelps, established one in his workshops in the centre of the town. A crowd of 500 gathered and demanded he take the machine down and make a public promise never to re-introduce it. Phelps refused to be intimidated and, when some of the crowd stoned his windows, fired shots into the crowd, killing three and mortally wounding two others. The crowd, outraged, continued their assault and Phelps' nerve broke. The machine was handed over, whereupon it was 'tried' and then ceremoniously burned on the town bridge. Attempts to reintroduce the engines in 1792 provoked further disturbances in Bradford on Avon and in Trowbridge and according to one report in 1795 they were still 'not allowed' there. In that year clothiers in Westbury tried to set them up. Again rioters smashed them and thoroughly intimidated the clothiers to the extent that no one could be taken up for their part in the disturbances. Westbury scribblers also threatened violence to John Anstie, a clothier who was setting up the machines in his Poulshot workshops some twelve miles away. Shepton Mallet clothiers needed troops to guard the machines they set up in that year from angry crowds. It was not until the end of the 1790s that scribbling engines were gradually introduced in numbers.

The flying shuttle loom encountered a parallel response. Invented in 1733, it was widely used in Lancashire from the 1760s onwards and spread into the Yorkshire woollen industry in the 1770s. Its major advantage was that it dispensed with the need for a second weaver on a broad loom. On its first establishment in Trowbridge in 1792, riots ensued and in 1803 a weaver employed by a Bradford on Avon clothier who had migrated to Malmesbury, far from the woollen districts, to establish their use in his factory, noted that 'Nobody else in Wiltshire uses them' as they were 'not allowed'. Attempts to introduce the loom led to riots in Chippenham in 1801 and few were established during the French wars. In 1816 riots greeted new attempts to introduce it in Bradford on Avon and Chippenham and as late as 1821–2 extensive riots took place in Frome when it was tried there.

Why did machinery evoke this sort of response? In part, of course, it was the labour-saving potential of the machine in question which triggered riot. But it was not simply this. In terms of mass redundancies, it was the spinning jenny which displaced most labour and hence women who suffered most from technological

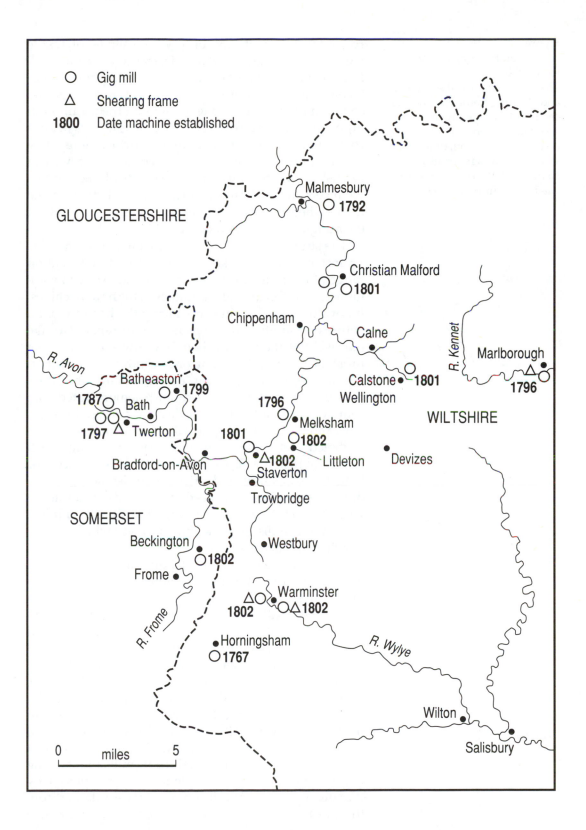

Figure 4.3
Attacks on finishing machinery in Wiltshire.
The introduction of the gig mill and shearing frame into the main centres of cloth production resulted in a series of disturbances, culminating in the Wiltshire Outrages of 1802.
Source: A. J. Randall, *Before the Luddites* (Cambridge, 1991).

Area of
main map

redundancy. But it was only where wives of textile workers were threatened that resistance was encountered. Rural labourers' families suffered just the same loss of income. Rural labourers, however, lacked the social cohesion or confidence engendered by the tradition of vigorous protest found in the woollen working communities and no resistance was forthcoming. Only one non-textile area saw violence and that was at Keynsham where miners' wives were displaced. Miners were certainly not afraid to riot but, distant from the towns where the innovators lived, their threats could not be brought to bear upon them.

The strong sense of community exhibited in the riots against machinery is shown by the wide occupation range of the rioters. It was not simply those who were immediately threatened who attacked the new machines. Innovators found themselves facing the hostility of an entire community. This is why few were prepared to take the risk. But the crowd, though a powerful agency of resistance, was a transient one. Clothiers found that introducing the machines in peripheral areas both put pressure upon the workforce and demonstrated that some workers at least might find advantages in them. For example, weavers gradually found that machine-scribbled and jenny-spun yarn made weaving much faster and their hostility to both machines dwindled. For long term hostility and effective resistance, a more organised response was needed. This was encountered when clothiers decided to introduce finishing machinery, namely gig mills and shearing frames, which would displace the shearmen.

The shearmen were the labour aristocrats of the woollen industry. Working together in small shops for master dressers, generally to be found in the main woollen towns, their skills and careful regulation of recruitment to their trade enabled them to form powerful combinations which in 1797 drew together with their counterparts in Yorkshire to form a single federal union, the Brief Institution. Highly organised though they were, faced with the threat of machinery, shearmen, like the scribblers, spinners and weavers, were well prepared to use force. This was well seen in the Wiltshire Outrages of 1802. While industrial action was employed against innovators who sought to introduce gig mills and shearing frames, this was often supplemented or replaced by threatening letters, attacks on property escalating from the destruction of dog kennels and rows of trees to

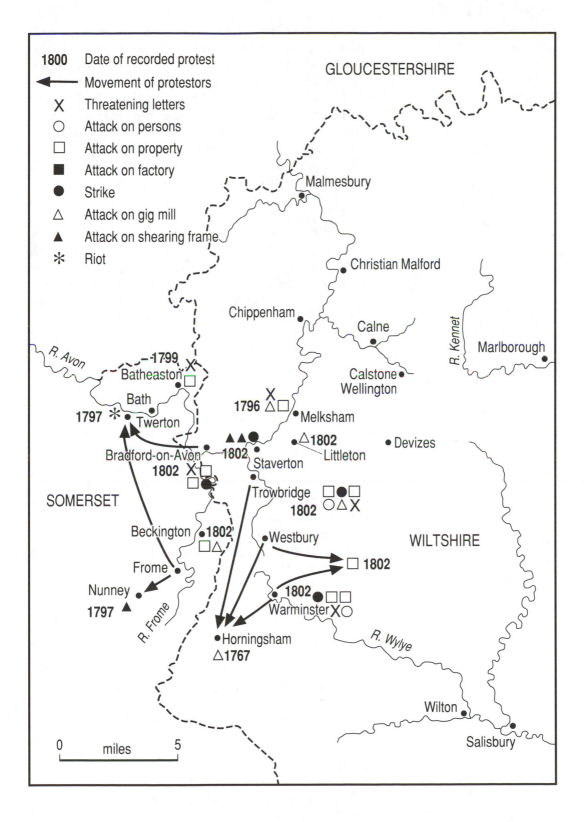

Protest against machinery in the west of England woollen industry, 1776–1802   29

outright assaults on mills, to arson and eventually even to attempted murder. Many of these attacks involved personnel from several of the main cloth dressing centres, indicating the coordination and control employed.

The Wiltshire Outrages brought to the fore the old regulatory legislation which had controlled the industry since the sixteenth century. Shearmen for example claimed that gig mills were proscribed by *5 and 6 Edward VI c 22* while weavers tried to prosecute clothiers who sought to concentrate weaving in shops under *2 and 3 Philip and Mary* and *Mary c 11*. Likewise, all the woollen trades appealed to the old Elizabethan apprenticeship legislation to protect their trades. Clothiers in the West, anxious to be rid of these legal impediments to progress, petitioned Parliament for their repeal in 1802 and Parliament obliged by suspending the legislation pending an enquiry. In fact two major enquiries were held, in 1803 and in 1806, which provide a detailed source of information on the industry at this crucial transitional period. Not until 1809 did Parliament decide. Then it chose to support the laissez-faire arguments of the innovators and, repealing most of the old legal framework which had for so long regulated the industry, forcibly precipitated the woollen industry into the new mechanised economy. This was a decision which had major significance for Luddism in Yorkshire in 1812.

The defeat before Parliament proved crucial for shearmen and, ultimately, weavers alike. But it is worth noting that even after 1809 clothiers in the West were slow to introduce finishing machinery, flying shuttle looms or loomshops. Fear of the violent response of their workers meant that gig mills and shearing frames began to be introduced in numbers only from 1816, flying shuttles from about the same time, while loomshops remained few even in 1830. Violence could not entirely stem the march of mechanisation but it provided many of the textile trades with a reprieve they would otherwise not have enjoyed. Paradoxically, however, the delay which gave these trades a prolonged life probably severely damaged the region's competitive position in the industry as a whole. Thus, while machinery was initially introduced in the West of England contemporaneously with that in Yorkshire, resistance in the West delayed its wholesale take up by up to twenty years on its northern rival. Thus the Yorkshire woollen industry continued to grow while that in the West had by 1826 ceased expansion and was commencing a slow but terminal decline.

Sources and further reading

J. de L. Mann, *The Cloth Industry in the West of England from 1640 to 1880* (Oxford, 1971).

A. J. Randall, *Before the Luddites: Custom, Community and Machinery in the English Woollen Industry, 1776–1809* (Cambridge, 1991).

5. The Luddite disturbances, 1811–12

Some of the most extensive and certainly the most famous industrial protests of the Industrial Revolution occurred in the Midlands and North of England in the years 1811–12. Beginning in Nottinghamshire, the 'Luddite' disturbances, drawing their name from the mythical Ned Ludd, spread into Yorkshire and across the Pennines into Lancashire.

The context of these disturbances was one of rapidly increasing food prices and of trade dislocated by the acute depression caused by the ill-judged 'Orders in Council' and by the short-lived war with the USA which they occasioned. But the motif of Luddism was hostility to machinery. In Nottinghamshire, Luddism was centred upon the hosiery industry where framework knitters, who worked in their own homes or in small shops upon rented frames, protested against wage cuts, the employment of 'illegal' apprentices and above all against wide frames and 'cut ups'. Whereas 'full wrought hose' was produced in the form of a tube on frames or stocking looms, some merchant hosiers recognised the advantage of producing stockings from widths of knitted cloth, woven, as was other cloth, as a sheet and then cut and sewn to shape. Cheaper and much less durable, the 'cut ups' and the wide frames that made them were resisted by the stockingers as debasing their trade and, they believed, as illegal under the ancient charter granted to the trade by Charles II which prohibited all engines that fabricate articles 'in a deceitful manner'. In Yorkshire Luddism centred upon the woollen industry and the cloth finishers, there called croppers, who found their trade threatened with destruction by the advent of gig mills and shearing frames. In Lancashire Luddism was much less clearly industrially centred, having significant inputs of both food rioting and popular radicalism, but at its core was the growing impoverishment of the cotton handloom weavers and the perceived threat to their trade from the new power looms.

The Luddite disturbances frightened the State far more than had any previous industrial protest. This was not only because of the geographical spread of Luddism but also because Luddism acquired a political, and perhaps even an insurrectionary, dimension. Historians continue to debate how far industrial and political grievances became intertwined in the years 1811–12 but it is clear that in all three regions the government and the political status quo was highly unpopular with those trades who made up the Luddite ranks. Framework knitters, croppers and weavers alike had experienced the consequence of the State's increasing absorption of the doctrines of *laissez faire* as their attempts to secure protection from innovating entrepreneurs were rebuffed. When the State flooded the north with troops to protect the property of those who were deemed by the local community to be riding roughshod over customary rights, this bitterness grew. In this climate, the radicals and the determined groups of revolutionaries who had planted the basis of a popular radical movement in the 1790s found fertile soil. While there is not space in this volume to do justice to the political dimensions of Luddism, we must beware assuming that those involved in the Luddite protests were narrowly 'industrial' in their outlook. Luddism continued to draw into question not merely the modernisation of various industries in the face of custom. It also focused attention on the whole character of the role of, and the accountability of the State.

Sources and further reading

For sources see the sources noted in the map captions. The foundation study is still J. and B. L. Hammond, *The Skilled Labourer* (see edition with introduction by Rule, London, 1979). The two major and contrasting recent accounts of Luddism are E. P. Thompson, *The Making Of the English Working Class* (Harmondsworth, 1968) and M. I. Thomis, *The Luddites* (Newton Abbot, 1970). J. R. Dinwiddy, 'Luddism and politics in the northern counties', *Social History*, 4, 1, 1979, offers a reinterpretation of the political aspects of Luddism which broadly sustains Thompson's case. A. J. Randall, *Before the Luddites* (Cambridge, 1991), examines the industrial and political background to Yorkshire Luddism.

5.1 Luddism in the Midlands

Luddism in Nottinghamshire has as distinctive a geography as its evolution. E.P. Thompson has noted the oscillation between Luddite activity and constitutionalist protest but the history of the protests is more complex than this. The disturbances in Nottinghamshire were marked by a number of phases.

The first phase took place in the opening months of 1811 when negotiations were held between a group of hosiers and their employees about wages. However, the resulting agreement, part of an ongoing process which went back at least to 1809, depended on the ability of the framework knitters to persuade the rest of the hosiers both to pay this newly agreed price and to discontinue the manufacture of cut-ups. Every time in the past, agreements had been made null and void by a minority of hosiers who would not abide by the agreed terms. When in turn the 1811 agreement was flouted, the framework knitters in the villages to the immediate northwest of Nottingham decided to take direct action against the recalcitrant hosiers. Their workshops were broken into and the jack-wires, a minor but essential part of the frame machinery, were removed and stored in the local churches. It was a simple task to refit the jackwires and no permanent damage was done to the frames. This type of coercion went on through February 1811 and into the first week of March but the undercutting hosiers held firm. Protest meetings began to be held by the framework knitters, culminating in a large demonstration of country workers in Nottingham market place on March 11th. They were dispersed by the military. No concessions, no offers of further agreements, were made to the men. The framework knitters, having failed to compel compliance, returned to their villages and that night escalated the violence by breaking at least sixty frames in Arnold. For several weeks this became a regular activity as the framework knitters sought out the frames of hosiers who had either not complied with the agreement or were known as bad employers. At the same time, Gravener Henson, a leading representative of the framework knitters, instigated legal proceedings against four of the rogue hosiers for illegal combination. The case was dismissed on a technicality. More military were brought in to the county, special constables were enrolled and two London police magistrates were sent to Nottingham.

A lull then followed with only a brief recurrence of frame breaking in July. In early November, however, frame breaking recommenced in earnest, initially in the district to the northwest of Nottingham, but thereafter major destruction occurred at Sutton-in-Ashfield, a centre of the trade to the north of Nottingham. Another pause followed in which the protestors waited to see if the hosiers would make concessions. This matched their methods in individual villages where offending hosiers were visited, given time to 'put their own house in order', failing which more of their frames were broken. Indeed, just as frame breaking recommenced and spread out from its original heartland, Derbyshire hosiers did make concessions to their men as did hosiers in a region from Nottingham westward to the Nottinghamshire-Derbyshire border.

Significantly, frame breaking now took place for the first time in Nottingham itself. The number of frames broken at any one time in the town was small but, given the level of surveillance there, these acts could be seen as both daring and as a pointed reminder to the hosiers that Luddism could take place at the very centre of the trade. Nottingham was not only the base of the major firms and the recognised meeting place between the two sides of the industry. It also accounted for well over a quarter of all of the frames in Nottinghamshire. By November 1811, that proportion had been inflated by the hosiers bringing country frames into the town for protection. A heavy capital investment was therefore located in Nottingham.

Response from the hosiers to these attacks was rapidly forthcoming. By 4 December negotiations between delegates representing the framework knitters and the hosiers had begun, initially under the auspices of the magistrates. These lasted through December and during this period there was a marked decrease in frame breaking. In this, the third, phase of the campaign, the hosiers had been brought to the bargaining table to negotiate for an agreement covering the whole trade. That agreement was published on 28 December. Average wages were raised by about 2 shillings a dozen, a rate which was to hold well into 1812.

However, some Nottingham workers remained dissatisfied, especially as a minority of hosiers again refused to accept the general agreement. Thus on 30 December, a fourth phase of the campaign began with a return to frame breaking. It was the immediate hinterland of Nottingham which was the main focus of the attacks. Two features characterised this phase. First, as before the pattern was one of an oscillation of frame breaking and then a respite to give recalcitrant hosiers an opportunity to come into line. Second, attacks were widened to include frames other than the wide frames used for 'cut-up' manufacture. Further concessions, however, were not forthcoming and another period of intense frame breaking followed in late January and early February 1812. The recalcitrant hosiers held out, which, given the level of troops now stationed in the region and the other protective measures adopted, was hardly surprising. The framework knitters had thus been unable to enforce the general agreement. Indeed, Felkin states that the rate of wages fell back.

The failure to secure their aims by coercion saw the framework knitters turn their attention to Parliament in an attempt to acquire legislation to regulate the abuses in the trade. Back in late November, the knitters had appealed to the hosiers for 'advice, aid, direction and support' on a similar approach to Parliament but the opening of negotiations in early December seems to have ended this initiative. Now the 'United Committee of Framework Knitters' turned to workers in the same trade in other regions to help coordinate their parliamentary campaign for regulation.

At the same time, however, the government was preparing a bill to make frame breaking punishable by death. Even though it was initially opposed by the Nottingham authorities, this bill made the chances of cooperation between hosiers and framework knitters increasingly difficult. The Act to make frame breaking a capital offence, passed in February, created an atmosphere of mistrust. In April an attempted assassination of a hosier took place and hosiers claimed that some of their numbers were too frightened to go to Parliament to state their case against the regulation of the trade. However, the great military camp which now stood just outside Nottingham and the new Act gave the hosiers confidence. They combined to oppose the parliamentary regulation of their trade. The framework knitters' bill failed.

There was a flurry of frame breaking activity in late November and December 1812, continuing throughout January 1813. In 1814 it recurred in Nottinghamshire but only as part of a lengthy strike. Finally, in 1816 frame breaking again reappeared, culminating in the notorious attack on the Heathcoat factory at Loughborough. In all

Figure 5.1.1
Luddite disturbances in Nottinghamshire and Derbyshire.
Sources: M. I. Thomis, *The Luddites* (Newton Abbot, 1970); F. O. Darvall, *Popular Disturbances and Public Order in Regency England* (London, 1934) chapters 4–6; W. Felkin, *A History of the Machine-wrought Hosiery and Lace Manufacturers* Cambridge, 1867); J. L. and B. Hammond, *The Skilled Labourer* (London, 1919).

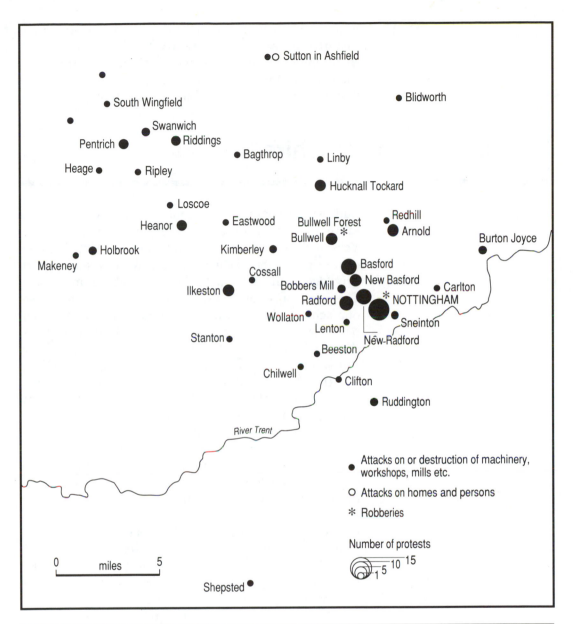

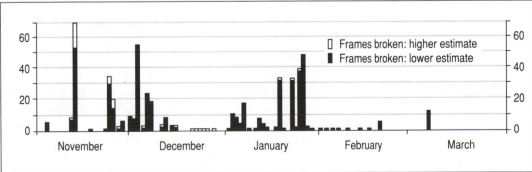

- Attacks on or destruction of machinery, workshops, mills etc.
- ○ Attacks on homes and persons
- ✱ Robberies

Number of protests

- Frames broken: higher estimate
- Frames broken: lower estimate

cases, the authorities acted quickly to suppress disturbances and check the spread. It also became clear that, while the frame breakers retained the support of their communities, frame breaking was a tactic that the majority of workers would no longer pursue.

5.2 Luddism in Yorkshire

Luddism in Yorkshire was centred in the woollen cloth industry and around the cloth dressers, known in Yorkshire as croppers. As with their West of England counterparts, the shearmen, they were a skilled and privileged elite with a tradition of labour militancy. Their grievances in 1811–12 sprang directly from the use of machines, the gig-mill and the shearing frame, which both they and their employers recognised would displace them. We have already recorded the struggle of the Wiltshire shearmen against such machines in 1802. It was the ultimate failure of that earlier campaign which brought matters to a head in Yorkshire. In 1809 Parliament had repealed all the old regulatory legislation governing the woollen industry, opening the way to those who wished to introduce cloth finishing machinery. At first entrepreneurs showed some reluctance to do this but, in the wake of the depressed trade that followed the Orders in Council crisis in 1811, some of the larger employers sought to install the new machinery in the hope of protecting or expanding their share of the market. This in turn put pressure upon all master dressers, who employed the bulk of the croppers, to follow suit or lose their trade. Increasing numbers began to introduce frames, though clearly with great trepidation. The Yorkshire croppers were a very powerful labour group and, other than around the Huddersfield district, had previously successfully defied all attempts by master dressers and merchants to introduce machinery. The stage was set for a major conflict.

At the point at which Nottinghamshire frame breaking began to reach its second peak in January 1812, the cloth workers of Leeds turned to direct action to protect their trade. On 15th January, a party of cloth workers, some with blackened faces and some armed with hammers or clubs, was surprised by the authorities on Leeds Bridge. Four days later an arson attack took place at a mill in the

Leeds environs. A lull followed but by the end of February the district around Huddersfield-Almondbury, where gig mills and shearing frames were most numerous, began to experience a series of nightly attacks on dressing shops. Organised groups, usually with faces blackened, would seek or force entry into the cropping shops and smash the hated machines. These attacks lasted until the end of March. As E. P. Thompson says, this campaign emerged 'already full grown, modelled upon the Nottingham discipline and tactics, but accompanied by a greater number of emphatic threatening letters' (Thompson, 1968, p. 609). Thus the form and tone of the campaign from the start differed decisively from that in Nottinghamshire. So did the response of the larger capitalists. From late February, merchants and manufacturers held meetings to coordinate their position. This was clearly stated in terms of the new political economy, denouncing the machine breakers and all who attempted 'to direct in this free state how capital shall be employed'. There was no attempt to negotiate as had been tried in Nottinghamshire. The innovators in the Yorkshire woollen industry believed they had through their Parliamentary campaigns of 1803 and 1806, already decisively won the right to direct the trade as they saw fit. Thus both parties conducted themselves in terms of threat and counter-threat.

In Yorkshire Luddism, industrial violence was increasingly coloured by political rhetoric. The tone of some of the croppers' leaflets was, as Thompson points out, 'very much more insurrectionary . . . than anything attributed to the Nottingham Luddites' (Thompson, 1968, p. 609). Radicalism of a Paineite hue had a much greater hold in the West Riding than in Nottinghamshire and central government certainly viewed the threat of political sedition with high alarm. As the conflict ran its course, these fears of political infiltration and of insurrectionary conspiracy grew more acute.

For a time, the threats and the frame breaking actions of the croppers appeared to bear fruit. Small manufacturers and master dressers began to destroy or to dismantle their frames rather than risk the croppers' wrath. Indeed, there is evidence to suggest that many master dressers were not displeased to see the apparent end of finishing machinery. However, some of the larger mill owners in the eastern districts were not so easily cowed and, as in Wiltshire in 1802, posted armed guards and began to turn their premises into small fortresses.

The croppers were faced with a difficult tactical choice. Through direct action they had succeeded in stemming the tide of machinery. The shearing frames in master dressers' workshops had, like the country frames in Nottinghamshire, proved easy targets. And many masters seemed willing to forego the use of machinery. However, while the large heavily fortified new mills continued to use their finishing machines, they would continue to put pressure upon all to follow suit or lose trade. The croppers believed that they had no choice other but to seek to close down their dressing activities too. Thus Yorkshire Luddism culminated in the massive night time attacks on Foster's mill at Horbury and on Cartwright's mill at Rawfolds near Liversedge. The attack on the first succeeded, that on the latter famously failed. For the first time, the Yorkshire Luddites encountered superior armed resistance and suffered their first real defeat.

With the reverse at Rawfolds, West Riding Luddism became more desperate. There can be no doubt that social relations came close to fracture. In spite of large offers of rewards, not a soul would impeach the mill's attackers. Arms were assembled and secret oaths and drilling increased. And, on April 27, Horsfall, owner of Otiwells mill and one of the most active opponents of the Luddites, was murdered on his way to his mill. A parallel attempt earlier on the life of Cartwright failed.

The murder of Horsfall marked the beginning of the end. While his assassins could not be identified for some time, the murder of a local employer, even one so widely hated, was not condoned by the working community and the heart went out of Luddite resistance. Their inability to coerce the large manufacturers in their fortress-like mills led Luddism in Yorkshire, as in Lancashire, towards a phase of renewed revolutionary plotting, arms raids and robberies.

Another factor in the decline of violence was the increasing presence of the military. Central and, to some degree, local government perceived a locality in almost open insurrection. Troops and militia were stationed in all the main centres with the deployment of special constables focused in a belt from Halifax to Wakefield. This not only formed a *cordon sanitaire* around what had been the main area of Luddite activity in the Huddersfield and Almondbury region but also put the weight of the State's preventative agencies in that part of the textile industry with the highest levels of fixed capital investment. These districts only suffered major

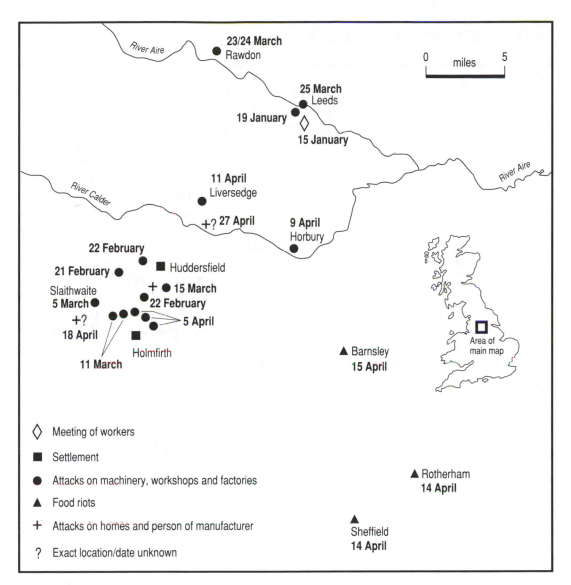

Figure 5.2.1
Luddite disturbances in Yorkshire.
Sources: M. I. Thomis, *The Luddites* (Newton Abbot, 1970); F. O. Darvall, *Popular Disturbances and Public Order in Regency England* (London, 1934) chapters 4–6; D. Gregory, *Regional Transformation and Industrial Revolution* (London, 1982) chapter 4; J. L. and B. Hammond, *The Skilled Labourer* (London, 1919); *Gentleman's Magazine*; *Annual Register*.

destruction in the early unguarded moments of the Yorkshire campaign. Ironically, by the time all this panoply of state repression was in place, Yorkshire Luddism was effectively over.

5.3 Lancashire Luddism

The third industrial region to experience Luddite disturbances in the years 1811–12 was the cotton industry of south east Lancashire and north east Cheshire. By 1812, illegal trade unionism was already strong in the cotton trades. Additionally, Lancashire had a longer radical political tradition than any other manufacturing county. Year by year the handloom weavers' fruitless agitation for a minimum wage had increasingly driven them in the direction of political agitation. As Thompson concludes 'when Luddism came to Lancashire it did not move into any vacuum. There were already, in Manchester and the larger centres, artisan unions, secret committees of the weavers and some old and new groups of Painite Radicals . . .' (Thompson, 1968, p. 651).

Stockport, a town that had seen the establishment of several steam-powered weaving factories, was the initial centre of Luddism in the region. During winter of 1811, there had been discussions at Stockport between weavers, manufacturers and magistrates concerning the level of wages and the effects of steam looms on employment but these had come to nothing. Failure to obtain redress of their grievances at local level led to two delegates from the weavers being sent to London to present their case to the Secretary of State. This too produced no satisfaction. By February 1812, rumours of impending attacks on weaving factories were circulating.

At the end of February/early March [the evidence as to date is not clear], two delegates from a secret committee at Stockport travelled to Bolton to attend a weavers' meeting there. It was agreed that the weavers must act themselves and Bolton weavers began to be sworn in to a secret organisation. A small secret committee was formed and nocturnal meetings took place on Bolton Moor. On 20 March, a warehouse owned by one of the first manufacturers to use steam looms was attacked in Stockport. Around the same time, Stockport delegates sought to establish another secret committee in the centre of the cotton industry at Manchester. This in turn led to the formation of a network of secret committees which by early April had spread throughout south east Lancashire and beyond.

On 5th April, a general meeting of delegates from towns in the Manchester region was held and it was

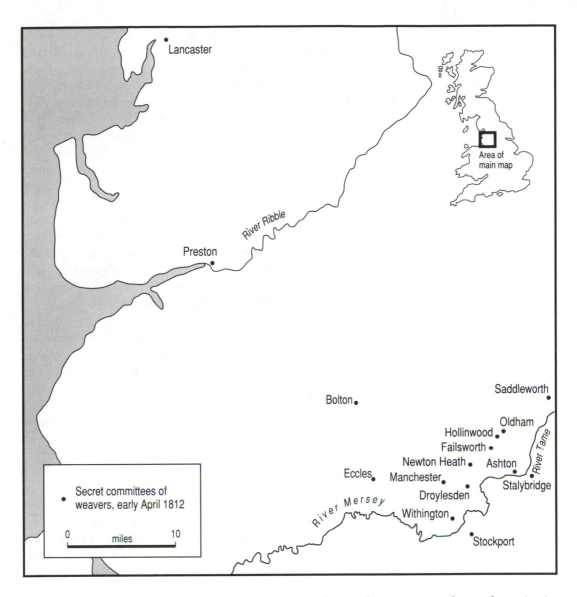

Figure 5.3.1
Secret committees of weavers in Lancashire and Cheshire 1812.
Source: E. P. Thompson, *The Making Of the English Working Class* (Penguin, 1968) p.618.

resolved to launch simultaneous attacks on factories in Bolton, Stockport and Manchester the following Thursday (9 April). This resolution was shortly after countermanded by a larger committee of representatives of the Manchester district.

However, that same week the Tory party in Manchester called a public meeting for April 8th at the Exchange Hall to send a congratulatory address to the Prince Regent for retaining his father's Ministers in office on his assumption of the Regency. Reformers sought to defeat the address. One of their handbills, headed 'Now or Never', with its complaints of rising prices, lack of employment and reduced wages and its call to action may well have struck a chord with the already-politicised weavers. Indeed, it was reported that the reformers even asked the Manchester weavers' secret committee to help them mobilise the opposition to the Tories. The Tories, realising that they had misjudged the popular mood, attempted to cancel the meeting but they were too late. Thousands of people gathered around the Exchange at the appointed time and, finding it locked, broke in and smashed windows and furniture whilst outside in St. Anne's Square an impromptu anti-Tory meeting of 3,000 people took place.

Thus, in the same week, plans to attack factories had been discussed, a crowd had vented their anger on that symbol of the cotton elite, the Exchange Hall, and the cause of reform received its most emphatic public endorsement yet in Manchester. Meanwhile, escalating food prices exacerbated social tensions.

Hopes that the cotton masters would be prepared to discuss wages and the effects of the steam looms on employment ebbed. With the cavalry patrolling the streets of Manchester at night, the industrialists made no moves to meet weavers' delegates. Thus, in the week of 13th April, workers took matters into their own hands. A series of protests swept through the region, combining protests over food prices with attacks on factories and on the homes of factory owners. Once more, the initiative came from the Stockport textile workers. On April 13th, Stockport spinners marched to Macclesfield, combined with colliers and carters from Bollington and Rainow, and, with the local workers, staged a food riot. They then went on to attack a factory and the house of a factory owner. On 14th April, the Stockport workers marched around their local area, led by two men dressed as women calling themselves 'General Ludd's wives', attacking looms and the houses of factory owners. The next day the crowd moved about the district obtaining money and provisions from houses they passed.

On April 15th, a food riot broke out Manchester. For the next five days similar protests occurred at different locations in the town, the worst outbreaks occurring on the 20th. These riots were followed by parties of the 'disaffected and disorderly' marching out into the country districts, demanding money and provisions. On April 20 and 21, major food riots occurred in the surrounding weaving towns. Led by 'General Ludd', riots broke out at Bredbury, Gee Cross and Stalybridge. Colliers and weavers from Ashton, Hollinwood and Saddleworth

Figure 5.3.2
Luddite disturbances in
Lancashire and Cheshire 1812.
Sources: M. I. Thomis, *The
Luddites* (Newton Abbot, 1970); J.
R. Dinwiddy, 'Luddism and
politics in the northern counties',
Social History, 4, 1, 1979; S. I.
Mitchell, 'Food shortages and
public order in Cheshire 1757–
1812' *Trans. Lancs. & Ches. Antiq.
Soc.,* 81, 1982; R. Glenn, *Urban
Workers in the Early Industrial
Revolution* (London, 1984); V. C.
Burton 'Popular Unrest in South-
east Lancashire and North-east
Cheshire during the Luddite
Period', Unpub. M.A. thesis,
University of Lancaster 1976; J. L.
and B. Hammond, *The Skilled
Labourer* (London, 1919);
*Gentleman's Magazine; Annual
Register.*

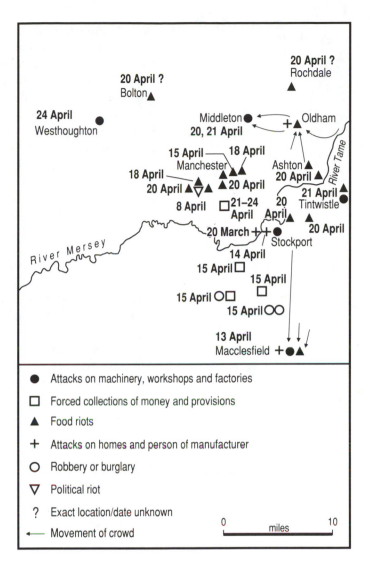

joined with Oldham workers and rioted over food,
proceeding thence to Middleton to attack a steam loom
factory. The attackers were beaten off but returned the
next day, having first tried unsuccessfully to seize arms
at Oldham. Outhouses and the house of the steam loom
factory owner's son were burned down. At Tintwistle on
April 21, food protests were combined with attacks on
textile machinery. The rioters' greatest coup, however,
was to come three days later when the large steam loom
factory at Westhaughton was destroyed by fire following
two previously unsuccessful attempts.

The Westhoughton incident marked the beginning of
the end of the industrial disturbances. The mill's
destruction had resulted from a misjudgement on the

part of the authorities. Better coordination of the forces of law and order thereafter made such attacks harder since, as in Yorkshire, the largest mills were now carefully protected and the military very much in evidence. Divisions arose in the secret committees centred on Manchester. Direct action had produced no concessions on wages or on power looms. During May, the emphasis switched back to petitioning and the practice of oath-taking came to a halt. The committee of trades was reassembled in Manchester and the attempt, shelved in March, to organise a petition for peace and parliamentary reform resumed. This activity continued into June with a series of meetings held openly in and around Manchester. While, at the same time, the revolutionary wing of the movement recommenced their activities with a spate of arms-stealing from private houses to the east of Manchester, by the late summer the 'moral force' element, which had always been the more widely supported, was clearly dominant as petitioning gained in momentum. In this respect, Lancashire Luddism saw the clearest emergence of a growing tendency for working people to look to political agitation as a means to alleviate their grievances.

6. The disturbances of 1826 in the manufacturing districts of the north of England *by David Walsh*

Throughout the spring and summer of 1826 there occurred a series of disputes centred on the textile districts of the North which included all the classic elements of nineteenth-century industrial disturbances. There were elements of Luddism, the battle for trade union recognition, reaction to the loss of worker independence, radical libertarianism, hostility to the Corn Laws, conflict over poor relief and a general and widespread hostility to the unremitting and unfeeling advance of the capitalist process of industrial production centred on the factory and rising theory of political economy.

The impact of the disputes was widespread. Even the financial heart of the nation felt the shock waves. For example, *The Times* reported on April 27 that; 'the City was thrown into much alarm by intelligence that the working classes at Blackburn and its neighbourhood had broken out into actual violence, and were committing their outrages with impunity.' The same source reported on Monday, May 1, that: 'Ministers were actively engaged Saturday and yesterday in devising measures for the restoration of tranquillity in Lancashire.' For a full Cabinet Council to sit on a Sunday in peace-time suggests that the officers of the State at the very highest level were extremely alarmed by the developments in the North.

The disputes appear to have been initiated by the handloom weavers of East Lancashire and came at time when the textile industry throughout the region was facing the worst slump since the end of the Napoleonic Wars. Of those working in the calico trade in Blackburn for example, out of a total workforce of 10,670, 2,807 were working full-time, 1,467 half-time and over 6,400 were unemployed. This massive recession has to set against a background in which the employers, apparently far from suffering with their workers, were embarking on some of the most expansive and costly projects of capital expansion seen thus far in the century. The power-looms which the weavers were destroying were not only a very real threat to their trade. They were also a symbolic one, in that employers seemed more concerned with machines than with people.

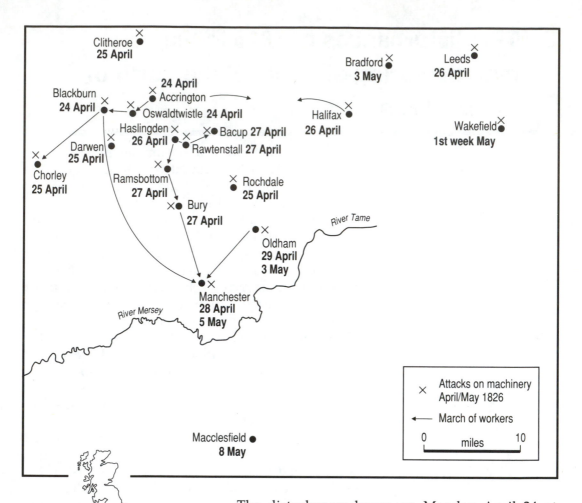

Figure 6.1
Machinery disturbances in Lancashire, Yorkshire and Cheshire 1826. For sources see the author's article 'The Lancashire "Rising" of 1826' *Albion* (forthcoming).

The disturbances began on Monday April 24 at Accrington. Early that morning, a meeting of weavers took place at Enfield, a place the *Annual Register* described, 'where the four roads leading to Blackburn, Burnley, Whalley and Haslingden meet'. During the previous week there had been skirmishes. On the Tuesday a coach carrying financiers from Manchester to view Syke's power-loom factory in Accrington had been stoned and it was this factory which was first to be attacked on the Monday morning. It was completely demolished. The crowd then moved on to weaving sheds which used the new looms. Factories at Wood Nook on the outskirts of Accrington, at Rough Hay and White Ash in Oswaldtwistle were systematically destroyed. They then marched on Blackburn. One contemporary in a letter described the scene thus. 'They marched 7 abreast, for about a mile long (many of whom were women) . . . at Park Place the military was completely beat off.' A report from Preston ran: 'The mob supposed to be about 10,000 had rather a terrific appearance as they marched through the streets, about 300 having pikes on their shoulders. Many said to the shopkeepers who were shutting up their shops: "never mind yer shops folk, we shallna meddle whe yo".' At Blackburn three mills were attacked. At Eccles's and Houghton's all the looms were destroyed, and at Fielden, Throp and Townley, the mills were entered but on finding no looms the building was left intact. On that first day in Blackburn, three people were killed and five seriously wounded. Ten thousand workers paraded the streets in triumph throughout the evening in defiance of a twice-read Riot Act, the town completely under their control.

The following day the disturbances spread dramatically. Groups moved east, north and south. At Chorley, a crowd from Blackburn destroyed Hilton's factory. An eye-witness described the scene. 'I saw the rioters at work, and the coolness and determination with which they destroyed everything was surprising. There was no appearance of haste, but on the contrary, the greatest serenity . . . there can be no doubt a great multitude of the townspeople were their friends. The women supplied the rioters with stones, concealing the missiles under their aprons.' That day mills were also attacked at Darwen and Clitheroe and the first sign of trouble occurred at Manchester. In the days following the disturbances moved to Haslingden, Rawtenstall, Ramsbottom, Bacup, Rochdale, Bury, Oldham and to the weaving communities in and around Manchester. In the first weeks of May, Macclesfield, in the far south of the region also witnessed machine breaking riots as did Wakefield in Yorkshire, while in that same county the factories of one Horsefall (a name synonymous with blood from the earlier outbreaks of Yorkshire Luddism) were attacked.

Later that summer the weavers' dispute erupted once more to include the spinners of East Lancashire, the strike holding firm until the onset of winter. The weavers' disputes were quelled by the authorities by the introduction into the region of a massive military force led by General Sir John Byng and by the arrest of suspected leaders. One local manufacturer, David Whitehead, recorded in his diary: 'In the morning the inhabitants were all an amazement, one telling another that such and such had been fetched out of bed in the dead of night . . . . It put such a terror upon the inhabitants . . . The rioters of Lancashire were so frightened that a-many of them durst not go to bed in their own houses. Some left the country; others hided them for weeks, some in one place and some in another, some in coal-pits . . . few, if anybody, would have thought they would have been guilty of such a crime.' (Diary of David Whitehead, n.d., p. 78).

There are two striking features regarding the disturbances of 1826. The first is the spread and sense of organisation of those involved. There is evidence of concerted action on the part of the weavers with groups moving across the region in a systematic way. Furthermore, widespread sympathy for the weavers of Lancashire manifested itself in the form of financial support from Liverpool, London, Bristol and even as far as Yeovil in Somerset. The second is the aspect of solidarity and sense of community displayed by working people at this time which cut across gender and trades. Taking a cross-section of those arrested at Blackburn, as well as handloom weavers there were power-loom weavers, spinners, a butcher, a farmer, a confectioner and several simply described as labourers. Of the 26 arrested at Blackburn six were women.

Sources and further reading
For sources see map caption. Further accounts of the protests can be found in J. L. and B. Hammond, *The Skilled Labourer* (London, 1919); *The Diary of David Whitehead* (n.d.) (typed manuscript, Rawtenstall Public Library); H. A. Turner, *Trade Union Growth, Structure and Policy; a Comparative Study of the Cotton Unions* (London, 1962); D. Bythell, *The Handloom Weavers* (Cambridge, 1969).

7. The General Strike of 1842

In the late summer of 1842, a great wave of strikes broke out in the industrial districts of midland and northern England. Within six weeks, strikes had spread to include fifteen English and Welsh counties and eight Scottish counties. More extensive than Luddism and more destructive than the Swing Riots of 1830, the strikes for a time in August 1842 seemed to pose a threat not only to capital and to property but also to the very security of the State as industrial grievances and political radicalism came together to create what many historians have seen as the first general strike.

The context of the strike lay in two related phenomena: a major depression of trade, one of the most severe downturns of the century, and the Chartist Movement. Since the publication of the People's Charter in 1838, Chartism had exercised a profound influence over the working people of the country, its demand for manhood suffrage proffering a clear solution to the ills of economic exploitation and political oppression. All Chartists recognised that petitioning alone was unlikely to persuade the ruling classes to surrender their command of the legislature by granting the Charter and, to this end, the first Chartist Convention, meeting in Birmingham in 1839, endorsed the policy of the so-called 'Ulterior Measures', a set of sanctions which the Chartists would implement should their demands be rejected. The most potent of these measures was to be the Grand National Holiday, a general strike which would last until the Charter was the law of the land. The first great wave of Chartism in 1839 foundered on the rock of governmental intransigence and repression and upon its own internal dissentions, and the strike call, half-heartedly made and then withdrawn in August, came to nothing. With hopes of a successful insurrection dashed by the Newport Rising's disastrous outcome in November 1839, the General Strike remained the only significant weapon Chartism had left in its armoury when in 1841 the movement revived. Nonetheless, the Chartist leadership remained wary of utilising a weapon it feared it could not control. The popular movement, determined that, after the great petition of 1842, there should be no more petitions, was of a more militant persuasion.

The disturbances of 1842 did not suddenly appear on

a landscape of industrial peace. In response to wage reductions and increasing unemployment, strikes had occurred from January onwards throughout Lancashire. Moreover, in the months prior to August, many trade unions in the Manchester region had become converted to the idea that their members' economic difficulties could be solved only by a political solution. They became an attractive recruiting ground for the Chartists. Thus the link between economic distress and political action was already forged before the summer of 1842.

Throughout the spring, Chartist agitation developed, often characterised by large Sunday camp meetings, and popular militancy increased. By May there was growing talk of 'a general rising among the people'. Unemployment meant that, by the end of May, large numbers of men were moving around the Lancashire-Yorkshire border demanding relief at country houses. Men were parading the streets of Burnley and a Chartist leader attempted to provoke a riot at Colne. On 12th June at a meeting on nearby Pendle Hill, William Beesley offered to lead the people if they were resolved on 'physical force.' The next day, Preston Chartists were said to be advocating the destruction of mills and factories in order that those so thrown out of employment would

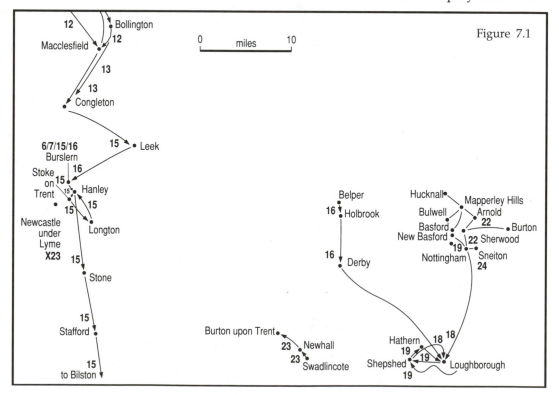

Figure 7.1

join them. Two days later a factory at Colne was destroyed by an arson attack.

This was not all. Hopes of significant modification to the Corn Laws had been rebuffed by Peel in February and the Anti-Corn Law League, a militant middle-class radical organisation dominated by Manchester cotton lords, had increased the tempo of its agitation. Peel's effigy had been burned at towns throughout south east Lancashire and meetings were held to begin a campaign to 'stop the supplies'. Warning that 'the country was on the eve of a revolution', the Anti-Corn Law League sought to create a sense of a political crisis, to which in July they added by orchestrating the mass signing of memorials to the House of Commons in which they combined the demand for Corn Law repeal with the threat of 'stopping all the mills' if this were not granted. There was, however, no love lost between the League and the Chartists, despite some unsuccessful attempts to present an united front against the government. It was the view of many Chartists that, if repeal brought cheaper food, their employers would use this as a pretext to cut wages.

The first serious industrial unrest occurred amongst the miners of the Potteries. Against a background of rising unemployment, short time working and wage reductions, miners from June onwards began to parade demanding money or food. On Monday, 11th July, a meeting of colliers in Hanley agreed to call out all the pits in North Staffordshire. A central Committee of Operative Colliers was set up and throughout the next fortnight colliers roamed the district in bands, 'turning out' their fellow miners. Support was also given by the potters. Then the turnout was extended northwards, being blocked only at Poynton, some thirty miles away, by troops. Delegates were also sent to Shropshire and to the Black Country where miners also went on strike. Troops were rushed in and this, combined with the impact of empty bellies, led to a general drift back to work. Nevertheless, a delegate meeting of Staffordshire, Shropshire and Cheshire miners was called by the Hanley miners for 31 July to consider calling a national delegate meeting of the miners of England and Wales. This was three months before the foundation of the Miners' Association in Yorkshire. Thus even before the workers of southeast Lancashire had set on course a general strike, the North Staffordshire miners' leaders had turned a local struggle into a national one.

Figures 7.1 and 7.2
The spread of the General Strike of 1842 in the North West and north Midlands.
Sources: A. G. Rose 'The Plug Riots of 1842 in Lancashire and Cheshire' Trans. *Lancs. & Ches. Antiq. Soc.*, 67, (1957); M. Jenkins *The General Strike of 1842* (London, 1980); R. Fyson 'The Crisis of 1842' in J. Epstein and D. Thompson (eds.) *The Chartist Experience* (London, 1982); F. C. Mather 'The General Strike of 1842' in R. Quinault and J. Stevenson (eds) *Popular Protest and Public Order* (London, 1974); D. Thompson *The Chartists* (London, 1984); The *Northern Star.*

As can be seen from the text the strike was a complex movement of marches, strikes and mass meetings with factories turning out to support the strike and being visited and revisited to make sure the strike held. A map cannot hope to catch this complexity completely. For clarity only the first marches in August in each area have been marked so that the spread of the strike can be discerned. Meetings have only been shown where no workers from other places marched into the particular settlement.

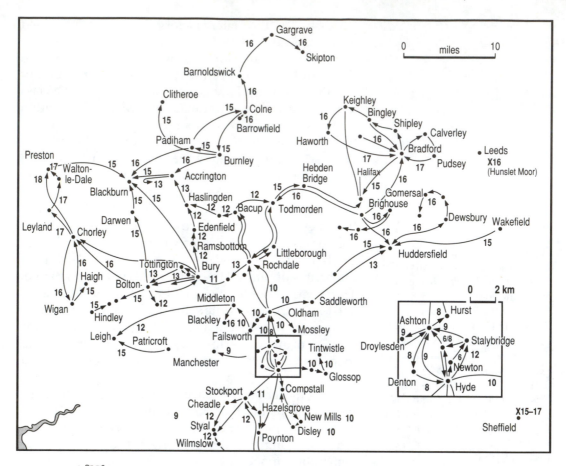

Figure 7.2
The spread of the General Strike
of 1842.
For sources see figure 7.1

The focus of unrest now shifted to southeast Lancashire. By early July, the first firms were beginning to give notice of wage reductions. These continued throughout the month. A meeting was called by weavers on 26 July at Ashton-under-Lyne to consider striking until they got 'a fair day's wage for a fair day's work'. At that meeting, local Chartist leaders spoke vigorously and resolutions were passed in favour of the Charter. Similar meetings were held at towns around Ashton during the next week, at each the wage demands and the demands for the Charter being linked. Strikes began and some employers restored the old rate. Bayley at Stalybridge refused, his workers turned out and then were supported by other turnouts in Dukinfield, Hyde and Newton. Local Chartist leaders then called for a general strike for the Charter at a large meeting on Mottram Moor on Sunday, 7th August. This meeting also resolved to march to Manchester on the Tuesday to stop all labour, visit the Exchange and teach 'the merchants how to give better prices for goods'. On the

Monday, men from Stalybridge marched to Dukinfield and Ashton, with one party going over to Denton and Hyde and the others to Oldham. Both marches ended with meetings which resolved to continue the strike for both fair wages and the Charter. The next day the march on Manchester took place. Mather suggests that, up till 12th August, the strikes and turnouts were largely non-political. This view may have come about partly because of what happened in Manchester. In negotiations with the authorities who met the crowds en route, their leaders talked only of their wish to turn out all the mills, to get bread and to see the masters at the Exchange - the meeting place of the region's cotton mill owners - over the wage reductions. Both sides were conscious of the forthcoming anniversary of Peterloo on August 16th and of the effects that openly provocative actions against the state on the part of the workers and against the strikers on the part of the authorities might have on subsequent events.

Over the next few days crowds of workers moved around the Manchester area, frequently skirmishing with the forces of law and order. Meanwhile, on 9th August, strikers, on their return to Ashton, Oldham and other towns, held meetings and decided to send delegates to spread the turnout throughout the large towns of Lancashire and Cheshire. In these counties and in Yorkshire and Staffordshire, this largely took the form of crowds of strikers marching to neighbouring towns where they drew the plugs from the factory boilers, thereby stopping all work. It was this tactic which christened the strikers 'plug dragoons' and the strike of 1842 the 'Plug Riots'.

On 12th August, two hundred trade delegates from the Manchester region and beyond met in Manchester and resolved to strike for the Charter. On the same day, delegates from Ashton arrived in Preston. The workers there declared a strike for both increased wages and the Charter. The 12th August strike call was responded to in West Yorkshire, Derbyshire, Nottinghamshire, Leicestershire and Staffordshire. In the Potteries on 15–16th August, the turnout became a riot of escalating destruction and looting in which a whole series of unpopular targets attacked. The leaders completely lost control of their followers and some of the attacks had overtones of a jacquerie. The troops at one point left the area to the mercy of the crowd. The depth of antagonism revealed by the 'Potteries Riots' may be due to the lengthy struggles by the colliers of the area. Coal miners formed a disproportionately high number of the arrested ringleaders. On the other hand, in the Chartist stronghold of Halifax, the second turnout on 15th August was led by women and accompanied by the singing of Chartist hymns and the One Hundreth Psalm. But even here, after strikers were arrested, a violent attack was launched on the soldiers who had carried out the arrests, an attack which was met by an equally violent response by the military.

Many more workers, both those already on strike and those not, throughout northern England and beyond waited on the meeting of the trade delegates' conference called for 15th August in Manchester. Here, out of 85 trades represented, 58 voted to go on strike until the Charter was the law of the land. This decision emphasised that it was the trades who provided the true leadership of strike. Outside their meeting place, crowds swarmed about, awaiting news, reflecting the strong community nature of the strike's support.

The Chartist national leadership meanwhile found itself trailing behind these events. The National Charter Association had failed to come out with a clear line and the Chartist National Convention which met, also in Manchester and on same day as the meeting of the trades' delegates, exhibited real reluctance to give the strike for the Charter a clear endorsement. Many feared that the strike would fail or lead to violence. O'Connor feared a plot by the Anti-Corn Law League. Indeed, after the failure of the strike he continued to assert that the 'Plug Plot' had been a deliberate snare to destroy the Chartists. However, with enthusiasm for the general strike spreading, the Convention found it had no choice but to endorse it and, on 17th August, it recommended that the strike be extended throughout the whole country.

The conversion of strikes from industrial to political aims had alarmed the government. The open endorsement of a general strike by the Chartists brought swift response. The meeting of trade delegates on 16 August in Manchester had already been broken up by magistrates. Now the government issued instructions to magistrates to suppress all such meetings in the disturbed areas. Arrests of many leading trade delegates and Chartist leaders quickly followed as the State acted with determination and speed to crush the strike. In such a changed atmosphere, troops began to attack peaceful meetings, as at the 'Battle of Mapperley Hills' on 20th

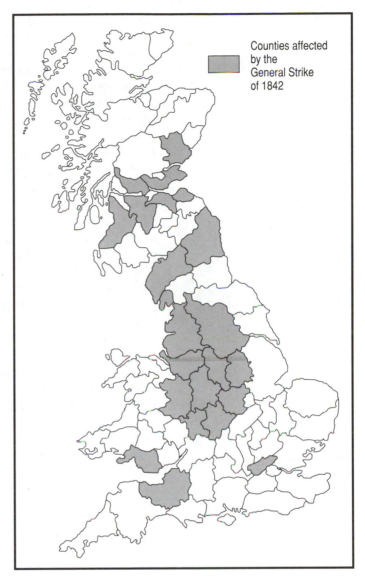

Figure 7.3
Counties affected by the General
Strike of 1842.

Counties affected
by the
General Strike
of 1842

August at Nottingham. The loss of their platform
deprived the Chartists of the means to maintain the
political momentum of the strike. Moreover, the overt
political nature of the strike also lost support for workers
amongst shopkeepers and tradespeople who had, not
entirely altruistically, lent their support to the stoppages
for increased wages.

Even so, the turnout continued to spread, northwards
to Lancaster, Carlisle and as far as Dundee as early as
16th August and eastward to Norwich, where Jacquard
weavers struck on 29th August. Ripples of the main
wave were felt in Glamorganshire and on Tyneside and
in the south even reached Chard in Somerset. But with

the centre of the general strike now the target of the state's repression, it was too late for these strikes to affect the course of events. By Tuesday 23rd August, the return to work in Manchester had become a flood, though the power loom weavers held out and did not give in until 26th September. The towns to the east and southeast of Manchester stood firm, but those to the west and north of Manchester witnessed the resumption of work in that last week of August. Inexorably the striking workers in south east Lancashire were forced back to work.

Throughout the strike, internal divisions threatened to undermine it. Divisions existed within the ranks of the Chartists, between the majority of the national leadership and many local leaders and supporters who sought to use peaceful methods for political agitation and who feared the use of the strike weapon for political purposes and those many rank and file Chartists who were quite prepared to use the turnouts to achieve the Charter. Divisions amongst the workforce also existed. The delegates to the Manchester trades conference were drawn disproportionately from certain industrial sectors with more than half coming from the skilled handicrafts and the mechanical or engineering trades. Divisions also occurred between different localities. In some places the strike was mainly a political action. In others it remained primarily a struggle for income.

For the men and women who took part in the strikes in order to achieve political reform, as Fyson concludes, 'it had been the point at which history failed to turn' (Fyson, 1982, p. 216). Chartism never again commanded such popular commitment. In the end the strike failed in both respects. On wages, the overwhelming majority went back at the old rate and some, like the Poynton colliers, even suffered a reduction.

Sources and further reading
For sources see the map caption. The best short account is F. C. Mather, 'The General Strike of 1842' in R. Quinault and J. Stevenson, (eds) *Popular Protest and Public Order* (London, 1974). Written with more verve is M. Jenkins, *The General Strike of 1842* (London, 1980). For the wider context see D. Thompson, *The Chartists* (London, 1984).

Section B: 1850–1900 *by Humphrey Southall*

Industrial protest: 1850–1900

The Industrial Revolution had supposedly transformed Britain and in the half-century from 1850 to 1900 the country became the 'workshop of the world': from her factories, shipyards and mines came the means of production, transport and energy which similarly transformed much of the rest of the world. The construction of heavy capital goods such as steamships or railway engines necessitated large industrial enterprises, and our notions of Victorian industry reflect this: Lowry-like matchstick men pouring out of the factory gates, workers' houses dwarfed by mill buildings, the pit-head or ships under construction. This is a striking contrast both with the eighteenth century, where the archetypal manufacturing workplace was either deep in the countryside or a room behind a shop, and with the late twentieth century when factories have been banished to industrial estates and town centres given over to shops and offices.

Raphael Samuel has anatomised the employment structure and nature of work in Britain in 1851. The largest single sector remained agriculture which had expanded in absolute size during the first half of the century and employed 1.5 million workers. Next came domestic service with over a million workers, overwhelmingly women. Third was construction (c. 700,000 workers), but here technology had changed little in centuries. Cotton employed about half a million workers and was of course the classic factory-based industry. However, another half million were employed in other branches of textiles where many still worked from home, and three-quarters of a million in clothing and footwear, which were entirely based at home or in small workshops. Woodworking (160,000 workers) and printing (80,000) were similarly un-mechanised and workshop-based.

This left three sectors where, together with cotton textiles, the Industrial Revolution had greatest impact. First was transport (450,000 workers), where the railways were a creation of the machine age and had a large workforce organised on military principles by former army officers. However, this sector also contained road transport and the docks, dominated throughout the period by small employers and casual employment. Second, in coal mining (400,000 workers) the need to drain, ventilate and keep dry ever-deeper pits required mechanisation and encouraged an increase in the size of pits. However, the work of the miner at the face had changed little, mechanised mining accounting for only 1.5 per cent of output even in 1901, and the isolation of the coalface from the manager's office meant that the workforce was controlled indirectly through piece-rates and small-scale sub-contractors. Third were engineering and the metal trades with 570,000 workers. This sector served a new global market for capital goods and large enterprises were common but, even here, handicraft methods survived. The new craft of engine-making borrowed many of its traditions from the far older craft of the millwright and highly-skilled fitters assembled steam engines by hand-filing rough metal castings. Ironfounding involved stirring hot metal by hand.

The years from 1850 to 1900 of course saw important changes. Some were in the direction of mechanisation and larger scale production. Wool textiles, carpet-making and some parts of the clothing industry moved into factories. New 'science-based' industries made their appearance in the shape of chemicals and electrical engineering. Machine tools replaced handicraft methods in engineering (see the case study of lock-outs in the industry). However, other sectors saw great increases in output without major changes in technology or the organisation of production. In coal mining, the growth of the workforce to almost a million in 1901 was proportionate to the rise in the tonnage produced. In clothing, demand from new working class consumers was met not from factories but by a shift from traditional tailoring to a highly developed division of labour based on small workshops and home-working, as found in the sweated trades of London's East End.

Above all, the period was marked by growth in the service sector and in consumer goods manufacture. According to calculations by Clive Lee, the British economy created upwards of 6 million new jobs between 1841 and 1911 and of these at least 52% were in services and construction. Many more were in manufacturing industries serving domestic consumers: paper, printing, and publishing; timber and furniture; clothing. If northern Britain was the workshop of the world, the south was perhaps the first consumer society and this was reflected in employment growth: of the new jobs created 1841–1911 in the south-east, 66 per cent were in services, and most of the rest in consumer goods. Commentators on modern Britain note the size of the service sector, which today comprises at least two-thirds of all employment in the UK, and speak of the eclipse of manufacturing. However, Britain arguably never was a predominantly manufacturing nation: if we include women workers and make some allowance for the tendency of

nineteenth-century census statistics to lump together those selling a product with those making it, by 1851 the country had already moved directly from an agricultural economy to one dominated by services.

Labour protest, and the records of labour protest, developed against this background. Farm workers were almost powerless both because they lived in isolated communities dominated in every sense by their employers, and because of a near-permanent labour surplus. Miners were almost as hard to organise, the isolation of the pits compounded by the rapid growth of the workforce which created communities consisting largely of in-comers with weak traditions of collective action. The majority of textile workers were women and children, repressed by their own men-folk as well as the employers. In the casual trades of the great cities, the work force was so fluid and barriers to entry so limited that any attempt to push up wages was easily defeated by blackleg labour — though the casual sector included groups such as the stevedores of the London docks with more specialised skills. This was a period when lock-outs were common and disputes frequently ended with the hiring of a replacement workforce.

Only the urban artisan trades enjoyed real bargaining power relative to their employers in mid nineteenth-century Britain. Most prominent among these trades were engineering, building and printing but they included a very wide range of crafts producing consumer goods in workshops. Their power came from their control over training and so over entry to the trade, and this could only be maintained through general acceptance of certain norms, in particular the need for and nature of apprenticeship, together with limitations on the number of apprentices per adult worker. A major goal of the artisan trades was to create and police a rigid divide between the unskilled and those who had served an apprenticeship. The sons of existing craftsmen often had preferential access to apprenticeships and the trades took on some features of self-perpetuating castes, a permanent upper class within the working classes. However, so long as employers operated on a small scale, failed to organise among themselves and generally accepted craft traditions, the workers had little need for formal organisation beyond the individual workshop. Consequently, both trade unions and industrial disputes were generally too small to attract much attention unless they became swept up in wider political movements. The Webbs spoke of the 'strike in detail', by which individual workers simply left their jobs one by one and moved away, but this is hard to distinguish from the normal operation of the labour market.

Larger-scale movements of workers, bringing with them the potential for more extensive collective action, might emerge for a number of reasons. Firstly, large multisite firms might have created correspondingly large unions or disputes, but such enterprises were very rare before 1900. Secondly, effective regional or national employers' organisations would create a need for matching workers' organisations, but the case study of lock-outs in engineering shows that the former only emerged in the late 1890s. In practice, larger and more formal organisations developed for two rather different sets of reasons.

In the artisan trades, local trade clubs first formed regional and national organisations to pool resources in support of action at the local level. The classic artisan unions such as the Amalgamated Engineers or the Friendly Society of Ironfounders placed great emphasis on 'friendly' provisions including unemployment benefit, sick pay and superannuation. These lessened the workers' dependence on their employers and increased a union's control over its members, since a blackleg would lose his pension entitlement. Local clubs first came together in the pre-1850 period in support of one type of benefit, the tramping pay by which craftsmen from one town received assistance as they travelled the country in search of work. The clubs issued membership tickets to prevent vagrant labourers passing themselves off as artisans. Subsequently the high mobility of artisans meant they wanted to retain their membership and benefit entitlements wherever they travelled, which led to the larger artisan unions expanding beyond Britain to America and the colonies.

Wider organisation also brought advantages in a localised dispute, the case study of the 1871 Nine Hours movement showing how the Newcastle engineers relied on their national union for funds and to prevent either strike-breakers being brought in or work in progress being moved elsewhere. However, these latter advantages would seem to have been insufficient by themselves to sustain national organisations, which throughout the period were largely limited to the geographically-mobile artisans. The failure of the National Agricultural Labourers' Union in the 1870s demonstrated that the artisan model of unionism, with its strong emphasis on welfare benefits, was impractical among low income groups. This episode also showed that the artisans provided strong financial support to the unskilled outside their own sector, while in the late 1860s artisan leaders such as Applegarth of the carpenters and joiners had been deeply involved in the Reform League's agitation for the extension of the franchise as well as in lobbying the government for changes in the laws affecting trade unions. Their notions of 'respectability' and their privileged position within the workforce separated the artisans from other groups but also made them if anything *more* politically active at the national level.

If the artisans unionised to focus their bargaining power within the labour market, drawing on their collective strength across the country, other groups organised so as to balance their economic weakness with their political strength *within particular localities*. This strength could be used in two ways. First, the case studies include many examples of processions and public meetings as means by which a whole community might be drawn into support of industrial action, creating an environment where strike-breakers became stigmatised outcasts. Mass action of this type also attracted financial support from sympathisers, essential to sustain strikers who lacked the artisans' financial reserves and networks, and also gained support in the press and in Parliament. This strategy was clearly effective in the short-run but employers were frequently able to claw back much of what they had conceded once public attention had moved elsewhere.

Second, the granting of the vote to working-class household heads in the towns in 1867 and in the countryside in 1884 provided a new potential focus for the exercise of political pressure. Much of the country remained dominated by traditional oligarchies but where a particular occupation formed much of the electorate, as on the coalfields and in many textile towns, organised workers could wrest control of a constituency. This might have been used in two ways, in search of broad social change or to press for specific reforms. From the late 1880s, socialist groups such as the Social Democratic Federation were playing a significant role in industrial protests such as the 1889 dock strike and the early May Day celebrations. However, the labour movement had far stronger links to the Liberal Party and in 1892 trade union support secured 11 'Lib-Lab' M.P.s, mostly in mining areas. Support for the governing party could be traded for specific trade union objectives: legislation on safety, hours

of work and so on. By 1900, the state was playing a new role in disputes as arbitrator, exemplified in the 1893 miners' lockout.

By the end of our period, therefore, the labour movement was founded on two very distinct traditions. On the one hand were the artisans, with a total of some 517,000 unionists in 1892 in the metal trades, building, clothing, printing and wood-working, 42 per cent of the total. Here solidarity was with other members of the same craft and national unions had emerged at an early date. However, these groups' control of the labour process was increasingly challenged by mechanisation and 'scientific management'. The engineers' lock-out of 1897–8 was a turning point and subsequently artisan unions gave less emphasis to craft exclusivity and more to political action. In the early twentieth century, the creation of National Insurance made union welfare benefits less important and the distinctive artisan tradition faded. On the other hand, the miners and textile workers had 383,000 members in all, 31 per cent of the total, and were generally organised into coalfield or county unions. The restricted geographical mobility of the workforce reduced the practical advantages of belonging to a national organisation and increased the strength of local loyalties. In the South Wales coalfield, this created problems even in bringing together miners from the different valleys: their solidarity was place-based and rooted in community, not craft.

Transport and other sectors accounted for some 335,000 unionists in 1892, 27 per cent of the total, among whom were the 'New Unions' of the unskilled. Numbers here had perhaps trebled since 1888 but individual unions remained small: Arch's National Agricultural Labourers' Union had 15,000 members, Tillett's dock labourers had 23,000 members and the largest 'New Union' was Thorne's National Union of Gas Workers and General

Labourers with 36,000 members. The major artisan unions, the engineers, the carpenters and the boilermakers were all larger than any of these. Weak organisation among unskilled urban workers, farm-workers and of course among women explains why even in 1901 only 2 million out of a workforce of over 16 million belonged to a trade union.

The case studies which follow inevitably select episodes which were well-documented in either the press or the records of major unions. This emphasises well-organised sectors such as engineering or, in the latter part of the period, mining, and also those disputes which became major political events. However, the typical worker was not unionised and worked in a small workshop or the casual trades. Lacking either the industrial strength of the artisans or the political power of the miners, substantial improvements for these workers came only in the twentieth century. These sometimes resulted from tighter labour markets but more often from the intervention of the state as legislator, as direct employer of labour and, once the Welfare State supplanted the Poor Law, as an alternative source of economic support for marginal groups on the fringes of the labour market. Events such as the 1888 matchgirls' strike and the 1889 dock strike *were* important, but more for their role in building a mass movement which secured these changes through political rather than industrial action.

The existence of a labour movement that was respectable but still largely extra-parliamentary meant that the late nineteenth century was a unique period when industrial disputes played a central role in political life. In this light, the Nine Hours movement of 1871 should be seen not simply as an industrial dispute over hours of work but rather as a demonstration of the artisan unions' strength, which led directly to action by farm labourers the following year. The 'revolt of the field' was in turn as much concerned with the extension of the franchise as with labourers' wages. The matchgirls' and the dockers' strikes were fought mainly through public opinion and were ended through outside intervention. In purely industrial terms, the 'great victories' of the unskilled were pyrrhic, the advances won being subsequently whittled away and the unions seldom retaining their memberships. By the end of the century, organised labour was increasingly turning away from industrial protest towards political organisation as a more effective way of achieving its goals. Meanwhile, the majority of strikes had more modest aims and were concentrated into particular industries and localities, as discussed in the next essay.

Sources and further reading

For the nature of work and the structure of the workforce, see R. Samuel, 'The workshop of the world: steam power and hand technology in mid-Victorian Britain', *History Workshop*, no. 3 (1977), pp. 6–72. For the importance of service-sector employment, see C. H. Lee, 'Regional growth and structural change in Victorian Britain', *Economic History Review*, 2nd ser., XXIV (1981), pp. 438–52. Statistics are taken from C. H. Lee, *British Regional Employment Statistics 1841–1971* (Cambridge, 1979) and from B. R. Mitchell and P. Deane, *Abstract of British Historical Statistics* (Cambridge, 1971).

The pioneering study of systems of industrial relations was S. and B. Webb, *Industrial Democracy* (London, 1897). For more recent accounts of the evolution from formal to informal systems, see A. Fox, *History and Heritage: the social origins of the British industrial relations system* (London, 1985).

The classic history of trade unions in this period was again by the Webbs: S. and B. Webb, *The History of Trade Unionism* (London, 1894). Although H. Clegg, A. Fox and A. F. Thompson, *A History of British Trade Unionism Since 1889: Vol. 1: 1889–1910* (Oxford, 1964) presents itself as a sequel to the Webbs, a substantial first chapter covers the pre-1889 period. Union membership figures for 1892 come from the *Sixth Report on Trade Unions* (BPP 1894 XCIV 55–), while estimates for 1888 appear in Clegg, Fox and Thompson, p.1.

The notion of locality- and craft-based solidarities is further developed in H.R. Southall, 'Towards a geography of unionisation: the spatial organisation and distribution of early British trade unions', *Transactions of the Institute of British Geographers* (1988), pp. 466–83, while the relationship between geographical mobility, trade union development and political activism is explored in H. R. Southall, 'The tramping artisan revisits: labour mobility and economic distress in early Victorian England', *Economic History Review*, 2nd ser., Vol. 44 (1991), pp. 272–96.

A fascinating cross-national and cross-industry comparative account of the relative importance given to industrial and political action is provided by G. Marks, *Unions in Politics: Britain, Germany and the United States in the nineteenth and early twentieth centuries* (Princeton, 1989). Several recent studies describe the involvement of trade unions with political movements in different periods. Margot Finn, *After Chartism: Class and nation in English radical politics, 1848–1874* (Cambridge, 1993) examines the links between the artisans and the reform movement in the 1860s. Eugenio Biagini, *Liberty, Retrenchment and Reform: Popular Liberalism in the age of Gladstone, 1860–1880* (Cambridge, 1992) emphasises the transformation of the Liberal Party from a parliamentary faction to a mass movement in which 'Lib-Lab' unionists such as Arch played an important role. Duncan Tanner, *Political Change and the Labour Party 1900–1918* (Cambridge, 1990) shows that the shift in union loyalties from the Liberals to Labour at the end of the period was tentative and based on pragmatic considerations rather than an ideological transformation.

8. The records of industrial protest

John Burnett, the first Labour Correspondent of the Board of Trade, began his *Report on the Strikes and Lock-Outs of 1888*, the first ever, with some comments on the recording of industrial disputes:

> It is indeed true that when a great strike or lock-out takes place embracing the whole of a large industry, or . . . an extensive district, public attention is aroused for a few days, and the newspapers of the country find it profitable to supply news . . . As a rule, however, even the largest labour fights are little more than a nine days' wonder . . . In the case of lesser disputes, where the interest aroused is comparatively local, they break out, run on for weeks . . . and no-one outside the locality is aware that they have taken place. . . . Hitherto in this country very little has been done to collect information as to these disputes . . . (p. 3)

This lack of systematic information has determined the approach taken by this Atlas. We have concentrated on the well-known, best-reported disputes which were often those with a strong political dimension. These are generally reasonable and desirable emphases, but they lead to an inevitable neglect of those strikes and lock-outs which formed part of the routine processes of industrial bargaining and labour market adjustment. Further, without some more comprehensive source, we can explore the chronologies and geographies of individual strikes but not of strikes as a whole.

As we move into the later nineteenth century, two new sources become available which *routinely* record strikes: the records of dispute benefits paid by individual large trade unions and the Board of Trade's strike register commenced by John Burnett. These permit us for the first time to consider the extent to which disputes were concentrated into particular periods and, crucially, localities, but three caveats should be noted. The first is that these records document not conflict between workers and employers, which of course took many forms, but rather the loss of time which resulted from certain types of conflict. Second, even as a count of strikes and lock-outs these sources are problematic: do they record all disputes or only a fraction and, if only a fraction, how representative of the whole? Third, once we can

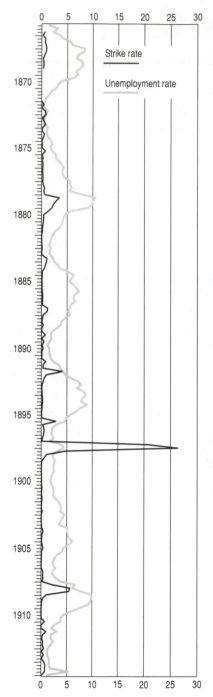

Figure 8.1
Numbers on strike pay in the Amalgamated Engineers, 1866–1914.

The graph plots the percentages of ASE members, less apprentices, in receipt of strike ('Contingent') and unemployment ('Donation') benefits, 1866–1914. These figures are totals for the union as a whole, including overseas branches. Numbers on Contingent were deducted from the Donation total in calculating the unemployment rate, as strikers usually received both benefits. Contingent benefit was suspended between August 1869 and October 1871.
Source: Amalgamated Society of Engineers, *Monthly Reports.*

systematically map the geography of strikes, we must be wary of easy claims that certain areas were 'strike-prone'. Certain industries organised their workforces in ways which made a large number of disputes inevitable and the geographical distribution of these industries will always explain much of the spatial distribution of strikes.

Trade unions had organised financial support for strikers from the earliest times, but unions only provide a useful source for the study of strike behaviour once well-defined benefit systems were operated over a series of years and a range of localities. Only large and well-organised unions could do this and they did not appear until after 1850. Even the largest, the Amalgamated Society of Engineers (ASE), was able to continuously operate a dispute or 'Contingent' benefit only from 1872 after a complex early history. Burnett's report on 1888 lists the expenditure on strike benefit of 39 unions. More details of the records of fourteen of these can be found in our *Guide to Trade Union Records*, but analysis here is limited to the ASE. This was the largest national union of the period and had the greatest expenditure in 1888. Unlike the major unions in mining and textiles, it provided national coverage and data for each branch was tabulated in its *Monthly Reports*. Lastly, as the following case studies show, it played a central role in many of the key disputes of the period.

Figure 8.1 plots numbers on benefit over time, while figure 8.2 maps the *average* pattern over the late nineteenth century. Little systematic pattern over time can be observed. Certainly, there is no evidence of disputes being concentrated into periods of high or low unemployment. However, despite this history of sporadic and apparently unrelated outbreaks, the geographical pattern over a period of years is remarkably consistent. Figure 8.2 includes the major lock-out of 1897–8 which significantly raises the average percentage on benefit but

Figure 8.2
Average percentage of A.S.E.
membership on dispute benefits,
1872–99.
The membership total excludes
superannuated and apprentice
members. These regional totals
were calculated from a very
large number of returns for
individual branches using data
from the January and July
Monthly Reports for each year.
The figures give the numbers in
receipt of Contingent and Full
Wages benefits on the last day of
the previous month.

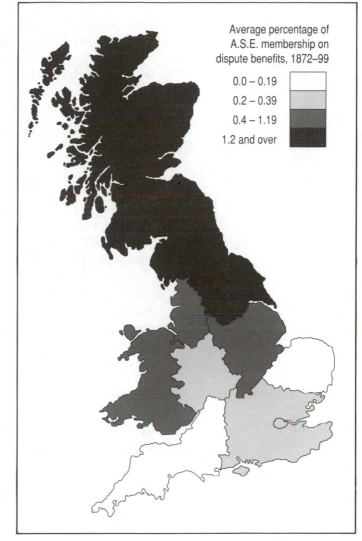

has little effect on the ranking of regions: for example, the average percentage for the North drops from 1.49 to 0.75 if 1897–9 is excluded, but it remains the top-ranked region.

These patterns are of considerable interest, the method of calculation meaning that they provide a reasonably accurate measure of the long-run average number of days lost and hence of the economic impact of strikes and of how this varied by region. However, they relate to a relatively narrow group of workers. It should also be noted that the ASE's strike pay was controlled by the national executive while branches or district committees could sometimes authorise payment of unemployment benefit to those involved in disputes. The ASE consisted of one type of worker — skilled engineers, particularly fitters and turners — but they worked in many diferent industries, and ASE members in southern England were more likely than those in the north to be involved in maintenance work rather than machine making, affecting the regional pattern.

Genuinely comprehensive strike data only become available from 1888. In 1886, the then-General Secretary of the ASE, John Burnett, was appointed Labour Correspondent with the principal mission of better aquainting the government with labour matters. One of his first jobs was to gather more accurate information on disputes and in early 1888 a questionnaire was sent out to employers and unions asking for details of disputes in 1887. This yielded only 32 reports of strikes and therefore a more elaborate system was implemented. Major newspapers from around the country were continuously monitored for reports of disputes which were noted in a register, and then questionnaires seeking information about each specific dispute sent to both employers and unions. The information sought covered both the factual outlines of a dispute and the parties' views on its cause, outcome, method of settlement and on what more might be done to prevent or settle disputes.

Consider, for example, one of the best known strikes of 1888. Entry 44 (p. 46) concerned 'Match girls' in 'London E.', the cause of the dispute being given as 'Employers desiring to obtain written statement controverting announcements in public press . . .' Settlement was described as being by 'conciliation' and the outcome as 'considerable concessions made by employers'. The questionnaires asked for beginning and end dates and for the numbers involved, categorised by skill, sex and age. In this case, the dispute is listed as beginning on 5th July 1888, ending on the 17th and with 1,200 women directly striking. A further 200 workmen (skilled and unskilled not distinguished) and 104 'young persons' were listed as being thrown out of work by the strike, leading to a total of 1,504 affected. Here we can make a direct comparison with our case study: the qualitative information is reasonably accurate, the dates are those of the walk-out and the return to work, but the number given as thrown out of work is misleading as it ignores homeworkers.

This was of course a very well-publicised dispute with an unusual cause. The report tabulates 509 strikes, of which 320 were for increased wages, 1888 being a year of reviving trade. The information gathered is of varying quality. Burnett sought information from both sides of each dispute and, where possible, commented on differences in their responses, but often received only one reply, or none. Some entries are based entirely on the original newspaper report and 156 entries lack information on numbers of strikers, although these are probably among the smaller disputes. Even the simple number of strikes is problematic: where several employers involved in the one dispute each sent in a response, they are usually listed separately. We can only guess at how many disputes were missed completely but in the ten years after 1893, when the office of the Labour Correspondent was expanded into the better-staffed Labour Department with a network of local correspondents, the average number of disputes per year was 724. Lock-outs were listed separately, but only five were reported involving a total of 985 workers.

We present a more extensive analysis of the post-1900 strike registers below, but the 1888 report was a worthy first attempt and deserves systematic analysis. No attempt has been made to analyse working days lost using the start and end dates, but figure 8.3 maps numbers of strikes on the left and numbers of workers affected by strikes on the right. The crude strike rates presented in the top pair of maps show a similar north-south divide to that seen for the ASE, but of course much of this reflects industrial structure. Strikes were reported from only fifteen of twenty-seven possible industrial sectors and over 90 per cent of strikes were in just six sectors. 184 strikes were in textiles and 137 were in mining, both sectors where piece work led to regular disputes. The graphs show rates adjusted for the size of each sector, the smaller shipbuilding industry emerging as the most strike-prone. Burnett commented, however, that the large number of disputes recorded for the cotton trade was partly a consequence of the thorough reporting of the *Cotton Factory Times*, while very large numbers of small disputes took place in clothing, printing and building without any press coverage.

The final pair of maps show rates adjusted to take account of the industrial structure of each region. This leads to a general reduction in rates, but northern regions remain markedly more strike-prone than those of the south. However, as with the ASE data, there may be marked regional variations in the nature of employment within particular sectors. For example, the construction of iron steamships in the great yards of the north led to

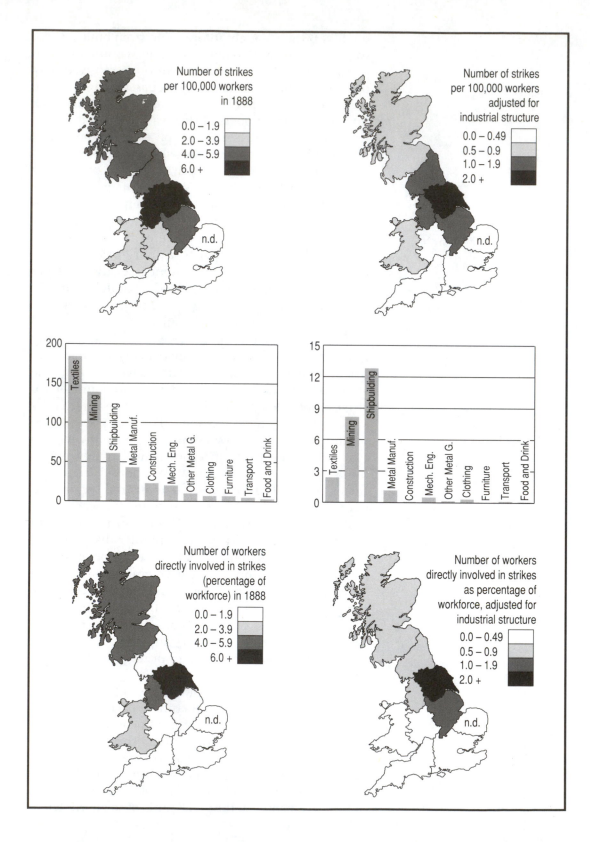

Number of strikes
per 100,000 workers
in 1888

0.0 – 1.9
2.0 – 3.9
4.0 – 5.9
6.0 +

n.d.

Number of strikes
per 100,000 workers
adjusted for
industrial structure

0.0 – 0.49
0.5 – 0.9
1.0 – 1.9
2.0 +

n.d.

Number of workers
directly involved in strikes
(percentage of
workforce) in 1888

0.0 – 1.9
2.0 – 3.9
4.0 – 5.9
6.0 +

n.d.

Number of workers
directly involved in strikes
as percentage of
workforce, adjusted for
industrial structure

0.0 – 0.49
0.5 – 0.9
1.0 – 1.9
2.0 +

n.d.

Figure 8.3
Strikes in 1888.
Source: Data for 508 strikes in
Great Britain and for 353 strikes
reporting 'general total of
persons affected' taken from
*Report on the Strikes and Lock-Outs
of 1888, by the Labour
Correspondent of the Board of
Trade*, BPP 1889 LXX, 703–.
Regional employment statistics
for 1888 estimated by linear
interpolation from 1881 and 1891
figures for 'total employment' in
C. H. Lee, *British regional
employment statistics 1841–1971*
(Cambridge, 1979); the regional
and sectoral classification of the
strike data follows Lee. The
method of adjusting regional
rates for industrial structure is
explained below; see p. 132.

quite different patterns of industrial relations to those operating in the surviving traditional yards of the south, and in general large scale factory-based methods were more likely to be found in the north. The different propensities to strike may therefore be a consequence of the resulting differences in the labour process, rather than some underlying cultural differences between north and south.

It will be clear that any attempt to identify systematic regional variations in strike-proneness for the pre-1900 period is fraught with difficulty and may well tell us more about the reporting system than about events in the labour market. Both analyses presented here, of the largest union in the country and of the first systematic government survey, point to a concentration of strike activity in northern Britain. This was clearly a consequence of the nature of these regions' economic development, but the degree to which industries and localities were associated makes attempts to distinguish the effect of one from the other ultimately futile: was mining strike-prone because the coalfields were entirely in the north and west, or was peripheral Britain strike-prone because mining and other strike-prone industries were overwhelmingly concentrated into these regions?

Sources and further reading
The strike pay statistics for the Amalgamated Engineers come from their *Monthly Reports* and were calculated using the large database of pre-1914 labour statistics assembled at Queen Mary and Westfield College as part of a research project funded by the Leverhulme Trust. More details of the database and of the records of strikes gathered by individual trade unions are given in H. R. Southall, D. M. Gilbert and C. Bryce, *Nineteenth Century Trade Union Records: an introduction and select guide* (Edinburgh, 1994).

The data on the strikes of 1888 come from the *Report on the Strikes and Lock-Outs of 1888, by the Labour Correspondent of the Board of Trade* (BPP 1889 LXX, 703–), which was the first in an annual series. The development of the Board of Trade Labour Department is described in Roger Davidson, *Whitehall and the Labour Problem in late-Victorian and Edwardian England* (London, 1985). The employment statistics and definitions of industrial sectors come from C. H. Lee, *British Regional Employment Statistics 1841–1971* (Cambridge, 1979).

9. Lock-outs and national bargaining in the engineering industry, 1852 and 1897–8

The two engineering lock-outs of 1852 and of 1897/8 are of importance in three ways. Both were very extensive and protracted disputes, among the largest of the period. Second, they symbolically marked the ascendancy of the artisan unions based on craft power and exclusivity. The 1852 lock-out advertised to the world the new national strength of the engineers' union which was to dominate the union movement until the twentieth century while their defeat in 1898, as much as the dock strike of 1889, paved the way for a new union movement, less concerned with the status of particular crafts and more concerned with achieving political change. Finally, the two disputes are even more important in the history of employers' organisations, and it is here that the greatest geographical interest lies.

Nineteenth-century employers had little need for formal industrial organisation: bargaining was strictly local, each town's major employers would associate informally and typically constituted a key element within the local oligarchy, and smaller employers followed their lead. The formation of the Amalgamated Society of Engineers in 1851, merging an older Lancashire-centred union with several London clubs, challenged this traditional system while carefully denying the political goals of the defeated Chartists. On 24th November the ASE demanded the ending of piece-work and systematic overtime across the country from 1st January 1852, expecting an easy victory.

The employers' resistance was initiated by John Platt, head of Hibbert and Platt's of Oldham, the largest engineering firm in Europe with nearly 1,500 workers. Platt, later the Liberal M.P. for Oldham, had clashed with the union in May 1851 on both the general issues of overtime and piece-work and two local demands, that labourers should not be allowed to work machine tools, and that a particularly obnoxious piece-master be dismissed. He had sought backing from other employers, but received only verbal support and was forced to make concessions. On 11th December he gathered the Lancashire employers at the Clarence Hotel, Manchester. This time, the union's concerted demands persuaded 34

'The document':

Declaration by the undersigned, on engagement in the employment of . . . .
I, A . . . . B . . . . do hereby honestly and in its simplest sense and plainest meaning declare that I am neither now, nor will, while in your employment, become a member of or contributor to, or otherwise belong to or support, any Trades' Union or Society, which, directly or indirectly, by its Rules, or in its meetings or transaction of its business, or by means of its officers or funds, takes cognisance of, professes to control, or interferes with the arrangements or regulations of this or any other manufacturing or trading establishment, the hours or terms of labour, the contracts or agreements of employers or employed, or the qualifications or period of service. I do also further declare, that I have no purpose or intention to call in question the right of any man to follow any honest calling in which he may desire to engage, or to make what arrangements, and engage what workmen he pleases, upon whatever terms they choose mutually to agree.

(Signed)

(Dated)

(Witnessed)

By demanding that their workers sign this statement, the employers hoped to destroy the Amalgamated Society.
(Source: Jefferys, 1945, pp. 40–41)

firms to form an association and to agree not only to lock-out their workers and subsequently to employ only non-unionists, but to pay forfeitable deposits to ensure they did not break ranks.

The Manchester Association of Employers then sent a deputation to London, and on December 24th persuaded the major London employers to join in their own association and to agree that both associations would organise lock-outs if workers in either centre struck. The employers appointed an agent, the lawyer Sidney Smith. He successfully presented their case in the media, emphasising the Oldham engineers' demand for the removal of labourers as if it were a general national demand by the ASE. *The Times* attacked the union as quasi-revolutionaries, while the engineers booed the Chartist leader Ernest Jones off stage rather than have his public support.

On 1st January unionists went to work normally but refused overtime. On 10th January the Lancashire and London employers closed their works, locking-out 3,500 ASE members, 1,500 other artisans and some 10,000 labourers. The union had to support both members and non-members, and their 'Trade Protection Fund' soon proved inadequate. £12,000 was raised from the membership by special levies, nearly £5,000 from other unions, and £4,000 from the general public. However, by mid-March lock-out pay was reduced from 15 to 10 shillings per week, on 24th March the ASE Executive agreed to reduce their demands, and on 4th April to abandon them. By then, the issue was the union's survival. On January 24th the employers announced they would reopen their works on 1st February but only to men who signed a 'declaration' abstaining from union membership, reproduced here. Thereafter men drifted back to work and the Executive conceded defeat on April 29th. Many unionists emigrated rather than sign the 'document', resulting in new branches in Canada and Australia. However, the majority signed while secretly remaining members.

The results of the 1852 lock-out are surprising. Despite its clear defeat, the ASE had demonstrated its financial strength and learnt the importance of limiting future disputes to one region at a time, as in 1871. Membership dropped during 1852, from 11,829 to 9,737, but then doubled by 1860. Conversely, nothing more was heard of the employers' organisation and the 'declaration' was quietly forgotten — although the ASE remained weak in

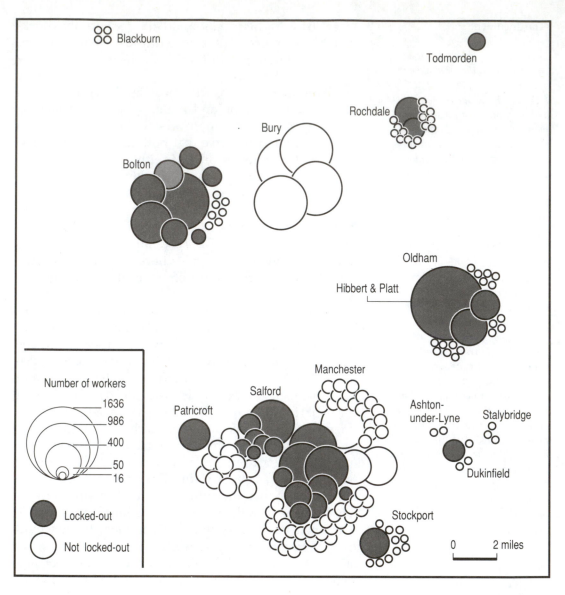

Blackburn

Todmorden

Rochdale

Bury

Bolton

Oldham

Hibbert & Platt

Manchester

Salford

Ashton-
under-Lyne

Stalybridge

Patricroft

Dukinfield

Number of workers

1636
986
400
50
16

Locked-out

Not locked-out

Stockport

0   2 miles

Area of
main map

Figure 9.1

Manchester-area firms participating in the 1852 lock-out.
The names of engineering employers joining the lock-out in
each town were listed in *The Times* of 14th January 1852, with
numbers locked-out for each, and the paper also listed the
names of non-participating employers in Manchester and
Salford with the total number they employed in each town. The
Northern Star of 17th January reprinted this information and
added the names of non-participating firms in other towns. This
map plots this information, dividing the totals for non-
participating firms in Manchester, Salford and Bury between
the named employers. The average size of non-participating
firms elsewhere was estimated by deducting the 34
participating firms with stated numbers locked-out and their

10,348 workers from the 287 employers and 14,298 workers listed by the 1851 census for engine and machine making in Lancashire and Cheshire: this implies an average of 16 workers in the remaining firms. Obviously, some of the non-participating firms will have been larger than this but the newspaper reports name 152 firms, over half of all firms in the north-west, and their size distribution must have resembled that of the industry as a whole: according to the census, over three-quarters of north-western engineering employers had under twenty workers. Equally clearly, the small number of employers in the lock-out were the largest firms in the industry and probably the most advanced technologically: nine of them had 300 or more workers, when the census claimed there were only ten firms of this size in the region. Overall, the locked-out firms employed more than half the engineering workers in the affected towns.

Oldham for many years. The lock-out was a dispute ahead of its time: the engineers' true strength lay in their control of the industry's technical base and no attack on their union could change this, even within the large and technologically-advanced firms which initiated the lock-out.

In 1872 the Iron Trades Employers' Association (ITEA) was created with Sidney Smith as its Financial Secretary and *eminence grise*, but Belfast, Glasgow and the north-east stayed outside, the Tyneside employers admitting they 'were still disunited as a district and had no prospect of being able to join the national association' (Wigham, 1973, p.12). By 1895 the ITEA had members in seventeen towns, mostly inland. It had no bargaining role, helping employers in disputes financially, supplying strike-breakers and black-listing strikers. In 1895 two other employers' organisations, one in the north-east and the other linking Belfast and Clydeside, agreed to a joint response to demands from the ASE and this led to the Employers' Federation of Engineering Associations being formed in April 1896, linking these centres of marine engineering with their generally larger employers.

The mid-1890s saw growing friction over the use of machinery and semi-skilled workers. In August 1896 the new Federation threatened a 'national' lock-out in response to a strike on Clydeside over a non-unionist working a lathe, and in February 1897 a series of similar incidents led to the first ever national conference between the union and the employers. This ended inconclusively and a trial of strength was clearly imminent. At this time the Manchester employers transferred their allegiance from the ITEA to the Federation, and on May 20th a joint deputation from the ITEA and the London employers sought the Federation's support in resisting union demands in London for an eight-hour day: thus the employers across the country were finally united. In June the Federation rejected the reduction in hours. The London unionists consequently decided to strike. The employers responded by threatening to dismiss 25 per cent of their entire workforces and the ASE in turn instructed that the remaining 75 per cent should then give notice. This concerted response by the employers led to a London-based dispute rapidly spreading across the country and acquiring a quite different geographical focus.

On July 3rd, work ceased at three London firms. By mid-July, 250 firms had joined the lock-out, affecting

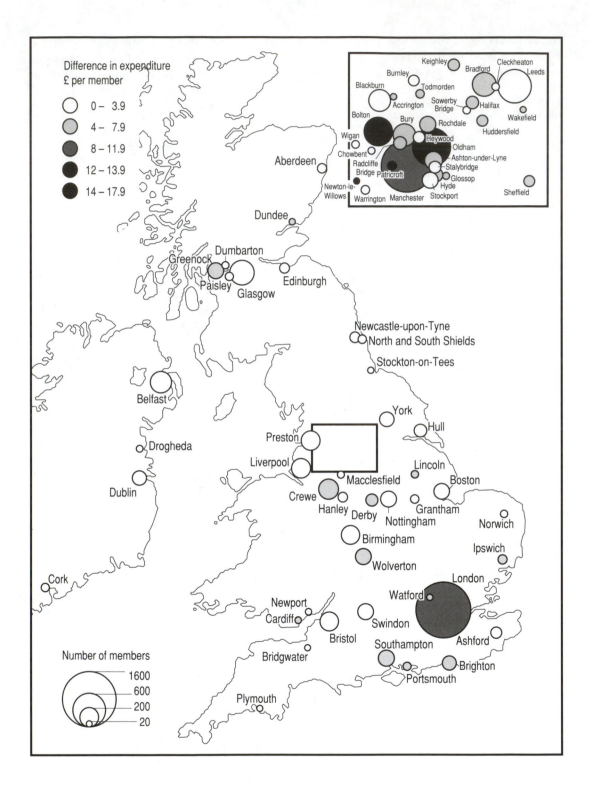

Difference in expenditure
£ per member

- ◯ 0 – 3.9
- ◔ 4 – 7.9
- ◒ 8 – 11.9
- ● 12 – 13.9
- ● 14 – 17.9

Keighley
Bradford
Cleckheaton
Leeds
Burnley
Todmorden
Blackburn
Accrington
Sowerby Bridge
Halifax
Wakefield
Bolton
Bury
Rochdale
Huddersfield
Wigan
Heywood
Oldham
Chowbent
Ashton-under-Lyne
Radcliffe Bridge
Stalybridge
Patricroft
Glossop
Newton-le-Willows
Hyde
Sheffield
Warrington
Manchester
Stockport

Aberdeen

Dundee

Dumbarton
Greenock
Edinburgh
Paisley
Glasgow

Newcastle-upon-Tyne
North and South Shields

Stockton-on-Tees

Belfast

York
Hull

Drogheda

Preston
Liverpool
Lincoln
Boston
Dublin
Macclesfield
Crewe
Grantham
Hanley
Derby
Norwich
Nottingham
Cork
Birmingham
Ipswich
Wolverton

London
Watford
Newport
Cardiff
Swindon
Ashford
Bristol
Southampton
Bridgwater
Brighton
Portsmouth

Plymouth

Number of members

- 1600
- 600
- 200
- 20

Figure 9.2
The wider impact of the lock-out is much harder to plot, the ASE's *Monthly Report* suspending publication for the months involved. Their *Half-Yearly Report* for January to June 1852 listed the total expenditure of each branch, and the impact of the lock-out was estimated by calculating the extra spent per member when compared with the equivalent data for the second half of the year. To this was added the direct expenditure of the special Finance Committees established in London, Manchester, Oldham, Bolton and Leeds (i.e. excluding the money they passed on to one another, the branches and the General Office). The expenditure is stated *per member*, but was not necessarily on the membership as it includes payments to striking non-members and for deputations, public meetings, 'posting placards' and so on. The result is inevitably approximate and probably little significance can be given to the difference between the two lowest bands. However, it broadly confirms the statement of William Allan, the ASE's General Secretary, to the Royal Commission on Trade Unions in 1867 that the lock-out 'was confined to London, Manchester, Liverpool, Bolton, Bury, and Oldham' (*Fourth Report*, p.64). The *Northern Star* of 17th January 1852 reported the lock-out in London as being limited to fourteen firms employing in total over 3,500 workers — as in Manchester, these were generally the largest firms.

about 25,000 workers, including 16,944 from the ASE. By mid-September, 34,000 were directly involved and the dispute became increasingly concerned with control of working practices. Negotiations led by the Board of Trade culminated in a conference between the two sides at the end of November. The employers' central principle was that they should be free to introduce into all workshops any condition which had previously been accepted by unionists somewhere in the country: levelling down rather than levelling up. The demand for an eight hour day was rejected. These terms were twice rejected by the workers during December, but a third ballot voted decisively to return to work on January 31st 1898, after seven months. The dispute's size meant that it took nearly six months for all involved to resume work. The Board of Trade estimated that a total of 6,849,000 working days were lost due to the strike.

Standard accounts emphasise that the dispute was national not local, but figure 9.3 shows that at its peak under 30 per cent of the ASE's membership were involved, and figure 9.4 that its main focus was in the north despite it having begun in London. Figure 9.5 shows that within the Northern region the lock-out was clearly concentrated in the big engineering firms around Newcastle, with many of the shipbuilding centres such as Jarrow little affected. The most affected areas were those where the Federation was strongest, and this geography indicates the degree to which they had redefined the central issue, from hours of work to control of the labour process.

The dispute was a defeat for the unions and particularly for the Amalgamated Society, to which four-fifths of the workers involved belonged. In June 1897 the union's funds stood at £361,140, but by March 1898 these had dropped to £134,000 despite income of £115,872 as donations from other unions and sources such as concerts and football matches. This was partly because the employers were able to widen the dispute geographically and so increase the drain on the union's funds, but also because the employers were simply more determined than previously and accepted the loss of orders and profit inherent in a lengthy dispute during a period of economic expansion. The union was also weakened by a lack of public support — as compared to the dock strike, it was the employers' demand for 'the right to manage' which captured newspaper support — and its poor relations with other unions. One indirect consequence of the dispute was the ASE leaving the TUC.

Figure 9.3
The 1897–8 lock-out is more easily charted, as the number of ASE members receiving 'Contingent' or dispute benefit in each branch at the start of each month was listed in the union's *Monthly Report*. The graph plots the percentage of the national membership locked-out, and between May 1897 and March 1898 adds the percentages in London and in the English counties north of Lancashire and Yorkshire, which principally covers the membership on Tyneside. This makes it clear that the lock-out's greatest impact was in the north, and that this became more marked as the dispute progressed.

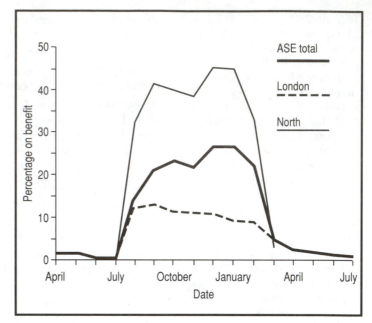

The central concern of craft unions like the ASE, and the source of their power, was the restriction of 'skilled' jobs to 'skilled' men, the former defined as much by tradition as by complexity, the latter as much by social origin as formal apprenticeship or other training since there was always a strong preference for the sons of existing artisans. This policy certainly pushed up wages and therefore benefited unionists at the expense of employers, but it also created a rigid divide between skilled men and the labourers who fetched and carried for them: once a labourer, always a labourer. Unsurprisingly, unionists from this tradition found more natural allies in the Liberal party than among the early socialists and had very mixed attitudes to the spread of unionism among the unskilled within their own sector.

By the 1890s, traditional notions of 'skill' were losing their meaning in engineering. The development of machine tools and the rise of the 'professional' middle class engineer meant the industry's technology was no longer embodied in the expertise of manual workers and was increasingly 'owned' by employers. Employers used this new mastery to create a new class of worker, the so-called 'semi-skilled', who worked the metal with machine tools set up by others and assembled the parts following blueprints from the office. Labourers, fitters and semi-skilled machinists all needed expertise as well as brute strength to do their work, but what distinguished the machinist was that their expertise was mostly specific to

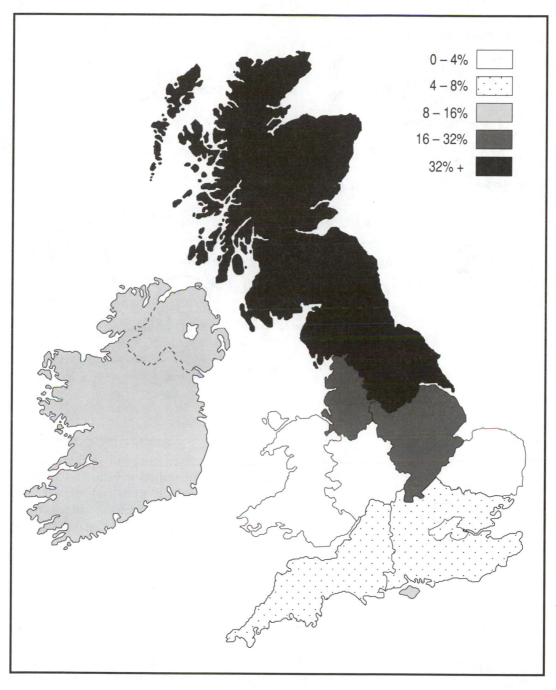

0 – 4%	
4 – 8%	
8 – 16%	
16 – 32%	
32% +	

Figure 9.4
ASE members on dispute pay by region at the height of the lock-out in December 1897. Calculated from the ASE's *Monthly Report*.

particular machines and blueprints, and so to a particular employer. The traditional artisan could always seek work elsewhere, but this independence was disappearing.

Until the 1890s, the union fought to keep these changes at bay but after 1898 it had to search for a new policy. In 1901, a new class of membership was created for machinists, although recruitment was slow and it was

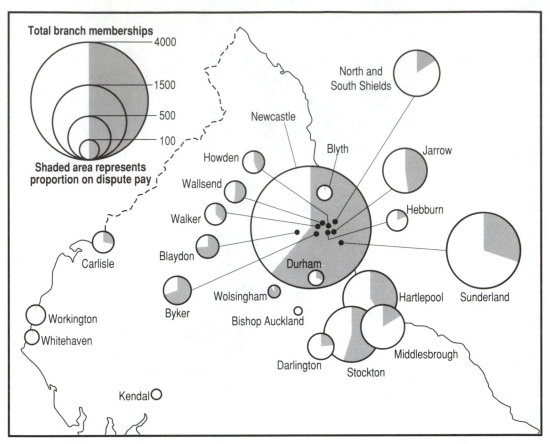

Figure 9.5
ASE members on dispute pay in
the North in December 1897.
Calculated from the ASE's
Monthly Report.

Area of
main map

not until the 1920s that numbers of semi-skilled workers in engineering exceeded the skilled. In industrial matters, the union maintained much of its aloofness and demarcation disputes remained common, such as those in the motor industry between the toolmakers of the Amalgamated Engineers and the production line workers of the Transport and General union. Other artisan unions, especially in building and printing, retained a pure craft basis far longer — there are obvious parallels between the 1897–8 lock-out and the Wapping dispute of 1986. However, the ten years following the 1897–8 lock-out saw the artisans losing much of their leadership role within the labour movement, a greater emphasis on a class- rather than craft-based solidarity, and a wider alliance between unionists and socialists. The emergence of employers' organisations such as the Engineering Employers' Federation as counterparts to the unions created a more clearly adversarial system of industrial relations. The alliance of factory owners and trade unionists within the Liberal party was no longer viable, and there are therefore close links between the industrial changes manifested in the 1897–8 lock-out and the political realignment of the early 20th century.

Sources and further reading
The standard history of the Amalgamated Engineers is James Jefferys' *The Story of the Engineers 1800–1945* (London, 1945) while Eric Wigham's *The Power to Manage: A History of the Engineering Employers' Federation* (London, 1973) was similarly commissioned by the employers. Engineering provides one of the case studies in Keith Burgess' *The Origins of British Industrial Relations* (London, 1975).

The most complete account of the 1852 lock-out is a pamphlet by the author of *Tom Brown's Schooldays*, Thomas Hughes, *Account of the lock-out of engineers, &c., 1851–2* (London, 1860). William Allan described the dispute to the Royal Commission on Trade Unions in 1867 (*First Report*, BPP 1867, volume 32). Set 58, volume 2, of the Francis Place collection contains newspaper clippings concerned with the strike. Keith Burgess, 'Technological change and the 1852 lock-out in the British engineering industry', *International Review of Social History*, vol. 14 (1969), pp. 215–236, mainly concerns the economic and technological background to the dispute.

The 1897–8 lock-out is documented in the Board of Trade's *Report on the Strikes and Lock-Outs of 1897, with Statistical Tables* (BPP 1898, volume 88, p. 423–) and the union's *Notes on the Engineering Trade Lock-Out 1897–8* (Amalgamated Society of Engineers, 1898), as well as in the union's *Monthly Reports*.

10. The nine-hours movement of 1871

Major disputes often become entangled with broader social issues, the right of workers to free association, the extension of the franchise and so on. However, if we exclude political strikes, the immediate origins of strictly *industrial* disputes must lie in some aspect of the bargain between employers and the employed — in this sense, strikes and lock-outs were an extension of collective bargaining by other means. In an evolving market-based economy, constant jostling between capital and labour was inevitable, as each group sought to take advantage of changes in labour supply or demand. However, this jostling was generally over the wage rate and other aspects of the employment bargain remained fixed over very long periods. Hours of work, fringe benefits, security of employment, matters of health and safety and so on have always been as much a matter for legislation as for bargaining.

The Nine Hours movement of 1871 is a relatively rare example of a successful attempt to redefine conditions of work through a purely industrial campaign, and provides a unique insight into the operation of Victorian labour markets. In a period when the setting of wages remained a matter for individual towns and often individual firms, what began as a conflict limited to the major engineering employers in the north-east of England became a bitter struggle indirectly involving the whole country and even foreign workers. However, once a settlement had been reached in the north-east, the new pattern of working rapidly spread to other regions and industrial sectors, and to smaller firms, through a remarkably rapid acceptance by both workers and employers that a systemic change had occurred. The latter stages of the Nine Hours movement were notable not for further strikes but for triumphal processions, as workers marched together to their factories to start work on the new basis.

The mid-Victorian period saw both rising real wages and an intensification of the labour process, reflecting greater mechanisation and scientific management techniques. Working days of ten hours or more were becoming unacceptable. Textile workers relied on community-based political action to secure the Ten Hours Act of 1847 which was limited to textile mills. In 1867, the Lancashire operatives resolved to agitate for an 'Eight

**The Nine Hours Movement
by a working engineer.**

*The Nine Hours' movement's on the move,
And spreading fast and a' that;
Nine hours a day and the same pay
Will be the thing for a' that.
For a' that and a' that,
It's coming fast for a' that,
When masters in a generous way,
Will yield the point for a' that.*

(First verse of a poem published by *The Beehive*, 11/11/1871, p. 5)

Hours Bill' and in 1872 established a Factory Acts Reform Association to achieve a fifty-four hour week. However, in the same period engineering workers and other skilled trades secured a nine-hour day and a fifty-four hour week by exploiting their control of the craft and their national organisation. There were moves towards a nine-hour day in the north-east in the mid-1860s and Tees-side engineers struck for it in 1866. However, the first yard to concede it went bankrupt and the campaign was defeated by the recession which began with the financial crisis of the summer of 1866.

By 1871, the recession was over and the economy of the north-east in particular was booming. Between 1851 and 1881, engineering employment in the region quadrupled and shipbuilding almost trebled in size. Labour shortages made it relatively easy for unions to establish wage increases. Figure 10.1 is taken from the study of the unemployment and wages which defined the well-known 'Phillips curve' trade-off. This relationship is usually considered as part of the dynamics of the economy as a whole, but the data used by Phillips for this period derive entirely from trade union reports: the unemployment statistics cover numbers on union benefit schemes, and mainly refer to the Amalgamated Society of Engineers (ASE), while the wage index is based on the 'standard rates' set down by skilled unions, principally in the metal trades and building. Wage increases were greatest in the north-eastern towns. For example, fitters' wages in Newcastle rose from 25s. per week in 1866 to 31s. in 1875, but dropped back to 28s. in 1880. London rates were a constant 36s. over this period.

Figure 10.1
Wage increases and unemployment, 1868–1879. This figure is reproduced from A.W. Phillips' classic article, 'The Relation between Unemployment and the Rate of Change of Money Wage Rates in the United Kingdom, 1861–1957', *Economica*, new series, Vol. 25 (1958), pp. 283–99. The derivation of the underlying data from trade union sources is further discussed in Humphrey Southall, 'Deconstructing the Phillips curve for pre-1914 Britain', forthcoming. The smooth curve is the relationship Phillips established using data for the entire period between 1861 and 1913. The sequence of data values shows wage increases accelerating as unemployment fell between 1868 and 1872, slowing down in the period of modest increases in unemployment between 1872 and 1875, and then wages being reduced as unemployment rates climbed towards the deep recession of 1879. Analysis of wage series for individual towns shows that these wage reductions were entirely concentrated into the industrial north.

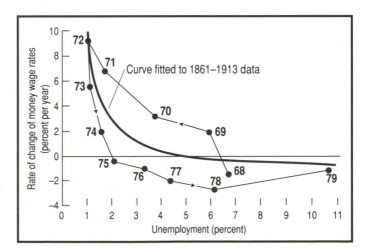

In late March 1871, the Sunderland engineers requested a reduction in hours from 59 to 54 per week. On 1st April they struck work. The Wearside employers were poorly organised and capitulated within a month, but meanwhile the Tyneside engineers had joined the campaign and established the 'Nine Hours League' on 29th April. Although many of the central figures were members of the ASE, including the League's principal spokesman John Burnett, the League was independent of the union. The League wrote to the Tyneside employers on 2nd May, but at a meeting on the 6th the masters agreed to reject the men's request. The master's resistance was led by Sir William Armstrong, whose factory at Elswick was the largest single employer, but Charles Palmer of Jarrow and G.R. Stephenson's stayed out of the dispute. Workers at one of the smaller firms then struck on the 15th and the remaining followers of the League followed them on the 27th, a total of 7,500 men at 12 firms including 2,700 at Armstrong's.

The north-east engineers' strike was a bitter war of attrition with both sides seeking outside support. The majority of strikers were non-unionists with no entitlement to strike pay and the ASE's Executive Council was initially very grudging in its support. It even censured the Oldham branch for holding a meeting in support of the Nine Hours movement. Some funds came from the miners' unions and the League began issuing strike pay on 6th June. On 11th July, they relieved 3,400 men but numbers dropped thereafter as strikers found other jobs. On 15th July, having turned down many similar requests, the ASE Executive finally agreed to circularise the branches for subscriptions in aid of the movement and in August they moved to re-establish a special strike pay fund. Support from union central funds was authorised fourteen weeks into the strike.

The masters were trying to send work elsewhere and bring in other workers. The ASE co-ordinated moves to stop work being transferred to Leeds and Sheffield. Finding black-legs with the necessary skills at a time of labour shortage was difficult, even paying premium wages. For example, 200 men were recruited in Dundee, but half failed to board ship for Tyneside and most of the remainder were persuaded to return home by the League. Some 1,000 workers were recruited abroad, notably Belgium. On August 8th Burnett visited London and the ASE Executive agreed to pay Cohn, the Danish secretary of the First International, to travel to Belgium to thwart this recruiting. Cohn returned from Belgium on 2nd September, having been expelled by the authorities, and was then sent to Newcastle to persuade the foreign workmen to return home. Although not encouraged by the League leaders, there was considerable harassment of the strike breakers and a large group were eventually billeted on Armstrong's Elswick site. The League responded with a mass meeting on the other bank of the river.

The strike held and the employers had grave problems recruiting and retaining replacement workers. They were also losing the battle for public opinion. They were seen to have rejected attempts at mediation — from the Mayor of Newcastle, from Charles Palmer and from A. J. Mundella, M.P. — and the national press was hostile. On 11th September, the *Times* supported the League, leading to letters appearing from Armstrong and Burnett. In his second letter, of September 28th, Burnett demonstrated the League's emphasis on better living standards rather than monetary gain by offering — without the League's authority — to accept reduced wages in return for shorter hours. Finally, at the beginning of October, two new mediators, the editor of the main Newcastle radical newspaper and the town clerk, proposed a new compromise, that a 54-hour week start only on 1st January, and this was accepted by both Armstrong and the League. A phased return to work began on October 9th.

So ended the strike on Tyneside, but this was only the beginning of the Nine Hours Movement which is much harder to trace. The League had garnered tremendous public support. On 15th September, public meetings were held in London, Birmingham, Glasgow, Leeds, Liverpool, Manchester and Sheffield. Further meetings, notably in Leeds and London, were held on October 9th, both to celebrate the Newcastle victory and launch new campaigns. The dispute in the north-east had become, in effect, a national dispute by proxy and its outcome led to capitulation by employers in many other districts. Burnett (1872, p. 74) commented:

> But what was more remarkable still [than the sudden collapse of the employers] . . . was the manner in which the movement began to spread — first over this district and then over different parts of the country.

In most cases, no strike occurred: the employers agreed to a request from their workers, or even volunteered a reduction in hours. By the end of October, *The Beehive*

Figure 10.2
The spread of the Nine Hours system.

This map is based on the first issue of *The Beehive* in which a town was mentioned in a report that the nine-hours system had been agreed. Obviously, the agreement might refer to a large number of firms or just one, the same town might appear again repeatedly (this is particularly true of London), and towns might have appeared earlier but in the context of a request for the system. *The Beehive* sometimes further reported that the Nine Hours system had become general for a given trade or industry within some locality. These dates are generally somewhat later than the first report. One example is Bristol, where the issue of November 4th reported that Fox, Walker & Co., an engineering firm, and the Bristol and Exeter Railway had introduced the Nine Hours system. The issue of 11th November described the system as in general use among newspaper compositors. However, it was not until December 16th that it was described as having been adopted by 'most large employers of skilled labour'. However, this information on general adoption is too unsystematic to be plotted.

reported that the Nine Hours had been 'largely conceded by employers in the North-east district of England' (28/10/1871, p. 5) and shortly after that it was almost general in Leeds:

> The whole of the engineering, machine, and tool shops are now working on it. It has also been adopted by the coach makers, bookbinders, printers, leather dressers, and several other trades. The woollen trade has advertised a meeting to be held in the Circus, on Friday next, to consider the question. (4/11/1871, p. 4)

Figure 10.2 attempts to trace the spread of the Nine Hours. It is tempting to see this as a geographical diffusion from one town to the next. Certainly, most of the earliest victories were in the industrial north and later reports come from the south. However, London provided both some of the earliest reports and the final skirmishes and the evidence shows that news of the Newcastle victory reached all parts of the country almost simultaneously. The most rapid successes came in large plants making capital goods, concentrated in the north. These needed to retain the best hands and were making good profits in an export-led boom. Smaller firms, and those mainly involved in maintenance work, were slower to reduce hours and expected to follow the lead of others. *The Beehive* reported that in London 'it is understood among the men that the engineering firms who employ but fifty hands, or any number under that, will at once concede the Nine Hours, when the larger houses have set the example' (11/11/1871, p. 11), while the directors of the Llynvi and Ogmore Railway gave as grounds for delaying granting the Nine Hours that 'they don't like to take the lead, their establishment being a small one' (23/12/1871, p. 5). In Lancashire and Yorkshire, the mill mechanics lagged far behind the engine makers in the same towns.

By the start of January, *The Beehive* could report that 'In nearly all the towns throughout the country the Nine Hours as a day's work came into operation on Monday, and the event has been celebrated by the workmen with processions through the towns with bands and banners' (6/1/1872, p. 5). There were significant laggards in Keighley, in Edinburgh and Dundee, and in particular in London where six firms were reported on 20th January as having locked out their workers. Many of these disputes concerned associated conditions, not the Nine Hours itself. The ASE Executive was also encouraging some branches to seek the Nine Hours. For example, on 11th

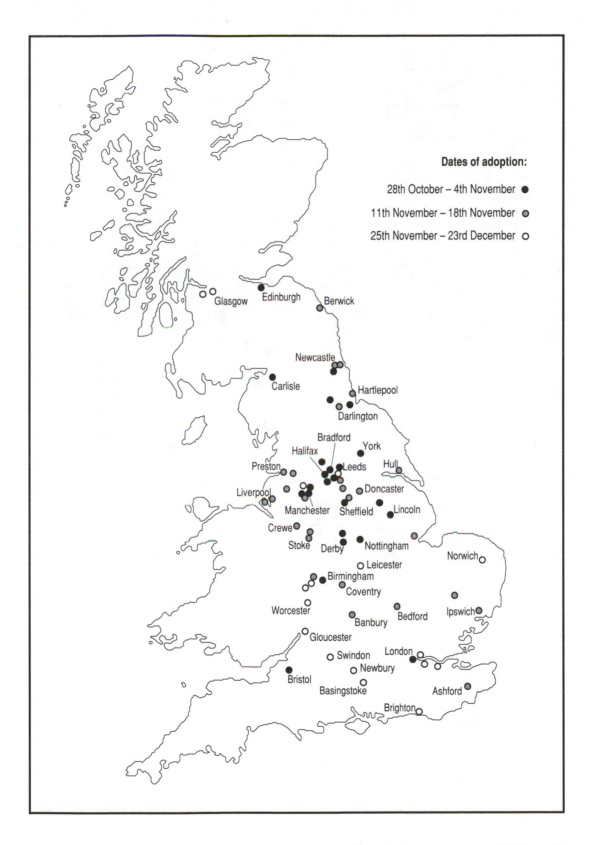

Dates of adoption:

28th October – 4th November ●
11th November – 18th November ◓
25th November – 23rd December ○

Glasgow
Edinburgh
Berwick

Newcastle
Carlisle
Hartlepool
Darlington

Bradford
York
Halifax
Leeds
Hull
Preston
Doncaster
Liverpool
Manchester
Sheffield
Lincoln
Crewe
Stoke
Derby
Nottingham
Norwich
Leicester
Birmingham
Coventry
Worcester
Banbury
Bedford
Ipswich
Gloucester
London
Swindon
Newbury
Bristol
Basingstoke
Ashford
Brighton

The nine-hours movement of 1871   87

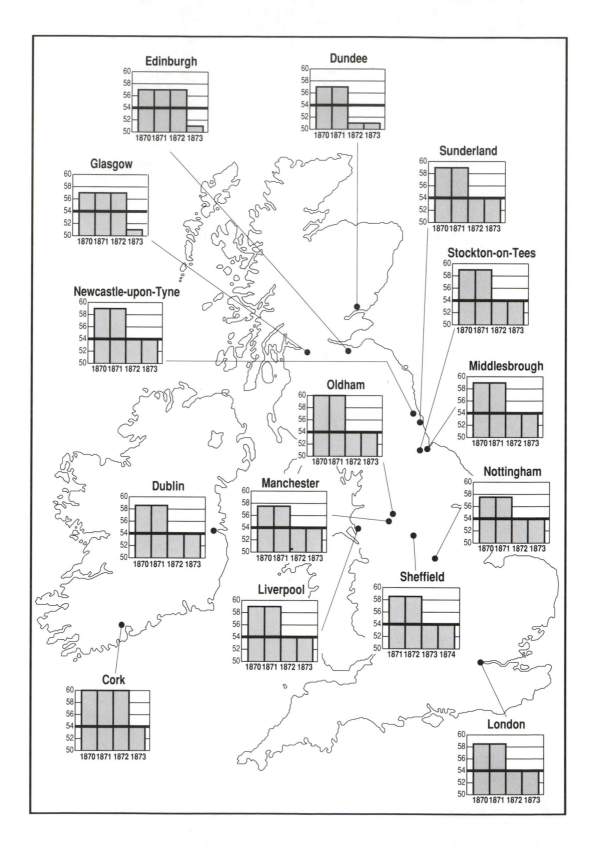

Figure 10.3
Normal hours of work for skilled engineers, 1870–73.
These data are taken from p.158 of the Board of Trade's unpublished 1908 report on 'Rates of wages and hours of labour in various industries in the United Kingdom for a series of years', available from the Department of Employment Library. The towns graphed are those for which data were available for all four years. Other towns could be included if we assume that hours were the same in 1870 as in 1866, but this seems questionable given the major recession which intervened. A number of towns have hours listed for 1872 and 1873 but not for earlier years, and in all cases hours were 54 or less by 1873.

February members at 'the extension works in Chatham' were instructed to hand in their notices if refused it. Nevertheless, on 2nd February, the Executive felt justified in proposing a national celebration of the Nine Hours System to be held at Whitsun at the Crystal Palace.

Figure 10.3 maps known reductions in engineers' hours during the early 1870s, and shows that hours were not merely reduced but standardised to 54 hours in all regions except Scotland. Although some of these gains were lost in the depression of 1879, the Newcastle strike was a famous victory for the skilled unions. The movement as a whole marked a new respectability, not merely for trade unions but for industrial action, as was demonstrated by the support from even Tory newspapers such as *The Times*. It is noteworthy that Burnett, who began the strike as a worker at Armstrong's Elswick site, became General Secretary of the ASE in 1875 and Labour Correspondent of the Board of Trade in 1886, setting up the reporting system on which later parts of this Atlas rely. The movement demonstrated very clearly the leading role of the engineers, for although they had the most noted victories the campaign spread far wider. The 6th January 1872 issue of *The Beehive* mentions the Nine Hours movement among builders in London, coach makers in Liverpool, packing-case makers in Bradford, colliers in south Staffordshire, shoemakers in Norwich and many other trades. As the next case study demonstrates, the success of the Nine Hours movement inspired even the most down-trodden workers to combine.

Sources and further reading
The Nine Hours strike in the north east is well-documented. John Burnett, *Nine Hours Movement: A history of the engineers' strike in Newcastle and Gateshead* (Newcastle, 1872) is a contemporary account by the strike's leader. A modern study is E. Allen, J. F. Clarke, N. McCord, and D. J. Rowe, *The North-East Engineers' Strikes of 1871: The Nine Hours League* (Newcastle, 1971). Unfortunately neither has much to say about the wider Nine Hours movement and the account given here was researched principally from the minute books of the ASE's Executive Committee, held by the Modern Records Centre at Warwick University, and *The Beehive*, a newspaper sponsored by the artisan unions which gave particular emphasis to industrial matters.

11. The revolt of the field, 1872–4

The agricultural labourers were as different a group from the engineers who led the Nine Hours movement as could be imagined: generally unskilled and those in southern England often living in communities dominated by the landowner or the parson. Some labourers had been swept up in the radical movements of the 1830s and 1840s but they developed little lasting organisation. During the 1850s and 1860s there was little activity. However, the economic upturn of the early 1870s, the new respectability of trade unionism and the spectacular success of the Nine Hours movement revived agricultural unionism. The National Agricultural Labourers' Union became, briefly, the largest union in the country and was a significant forerunner of the 'new unions' of the 1880s and 1890s. It was created through a strike in 1872 and all but collapsed following a lock-out in 1874.

There had been some signs of unrest among the labourers in 1871, notably new unions in Herefordshire and Lincolnshire, but what first attracted widespread public attention was the Wellesbourne strike the following spring. On January 29th 1872, a meeting of labourers was held at Harbury in Warwickshire to discuss a rise in wages. On February 7th, another meeting was held at Wellesbourne and Joseph Arch of Barford was asked to speak. Born in 1826, Arch had already distinguished himself as a champion hedger, as a Primitive Methodist preacher and as a campaigner for the Liberal party in a Tory region. Unusually, Arch was a freeholder and therefore a voter He was also a versatile worker, turning his hand to building work as well as farming, and travelling widely. His wide experience and relative independence from particular employers made him a natural leader, and at the Wellesbourne meeting he urged the formation of a new union. At a second meeting a week later, 200–300 men agreed to join up.

During the remainder of February, Arch travelled incessantly, giving up all other work to speak for the union. In early March, the Wellesbourne union circularised local farmers requesting reduced hours, a daily rate of 2s. 8d. and an overtime rate, and giving notice of a strike from March 9th if refused. The farmers made no response and on March 11th 200 men struck. Members in villages not involved in the dispute

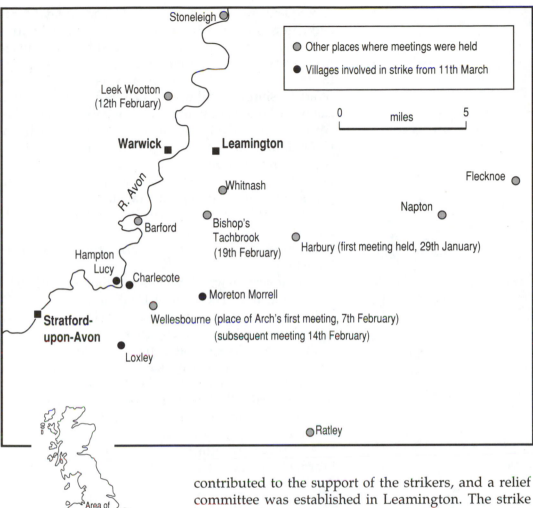

Figure 11.1
The Wellesbourne strike, 1872.
This map plots the villages
involved in the strike, based
mainly on the account given in
Horn's biography of Joseph
Arch. As can be seen, the dispute
was concentraded into a small
group of villages east of Stratford
and south of Warwick and
Leamington.

contributed to the support of the strikers, and a relief committee was established in Leamington. The strike immediately drew outside attention, being reported in *The Times* on March 14th. The strikers won assistance from the nearby radical centre of Birmingham, with a meeting in the Town Hall on April 3rd and pledges of support from leaders such as Joseph Chamberlain. The London Trades Council established a committee to aid the strike: William Allan of the ASE served as Treasurer and his union contributed £300.

The strike ended not through a settlement but because all of the strikers had emigrated or found other, better-paid employment. By April 6th, only 56 men were still out at Wellesbourne, 28 at Moreton Morrell and 10 at Loxley, and all these were sent to other work, 25 going to a soap factory near Liverpool. As figure 11.1 shows, the Wellesbourne strike was brief, highly localised and involved few workers. It would be of little significance were it not for its catalytic role in the creation and subsequent growth of the union. On Good Friday, March 29th, a great demonstration was held: 'The labourers with their wives and children, headed by their village drum and fife bands, marched into Leamington singing.' (Selley, 1919, p. 42) The union was named as the 'Warwickshire Agricultural Labourers' Union', and soon claimed 64 branches with 5,000 members. At the end of April they invited other unions to join them in a National Union and, at another meeting on May 29th, the National Agricultural Labourers' Union was established at Leamington. Arch became chairman and Henry Taylor, previously the Leamington branch secretary of the Amalgamated Society of Carpenters and Joiners, made secretary.

Arch described the spread of agricultural unionism in these terms:

> The movement was flowing across the country like a spring tide. The men of Denham in Buckinghamshire joined in hundreds. There was agitation in Norfolk, where the men struck for shorter hours; there was a lock-out at Long Sutton Marsh, and very soon the wages in that district advanced to two shillings and sixpence a day. Men in Dorsetshire were striking; the labourers about Shaftesbury and Blandford came out asking for a rise to twelve shillings a week. (Arch, 1898, pp. 55–6)

Arch played a central role in this, travelling incessantly in order to spread the union into the South East and East Anglia. Figure 11.2 reconstructs his movements during the last four months of 1872, when he addressed a total of 58 public meetings.

During the remainder of 1872 and 1873, the labourers appeared to carry all before them, but there were structural weaknesses to the movement. One was its concentration in southern England, as shown in figure 11.3. This is often explained through the higher wages of northern labourers, necessary as men might more easily move to work in nearby industrial towns and in mining. However, farming in the north was fundamentally differently organised: based more on animal husbandry than arable farming, hands were much more likely to be taken on by the year at hiring fairs at which wage levels were set, and then to live with the farmer. In the south and east, grain farming was more dominant, with larger farms and demand for labour concentrated at harvest. Union activity was associated with counties with few live-in farm servants, a high proportion of arable land

Figure11.2

The travels of Joseph Arch, September–December 1872. Arch's autobiography provides only a very general account of his activities , so this map is constructed from reports of meetings and announcements of future meetings in the *Labourers' Union Chronicle*. What cannot be shown is that Arch almost always returned to Leamington for the bi-monthly meetings of the union's executive committee every other Monday. The meetings plotted are a mixture of open-air mass meetings and evening meetings in public halls. On several occasions, Arch's speech took the form of a sermon within a Methodist service: as he himself put it, 'for more than 25 years I have been a Methodist local preacher, and I am not ashamed of my calling. I have travelled over 7,000 miles to preach the Gospel of Jesus Christ to my perishing fellowmen' (*Labourers' Union Chronicle*, 12/ 10/1872 , p. 4). Both visits to Bradford were to speak in support of the Land Tenure Reform Association, while he visited London to build outside support for the union: on the 10th of December, he shared the platform in the Exeter Hall with Daniel Guile of the Ironfounders' union, Robert Applegarth of the Carpenters and Joiners, Archbishop Manning and the prominent Liberal M.P. A. J. Mundella.

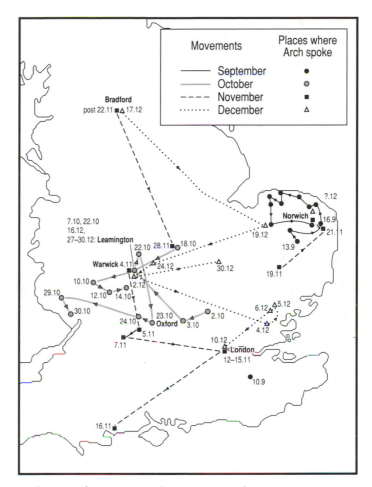

and many farmers employing more than ten men.

A second structural weakness was that, even in its strongholds and at its peak, unionists remained a minority: about half the male agricultural labourers in Warwickshire, under a third of those in Suffolk and Herefordshire, about a fifth in Dorset. This reflected great variation from one village to the next, hard to explain systematically although there is some evidence that unionism was concentrated in villages with a tradition of religious non-conformism and active friendly societies. Thirdly, the movement was divided, as many local unions refused to join the highly centralised NALU in which three-quarters of total income went to the central office in Leamington. Many of these unions joined the Federal Union of Agricultural and General Labourers, established in November 1873 with eight districts and c. 49,344 members. Finally, the labourers lacked the artisans' experience of organising and the NALU experienced many financial problems. The most basic was that the

Figure 11.3
Membership of the NALU.
The map plots the membership
of the NALU's districts, and of
the rival Federal Union, using
information tabulated in J. P.
Dunbabin, 'The incidence and
organisation of agricultural
trades unions in the 1870s',
Agricultural History Review
Vol.16 (1968), pp. 114–141. The
graph plots the union's
membership from 1873, the year
following its formation, through
to its final dissolution in 1895
Unfortunately, the union itself
provided a poor statistical record
and the series combines totals
give in Horn's biography of
Arch, Hasbach's *History of the
English Agricultural Labourer*, the
Sixth Report on Trade Unions [BPP
1894 XCIV 55–.], and the *Twelfth
Report on Trade Unions* [BPP 1900
LXXXIII 601–.].

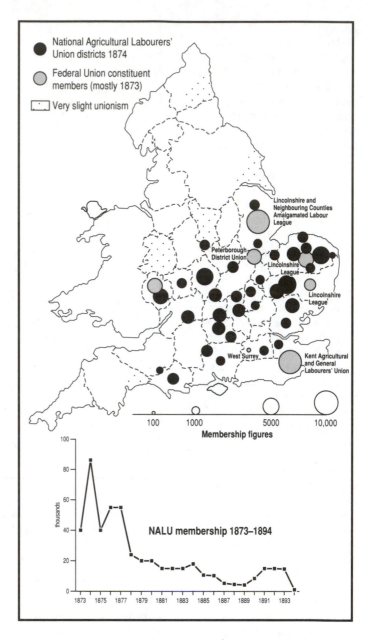

income to central funds during 1873–5 was only about
half of what it should have been, given the size of the
membership.

Once it was clear that the labourers had, at long last,
an effective combination, the farmers began to form
'Defence Associations'. The autumn of 1872 saw the
formation of both the Essex and Suffolk Farmers' Defence
Association, based at Sudbury, and the Newmarket
Farmers' Association. In the spring of 1873, the latter
officially ignored a demand from the labourers but

increased wages. The Sudbury farmers, however, initiated a lock-out involving about a thousand men in an area about 18 miles by 14 which ended with the men leaving the union and drifting back to work. At the end of February 1874, the Newmarket-area labourers again requested a wage increase and this time the farmers resolved to reject the men's demand and lock-out all union members. This lock-out began on March 21st and soon attracted national attention. Within a month, the lock-out had spread to five neighbouring counties and to Gloucestershire, Hampshire, and Warwickshire. By March 23rd, 2,000 men were locked out. By the beginning of May there were over 8,000.

The dispute was again a very public affair:

On market days, during the continuance of the lock-out, the Union delegates generally held outdoor meetings, to which the labourers came in hundreds from the neighbouring villages, often accompanied by their womankind. Sometimes they paraded the town with a band of music at their head, and a few blue banners. All the men wore bits of blue ribbon. The women were respectably dressed, and bore the same badge on their bonnets. (Clifford, 1875, p. 44)

The labourers were again dependent on outside support: this time, the ASE contributed £1,000. Arch toured not East Anglia but the north, raising funds. On June 30th, a 'pilgrimage' of labourers set out from Newmarket to tour the industrial towns, collecting £100 in Nottingham and £140 in Sheffield. However, the labourers were greatly weakened by their division into the National and the Federal unions, which failed to co-operate, while the farmers were organising across the region: a Defence Association was formed at Bury St. Edmunds on April 22nd and joined the lock-out. In July, an 'East Anglian Farmers' Central Board of Consultation' was established at Bury St. Edmunds and included the associations for West Suffolk, Newmarket, Norfolk, the Isle of Ely, Huntingdon, 'Essex and Suffolk', 'Colchester and East Essex', 'Saffron Walden', 'Wilford Hundred' and 'Saxmundham District'.

The men's determination crumbled in late July when they saw the harvest being gathered in without them. On the 27th, a sub-committee of the NALU Executive resolved that, as the men could not be supported by the union indefinitely, they be offered the choice of assisted migration or emigration, or of relying on their own

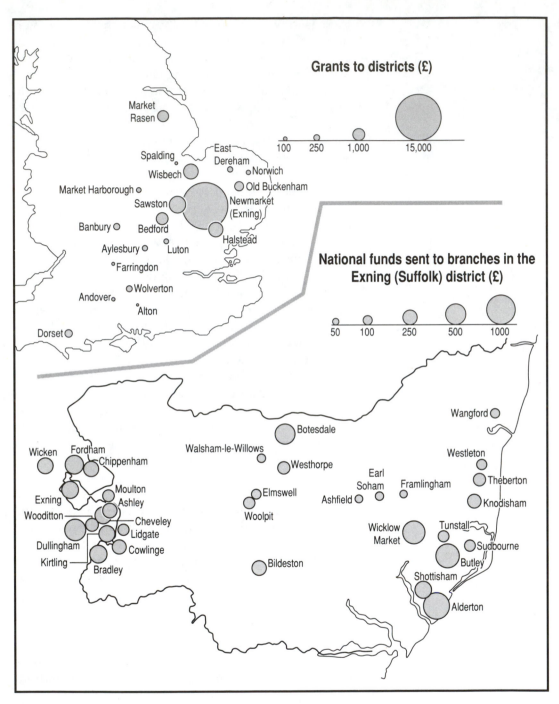

Grants to districts (£)

100   250   1,000   15,000

National funds sent to branches in the Exning (Suffolk) district (£)

50   100   250   500   1000

Market Rasen

Spalding
East Dereham
Wisbech
Norwich
Market Harborough
Old Buckenham
Sawston
Newmarket (Exning)
Banbury
Bedford
Aylesbury
Luton
Halstead
Farringdon
Wolverton
Andover
Alton
Dorset

Wangford

Botesdale
Walsham-le-Willows
Westleton
Wicken
Fordham
Westhorpe
Theberton
Chippenham
Earl Soham
Framlingham
Moulton
Elmswell
Knodisham
Exning
Ashley
Ashfield
Wooditton
Woolpit
Cheveley
Lidgate
Wicklow Market
Tunstall
Dullingham
Cowlinge
Sudbourne
Kirtling
Butley
Bradley
Bildeston
Shottisham
Alderton

resources. Two days later the Federal Union executive council in London resolved to end the lock-out. The NALU sought to claim a victory, arguing the union had grown in size, had raised over £20,000 to support its members and had become more truly national. However, during the following winter 112 branches closed and the

Figure 11.4
The Eastern Counties lock-out of 1874.
The only systematic information available to map the dispute are reports of national funds sent to the districts during the strike. The national map plots grants made between March and August 1874, listed in F. Clifford, *The Agricultural Lock-Out of 1874* (p. 21); the detail for Suffolk plots national funds sent to branches in the Exning district between April 4th and July 6th 1874, listed in the *Labourers' Union Chronicle* of the 8th of August (p. 7). The resulting maps are inevitably imprecise, as expenditure by the Federal Union is excluded as is any direct expenditure of income from the local branches on strike pay.

union lost 28,000 members. 1875 saw the onset of severe agricultural depression, as well as a down-turn in the national economy as a whole, and the union steadily lost members.

By 1889, the membership had dropped to 4,254, but the dockers' victory led to a revival and the NALU had gained ten thousand members by the end of 1891, mainly in Norfolk, Essex and Suffolk. In this period, socialist agitators of the Land Restoration League toured in 'Red Vans', 'containing beds for the agitators, and carrying thousands of pamphlets of all sorts in their capacious interiors, from which speeches were made evening after evening in village after village' (Hasbach, 1908, p. 301). During 1892, the dock-workers' agents were active in establishing unions in Oxfordshire and Lincolnshire, partly to reduce the threat of agricultural labourers working as black-legs in the docks. The total membership of agricultural unions rose to a new peak of 36,986 in 1892, but then collapsed in the recession year of 1894. By 1897, it had fallen to 3,879. By 1906 only two negligible unions remained.

The revolt of the field was no victory for organised labour, the economic forces ranged against the labourers being too strong. They worked in a declining sector, concentrated into declining regions. Thus, between 1871 and 1881, numbers employed in agriculture in Great Britain declined from 1,807,603 to 1,590,641; total employment in East Anglia fell from 448,446 to 320,370. Without the artisans' control over entry to skilled work, the men were almost always defeated by a permanent labour surplus. Even the Wellesbourne strike was not a conventional victory. The unionists recognised their weakness. During the 1880s there was a vigorous campaign for allotments on which labourers could become their own masters, leading to the Small Holdings Act of 1892, but the most effective remedy for individuals was migration and emigration. These the union actively promoted: Arch spent part of 1873 visiting Canada at the invitation of the colonial government, and in 1881 claimed that three-quarters of a million people had emigrated. This was an exaggeration, but the mid-1870s certainly saw a surge in emigration by male agricultural labourers. At the end of the 1874 lock-out, the NALU reported that, of the 3116 members involved, 694 had migrated and 429 emigrated. However, perhaps the union's real achievement was political. The Reform Act of 1867 had extended the franchise to male householders in boroughs, but in rural constituencies it was still restricted to freeholders. By giving voice to the voiceless, the agricultural unions paved the way for the Reform Act of 1884, which enfranchised all male householders. The first General Election held under the new franchise, that of 1885, secured a personal triumph for Arch when he was elected M.P. for North-West Norfolk.

Sources and further reading

The farm-labourers have been surprisingly poorly served by historians. J. P. Dunbabin, *Rural Discontent in Nineteenth Century Britain* (New York, 1974) is a series of case studies rather than a connected account; J. P. Dunbabin, 'The incidence and organisation of agricultural trades unions in the 1870s', *Agricultural History Review* Vol.16 (1968), pp. 114–141, usefully supplements this with a statistical survey and a discussion of why the NALU established itself in some villages but not in others. Pamela Horn's biography of *Joseph Arch* (Kineton, 1971) is the only general account, and can be supplemented by Arch's autobiography (London, 1898). Alun Howkins, *Poor labouring men: rural radicalism in Norfolk 1872–1923* (London, 1985) focuses on a particular county.

Three contemporary writers were used extensively: F. Clifford, *The Agricultural Lock-Out of 1874, with notes upon farming and farm-labour in the Eastern Counties* (Edinburgh, 1875) combines a narrative of the dispute with extensive descriptions of farming practices, based on Clifford's travels; W. Hasbach, *A History of the English Agricultural Labourer* (London, 1908) covers the background to the disputes and later developments; E. Selley, *Village Trade Unions in Two Centuries* (London, 1919) provides an outline history of the union. Further detail was taken from the relatively complete run of the *Labourers' Union Chronicle* held by the Warwickshire Record Office; the first issue, in June 1872, includes an account of 'what has been done in Warwickshire' covering earlier developments.

12. The strike at Bryant and May's match factory, East London, July 1888 *by Gillian Rose*

The strike of the women matchmakers at Bryant and May's factory in Bow, east London, in July 1888, is often described as a mere prelude to the strike of dock workers in the city a year later. In some ways it was just that: it was shorter, smaller, and had far fewer consequences for the history of trade unionism in Britain than the men's action in the docks. Nevertheless, the strike of women at Bryant and May's was larger and more complex than is often acknowledged and its geographies demonstrate a complicated and important series of linkages between workplace, neighbourhoods and homes.

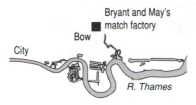

Bryant and May's match factory in Fairfield Road, Bow, was built in 1861 and extended in 1874, but its manufacturing processes were not confined to the factory buildings. Bryant and May's factory produced matches but making matchboxes was work contracted out to local agents. They in turn gave the materials to local women and paid them $2 \frac{1}{4}$ d. per gross of boxes. In their turn, they sub-contracted the actual construction of the boxes to women in their homes and paid them $1 \frac{1}{4}$ d. per gross. Located in a desperately poor area of London, Bryant and May's depended for much of its manual labour on these local women whose need for wages, no matter how low, forced them to accept the poor working conditions both of homeworking and in the Fairfield Road factories (including the risk of contracting 'phossy-jaw' from the phosphorous used in the matchmaking process). The strike had severe consequences for many homeworkers and some asked for money from the strike fund. Homeworking was thus one way in which the factory was connected to local neighbourhoods.

Homeworking was in fact what prompted the strike, in a roundabout way. On June 15, 1888, a meeting of the Fabian Society passed a motion condemning the low wages paid to women who worked at home making matchboxes. The socialist activist Annie Besant decided to investigate this matter further and on June 23, in her weekly paper *The Link*, she published an article entitled 'White Slavery in London'. This described the terrible working conditions in Bryant and May's match factory

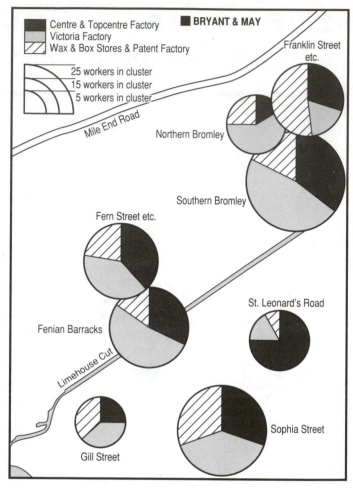

Figure 12.1
Neighbourhood clusters of
Bryant and May workers in Bow,
Poplar and Limehouse. These
have been identified and mapped
from the *Match Girl's Strike
Register* listing payments to
strikers.

and was, Besant said, based on information given to her
by three workers there. On June 27, *The Link* reported that
the factory was in uproar as foremen acting on the
instructions of the factory owners demanded the names
of the informants: three days later, Besant said that the
three had been sacked. On July 4, *The Link* described the
workers' refusal to sign a declaration of satisfaction with
their working conditions. The next day, the box-filler
who led the boycott was sacked when she protested at
being demoted, and all the workers walked out in support.
About 1,400 women were on strike at this point.

On July 6, one or two hundred women marched down
Fleet Street to the offices of *The Link* to ask for Besant's
help in publicising their cause (a previous strike two
years before had failed for lack of publicity). Besant
helped to organise a strike fund and a Strike Committee,
and a mass meeting took place on July 8 on Mile End
Waste. Four resolutions were passed: that Besant's article

on working conditions was true; that evidence of Bryant and May's illegal practice of levying fines for unsatisfactory work be reported to the Home Secretary; that the low wages and high share dividends of Bryant and May were unfair; and that the workers should form a union. The strikers also wanted the 'pennies' returned to one group of workers, the box fillers: these were the pennies the fillers once paid to younger women to carry their work to and fro for them, which had not been repaid to the fillers after the younger women were employed elsewhere by the management. The London Trades Council stepped in to mediate between the company and the Strike Committee and, on July 17, the demands of the workers were met. By July 21, all the women were back at work. On July 24, the Strike Committee met to draft the rules of the Union of Women Matchworkers and by early September the Union had 600 members.

The strike began in the Victoria factory, which contained Bryant and May's highest paid female workers: their weekly wages averaged 6s. 3d., compared to only 5s. for single women working in the Wax and Box Stores and Patent factory. The Victoria factory also contained the largest proportion of married women: about a fifth, compared to about a tenth in the other two factories. Married women often worked harder on piece rates to support a family and the average rent paid by women in the Victoria factory was certainly higher than in the others. But, unlike the other factories, there was no significant difference between the average pay of married and single women in the Victoria. Rather, it was supervisory men who were the most prominent well-paid group. Clara Collett heard these foremen described as brutal, and married women seem to have been less willing than the usually younger single women to put up with this sexual division of power. Collett described married women workers as 'frequently the most industrious, but they generally exert a most mischievous influence on their companions' by being 'coarse' (Booth, 1893, p. 315). Perhaps sexual barracking in the Victoria factory turned into something more serious during the events of July 1888, causing the women of the Victoria factory to start the strike.

Yet they were followed by the workers in the two other factories on the site. Why? In order to answer that question, the relationship between the factory and the women's domestic life must again be addressed. The solidarity among all the factory workers was evident

Figure 12.2
Bryant and May workers in the Eastward Street area of Limehouse, described by Booth as the 'Fenian Barracks', mapped from the *Match Girl's Strike Register*. The base map is the Ordnance Survey 5 feet to 1 mile map of London published in 1895, and house numbers have been assumed.

both inside the factory and outside it, in neighbourhood and leisure activities. Collet commented on the clothing clubs organised by the women in the factory, for example, and on their habit of parading arm-in-arm down Bow Road on Saturday nights and Sunday afternoons, 'without exception very expensively and gaudily dressed, from the hat, with its three, and in many cases four, long ostrich feathers of a brilliant red or royal blue shade, down to the high-heeled boots of the latest style', as the *Pall Mall Gazette* (11/7/1888) disapprovingly noted.

Bryant and May's workers very often lived close to each other too, in the poorest neighbourhoods of the East End. From the Strike Register, compiled in order to make payments from the strike fund, it is possible to estimate that, of the women whose addresses can be located, about one-third lived in eight neighbourhood clusters. One of these neighbourhoods was what Charles Booth described as 'the Fenian Barracks', a terrible slum occupied mainly by Irish families. Indeed, in the Victoria factory 'all our hands, men and women, hail from the Emerald Isle by birth or lineage' (*Girl's Own Paper*, 12/1895, p. 148) and at least one other cluster — that in Sophia Street in Poplar — was also an Irish neighbourhood. In a period of strong anti-Irish sentiment, the solidarity of living among an outcast community may also have contributed to the women's decision to strike as a group. All of such neighbourhoods were structured through a network of reciprocal borrowing and lending, however, as well as through a series of routine activities, out of which developed a certain solidarity too.

Neighbours depended on each other for survival and in the factories of the Fairfield Works it was likely that a co-worker was also a neighbour to be relied on and trusted. Two-thirds of the women on the Strike Committee lived in one or other of those eight neighbourhood clusters, suggesting that the strike depended on these neighbourhood networks for its success. Moreover, the routines of neighbourhood life disrupted the demands of the factory. Monday was often taken off, and the manager of the Fairfield Works complained to the *Girl's Own Paper* that 'we cannot, do what we will, make them understand the importance of regularity in labour' (12/1895, p. 148). Neighbourhood life affected waged work, even had priority over it, and this too may have influenced the decision to strike. It may also explain the short life of the Union of Women Matchmakers at Bryant and May's,

Legend:
● Worker in Centre and Topcentre Factory
■ Worker in Victoria Factory
▲ Worker in Wax and Box Stores and Patent Factory

which seems to have survived for only one or two years.

In order to understand the strike at Bryant and May's in 1888, then, it is also necessary to consider the complex intersections of class, gender and ethnicity both in the workplace and in the surrounding neighbourhoods and communities.

Worker in Centre and Topcentre Factory

Worker in Victoria Factory

Worker in Wax and Box Stores and Patent Factory

Figure 12.3
Bryant and May workers in Sophia Street, Poplar, mapped from the *Match Girl's Strike Register*. The base map is the Ordnance Survey 5 feet to 1 mile map of London published in 1895, and house numbers have been assumed.

Sources and further reading

Accounts of the strike are provided by Ann Stafford, *A Match to Fire the Thames* (London, 1961) and Reg Beer, *Matchgirls' Strike, 1888: The struggle against sweated labour in London's East End* (London: National Museum of Labour History Pamphlet No. 2, n. d. (1979)). Details of women's work appear in the *Report to the Board of Trade on the Sweating System at the East End of London* (BPP 1887 LXXXIX) and in chapter 9 of Charles Booth's *Life and labour of the people in London. Vol. 4: The trades of East London* (London, 1893), written by Clara Collett. The *Match Girl's Strike Register* was reprinted by the National Museum of Labour History (London, n.d. (1980)), and other contemporary material comes from *The Link*, *The Pall Mall Gazette*, and the *Girl's Own Paper*.

13. Organising the unskilled: the 1889 dock strike

The importance of the 1889 dock strike lies in its successful long-term mobilisation of the unskilled, for out of it eventually emerged the Transport and General Workers Union, a general union which came to replace the Amalgamated Engineers as Britain's largest union. It was also notable for the effective links formed between trade unionists and socialist groups, particularly the Social Democratic Federation. Within the history of the dispute, geographies can be distinguished on three distinct scales: the complex internal geography of the London dock system; the geography of London as a symbolic space; and a much wider geography of trade union solidarity which proved decisive for the immediate outcome of the strike.

The development of the strike reflected the structure of dock employment. It began among the hourly-paid casual labourers employed by the dock company at the South West India Dock, and as a dispute over the 'plus' system of bonuses paid for rapid unloading, in this case of the *Lady Armstrong*. Although Ben Tillett, leader of the then-tiny Tea Operatives' and General Labourers' Union, was involved from the start of the dispute on Monday 12th August, the initiative seems to have come from the men, for whom the *Lady Armstrong* was only a pretext. Trade was booming and the plus system of arbitrary bonuses gave ample opportunities. Tillett had to persuade the men to stay at work on the 13th, and the West India Docks struck on Wednesday the 14th. Their demands were that no man was to be employed for less than four hours at a stretch; contract and piecework were to be abolished; and wages were to be raised to 6d. an hour (the 'docker's tanner') and 8d. overtime.

Tillett had led an abortive strike at Tilbury in October 1888 and this had convinced him that localised strikes by unskilled workers were easily defeated by imported black-legs. He therefore moved rapidly to widen the dispute and recruit allies. The dockers lacked organising experience and the two other principal leaders of the strike came from outside the industry: Tom Mann and John Burns were both engineers, members of the ASE who had joined the Social Democratic Federation and

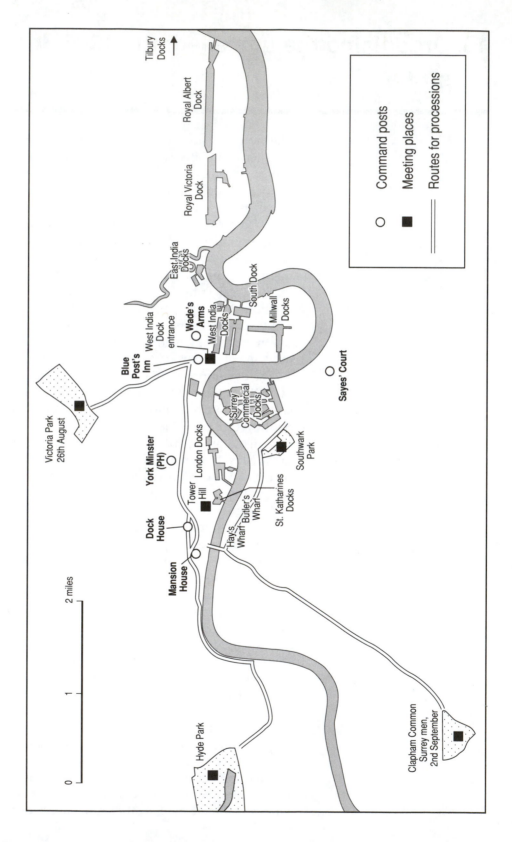

become active socialist agitators. The remainder of the first week was spent organising and holding meetings, and on the Friday evening the Victoria and Albert dockers joined the dispute. The London and St. Katharine's men stayed aloof, still angry at the refusal of the West India docks to join their strike in 1880: they joined the dispute on the Monday, following effective picketing led by Burns. On Monday also, Tillett went to Tilbury, accompanied by Harry Orbell who organised the strike there.

Each of these groups of docks was controlled by the Joint Committee. The London and St. Katharine Company had opened the Victoria (in 1855) and Albert (1880) Docks to accommodate larger steamers and the East and West India Company competed with Tilbury Docks (1886), twenty miles down river. This competition proved ruinous and in 1888 the two companies agreed to work together. The resulting Joint Committee controlled all the enclosed docks handling general cargo and were consequently able to double the fees charged to ship owners.

However, they were by no means monopoly employers of dock labour. Firstly, the Millwall and Surrey docks were more specialised: the former handled grain and timber, using more machinery and a largely country-born workforce; the latter dominated the timber trade. Both relied on sub-contractors, paid by the piece, to employ labour. Secondly, while unloading ships required little skill and the only concern was a rapid turn-round, how a ship was loaded affected both how much cargo it carried and its sailing properties. This work was therefore in the hands of skilled stevedores, employed by the ship owners and earning about 36s. a week. They had been effectively unionised since the 1870s. Thirdly, the enclosed docks were in active competition with the riverside wharves which took most of the coastal trade and an increasing share of foreign trade. By 1900, these handled just over half the total tonnage of the port and employed 41 per cent of the labour force. Finally, there were the sailors and lightermen. The latter had a legal monopoly, earned 40 to 60s. per week and rigorously controlled entry through apprenticeship.

The second week was spent involving these other groups. On Saturday, Tillett persuaded a joint meeting of the councils of the two stevedores' unions to join the strike and establish a strike committee based at Wade's Arms in Poplar. On Monday 19th, some 300 men from Millwall joined the strike procession, but Tuesday

Figure 13.1
London and its river in 1889. This map surveys the cultural landscape on which the dockers' struggle was played out: the river and the docks themselves, although inevitably Tilbury is excluded and the riverside wharves are less identifiable than the enclosed docks; the command posts of the various factions, mainly public houses in the case of the men; the public spaces where the major meetings were held; and the routes of processions in so far as these were recorded.

morning was spent 'tramping the wet and sodden roads of Millwall to get out the remainder of the men' (Smith and Nash, n.d., p. 66). On Wednesday, the lightermen came out and added their own set of demands, while on Thursday the Surrey Commercial docks stopped work. By the end of the week, all the main docks had stopped. The third week saw other riverside workers becoming involved: biscuit makers in Bermondsey and gas workers at Greenwich. On Wednesday 28th, a thousand men marched to Erith to picket an isolated wharf. In essence, the dispute began at the heart of the docks and its leaders had then to involve those on the fringes, defined both economically and geographically.

The second geography becomes apparent in the actual conduct of the strike. Unlike skilled unionists, the dockers scarcely possessed a monopoly of their trade and there was a constant threat of blackleg labour. Picketing offered only a partial solution, making it necessary to unite the riverside communities in support of the strike. Further, they lacked the resources for a long drawn-out stoppage and therefore needed to demonstrate their strength, maximising the pressure on the dock owners to settle. As a result, very public demonstrations played a central part in the dispute, taking it out of the relatively isolated docklands communities to the wider metropolis. Almost every day, starting on the 14th, saw a procession from the docks to the City, marching past the Joint Committee's headquarters at the Dock House in Leadenhall St. That of the 19th 'first thoroughly aroused the City to the fact that something unusual was going forward in the unknown country to the east of Aldgate pump' (Smith and Nash, n.d., p. 65), and this soon settled into a ritual:

> Every morning of the strike saw a great gathering on Tower Hill . . . the Trafalgar Square of East London . . .; and every day . . . the City was paraded by a procession. . . . It was disquieting to have the "degraded dockers" marching past your offices in tens of thousands, . . . while the windows rattled with the "Marseillaise". . . . On Sundays, the processionists would penetrate as far as Hyde Park — the great centre of political and social demonstrations — and return eastward, refreshed and stimulated by platform oratory. . . . In high spirits at the approaching victory, the dockers let the City know they "weren't starved yet". (Smith and Nash, n.d., p. 68, 78, 83, 84)

On the 26th, the procession went north to Victoria Park, while the Surrey-side men held their own celebrations: meetings in Southwark Park and, on the 2nd September, a procession to Clapham Common. These processions were not merely marches but celebrations. Led by Tillett and Burns, whose straw hat became a trademark, with three or four brass bands, a crowd of 50–80,000:

> burly stevedores, lightermen, ship painters, sailors and firemen, riggers, scrapers, engineers, shipwrights, permanent men got up respectably, preferables cleaned up to look like permanents, and unmistakable casuals with vari-coloured patches on their faded greenish garments; . . . Doggett's prize winners, a stalwart battalion of watermen marching proudly in long scarlet coats, pink stockings, and velvet caps, with huge pewter badges on their breasts; . . . Father Neptune on his car in tinsel crown and flowing locks, surrounded by his suite, — Britannia in a Union Jack skirt, the doctor in a faultless hat . . . and the barber brandishing a huge razor . . . Such was the strike procession. It had its moods — was merry on some days, taciturn on others, laughed at the Dock House sometimes, howled at it at others, but it never lost command over itself. (Smith and Nash, n.d., pp. 85–6)

This was above all a demonstration of power and discipline by the previously powerless and disorganised. Further, it was a march out of 'darkest London' to the great meeting places of the west. By meeting at Clapham Common and Hyde Park, the strikers were placing themselves in a *political* tradition running back to the Chartists and before. Only by converting a set of economic demands by an occupational group into a political movement sweeping up an entire community could such a disparate and poorly defined group be held together.

Even so, the strike represented a desperate economic struggle. Unlike artisan unions, the dockers began with minimal strike fund and scant personal savings. Unlike the match girls, the numbers involved placed tremendous demands on outside sympathisers. Fortunately, the stevedores were already well organised and provided the backbone of the strike committee. A relief committee was established from 21st August, and created a system of union cards to identify those entitled to benefit and tickets which could be exchanged for a shilling's worth of groceries. However, initial funds were limited — the stevedores' joint reserves were about £3,000 — and by

29th August relief was being restricted. This led to Burns and Mann urging that the strike be broadened into a general stoppage across London, hoping for a speedy settlement despite the likely loss of public support. This was a desperate measure, but it was agreed that a 'No-Work' manifesto be circulated calling for a general strike on 2nd September.

Financial assistance from beyond the local community had been limited. Total donations from other British unions were £4,234, with even the ASE giving only £670. However, on Friday 30th funds were telegraphed from Australia by the wharf labourers and seamen of Brisbane. Coupled with vigorous lobbying, this transfusion led to the abandonment of the No-Work manifesto and by the end of the strike over £30,000 had been sent from Australia, nearly two-thirds of all relief funds. A network of support on the largest possible geographical scale saved the strike and perhaps reflected London's position in the global trading system. On Monday 2nd, a threat of rebellion by the Surrey-side men was dealt with by Tom Mann being sent south of the river, a series of public meetings and a separate committee being set up. By Wednesday, it was the dock owners who were under strong pressure to settle: public opinion was against them, their customers, the ship owners, preferred concessions to continued stoppages, and many of the river wharf owners, led by Lafone of Butler's Wharf, were seeking a separate settlement.

On Thursday 5th September, the Lord Mayor of London intervened and a Conciliation Committee met at the Mansion House next day. The employers offered to pay 6d. per hour, but only from January 1st, and ignored the men's demands on overtime. This was rejected by the men and the following Tuesday Cardinal Manning met the strike committee who agreed to the pay increase being delayed until November. On 12th and 13th, the Lord Mayor, Manning and Sidney Buxton, M.P. for Tower Hamlets, persuaded the employers to accept the same compromise and the agreement to end the strike was signed on 14th. On Sunday 15th, there was a final procession to Hyde Park Corner, 'to the spot which had seen the beginning of so many labour movements and had celebrated the triumph of so few' (Smith and Nash, n.d., p. 155). Work re-started on the Monday.

Although the immediate outcome of the strike was near-total victory for the dockers, in the long term their gains were hard to sustain. The spring of 1890 saw a refusal to pay men during meal breaks, led by the Hay's

Wharf Company, and the men were defeated in the subsequent strike. By November 1890, the economy had turned down and the demand for labour was weaker, and the Joint Committee took the opportunity to repudiate much of the previous year's agreement. The more positive legacy of the strike was in the development of the dockers' union. In September 1889, the Tea Operatives and General Labourers renamed themselves the Dock, Wharf, Riverside and General Labourers' Union of Great Britain and Ireland, with Tillett as general secretary, Mann as president and 30,000 members by the end of November. Tillett went on an organising tour of the provinces. 63 new branches formed in the first three months of 1890, and there were branches in Rotterdam and Amsterdam. Union was far from complete. The separate strike committee for the Surrey dockers continued as the South Side Labour Protection League and the National Union of Dock Labourers, based in Liverpool, dominated Britain's second port. Only in 1910 did these group together into the Transport Workers' Federation, and the Transport and General Workers' Union was formed through a merger in 1922. However, despite the limited practical achievements of the strikers and the long subsequent struggle to build effective unions of the unskilled, it was arguably the 1889 dispute which showed that such unions were possible and that the blackleg problem could be overcome if organisation and community involvement were on a sufficient scale.

Sources and further reading

All modern accounts of the dock strike rely on the narrative provided by Hubert Llewellyn Smith and Vaughan Nash, *The Story of the Docker's Strike. Told by two East-Londoners* (n.d. (1890)). Terry McCarthy's *The Great Dock Strike 1889: the story of the Labour movement's first great victory* (London, 1988) is a lavishly illustrated compilation quoting extensively from newspaper reports and the memoirs of leading figures in the strike. Jonathan Schneer's *Ben Tillett : portrait of a labour leader* (London, 1982) is a biography of the dockers' own leader, while John Lovell, *Stevedores and Dockers: A study of trade unionism in the Port of London, 1870–1914* (London, 1969) covers a longer period. The broader history of employment practices in the docks is covered in Gordon Phillips and Noel Whiteside, *Casual Labour: the unemployment question in the port transport industry 1880–1970* (Oxford, 1985).

14. The early May Days: 1890, 1891 and 1892

by Chris Wrigley

The early May Days saw massive crowds turn out in Hyde Park, London. Engels, who was on one of the platforms for the first international May Day in 1890, wrote afterwards:

> The demonstration here on 4 May was nothing short of *overwhelming* and even the entire bourgeois press had to admit it . . . 250 to 300,000 people, of whom over three-quarters were workers demonstrating . . . All in all, the most gigantic meeting that has ever been held here.

(Engels to August Bebel, 9 May 1890; Kapp, pp. 378 and 380).

To Karl Marx's daughter Laura he wrote that he had

> 'heard again, for the first time since 40 years, the unmistakable voice of the English proletariat'.

(Engels to Laura Lafargue, 10 May 1890; Kapp, p. 380).

The equivalent demonstration in 1891 was roughly of the same size, but that of 1892 was even bigger.

The British demonstrations were a response to a call from a Marxist congress held in Paris in 1889 at the time of the centenary of the storming of the Bastille. This congress, later seen as the start of the Second International, called on

> 'workers in all countries and in all towns, on the same agreed day . . . [to] call upon the public authorities to reduce the working day by law to eight hours'

and to carry out its other demands (Panaccione, ed., 1989, p. 18).

The remarkable size of the London demonstration of 4 May 1890 was facilitated by three disparate groups coming together at Hyde Park on the nearest Sunday, not on 1 May a working day. The prime organisers were the members of the Central Committee for the Eight Hours legal Working Day Demonstration. The Central Committee included socialists and radicals, the most important of which were Eleanor Marx Aveling and the Bloomsbury Socialist Society and the Labour Electoral Association. Even more important, in ensuring the scale of the turn-out, was the support of the London Trades Council. But this still predominantly LibLab body would not declare in favour of achieving the eight hour day by statutory means, and insisted that it made its own separate arrangements including even marching to Hyde Park by a different route. The third group was the largest British Marxist organisation, the Social Democrat Federation (S.D.F), which initially had opposed participation in what its leader called 'The First of May Folly'. These were not the only divisions in London. Some on the Left tried to act on 1 May, regardless of the attitude of the Trade unions. Some 1,500 people joined a march to Hyde Park organised by a S.D.F. trade unionist and that evening 'several thousand' attended a rally at Clerkenwell Green organised by William Morris and the Socialist League. In 1891 a purist march to Hyde Park on 1 May only attracted some 200 people – but on 2 May there was a large demonstration by the carpenters and joiners union, who went their own way as they could not agree to a statutory eight hour day.

The size of the main 1890 London demonstration displayed the growing strength of trade unionism, especially among unskilled workers, and the liveliness of the metropolis' radicalism. At Hyde Park the crowds were most eager to hear the heroes of 'new unionism' – John Burns, Tom Mann, Ben Tillett and Will Thorne. There, and elsewhere in Britain, the banners of these unions were much in evidence. Yet the London Trades Council's contingent, which represented the older unions as well as many of the new, mobilised the greatest numbers on the day. The success of this and other early May Day demonstrations was also linked to a resurgent working class radicalism. With these demonstrations there was again pride in penetrating *en masse* into wealthy London, just as had been the case with the unemployed in 1886 and the dockers in 1889. The early May Days marked a widening political awareness that also manifested itself in Progressive support in London County Council and London borough elections. Moreover the size of the London demonstrations was enlarged by them not being gender-segregated events. Women were conspicuous participants in the demonstrations, with women trade unionists among those speaking from the platforms.

Elsewhere the presence of socialist activists often ensured that May Day events occurred. But it is noticeable that where the support of the trades council or prominent unions was not gained, the turn-out could be small. Thus in Edinburgh on 4 May 1890 four to five hundred people

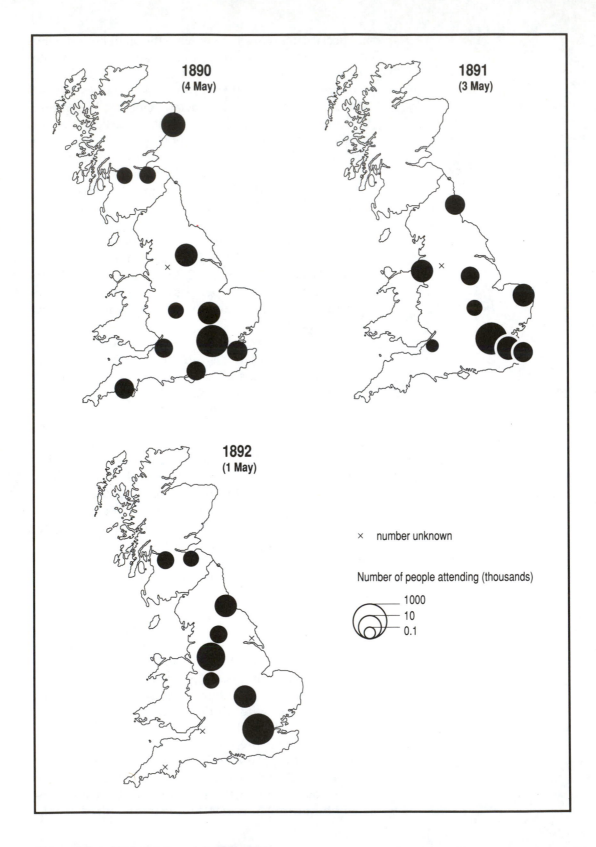

1890
(4 May)

1891
(3 May)

1892
(1 May)

× number unknown

Number of people attending (thousands)

1000
10
0.1

attended an S.D.F organised demonstration, and heard Keir Hardie regret that the trades council had narrowly voted not the participate (though one of its prominent members presided at the meeting). At Northampton, when – due to a misunderstanding between the May Day organiser and the trades council – the 1891 event failed to get trades council backing, only 500 attended. In contrast, when the trades council backed the demonstration, 10,000 turned out in 1890 and at least the same number in 1892.

Outside of London the strength of these demonstrations also owed much to the nature of the local labour markets and to local issues. 'New unions' were at the forefront in most places – notably the Gasworkers' Union and near the coast those for dockers and sailors. Also prominent were those groups which were particularly strong in the areas and which were then involved in struggles to improve their lot. Thus farm workers were conspicuous in Norwich and Jewish clothing workers in Leeds and Manchester in 1891. May Days were also used by trade unionists in dispute to highlight their cause; as in 1890 with London women envelope makers and in 1892 with Cardiff building workers and coal miners of eastern Durham County.

It was the size of the London May Day demonstrations which astonished and alarmed many of the propertied classes. Though they soon could draw comfort from the good humour and constitutional attitudes of these events. But also very notable was the spread of May Day demonstrations not only to other great cities but even to smaller towns such as Sittingbourne in Kent. This map provides some indication of the responses to May Day elsewhere, but fuller details will await future work of local historians.

Figure 14.1
Most of the information for this map stems from one or more issues of *Argus* (Norwich), *Bristol Mercury and Daily Post*, *Canterbury Journal and Farmers' Gazette*, *Chatham and Rochester Observer*, *Derby Daily Telegraph*, *East Kent Gazette*, *Economist*, *Edinburgh News*, *Jarrow Express*, *Leeds Mercury*, *Leicester Daily Mercury*, *Manchester Examiner and Times*, *Manchester Guardian*, *Midland Counties Express*, *Newcastle Daily Leader*, *Nottingham Daily Guardian*, *Northampton Daily Reporter*, *Sevenoaks and Kent Messenger*, *Sheffield and Rotheram Independent*, *Star* and *Times*. See also Wrigley in Panaccione (1990).

Sources and further reading
For the newspaper sources see the caption for Figure 14.1. On the background see A. E. P. Duffy, 'The Eight Hours Day Movement in Britain 1886–1893', *Manchester School of Economic and Social Studies*, 36, 1968, pp. 203–22 and 345–64, and P. S. Foner, *May Day* (New York, 1986). On European and wider responses see A. Panaccione (ed.), *The Memory of May Day*, Venice, 1989, and E. J. Hobsbawm, 'Birth of a Holiday: the First of May' in C. J. Wrigley and J. Shepherd (eds.), *On The Move*, 1991. For fuller details of Britain see Wrigley in Panaccione (1989), pp. 83–108, in A. Panaccione (ed.), *I Luoghi E I Soggetti Del I Maggio*, June 1990, pp. 35–41. For the Central Committee, see in particular Yvonne Kapp, *Eleanor Marx*, Vol. 2 (1976).

15. The coal lock-out of 1893 *by Chris Wrigley*

Figure 15.1
Figure 15.1 is based on MFGB data from the delegate meeting held at the Hen and Chickens Hotel in Birmingham on 19–20 July 1893. Clearly the data were generally rounded for delegation purposes, but they do give a good impression of the location and strength of the MFGB shortly before the great lock-out. The Monmouth and South Wales figures represent William Brace's work in the area; the bulk of the miners remained supporters of William Abraham ('Mabon'). The other notable gaps in coverage include the Scottish miners (who affiliated as a federation in 1894), the South Staffordshire miners and some Lancashire miners. The original hub of the MFGB was Yorkshire and Lancashire/ Cheshire. Details from the Credential Committee's report at the Hen and Chickens Hotel are printed in Page Arnot, 1949, pp. 227–8.

The 1893 coal lock-out was in its time the greatest industrial dispute in British history. It was a large but not a national affair. Some 300,000 miners were involved and some 24.4 million working days were lost in this dispute which ran from the last week of July until 17 November. Then it was brought to a close by the unprecedented intervention of the government.

The dispute affected most areas covered by the Miners Federation of Great Britain (MFGB). This had been formed in 1889 in the midst of an upturn in the economy. The favourable economic circumstances had encouraged concerted action to press for higher wages as the selling price of coal rose. Between 1888 and 1890 the MFGB areas had gained 40 per cent increases in wages. The main 1893 lock-out followed on from the price of coal falling 35 per cent from its 1890 peak, the employers calling for a reduction of 25 of the 40 per cent gained in 1888–90 (representing a 17.75 per cent reduction on July 1893 rates) and a lock-out of miners in some of the Midland Federation coalfields. As Keith Burgess has commented, the scale of the reduction demanded by the owners 'suggests that at least some of them were deliberately looking for an excuse to stop production in an effort to force up prices' (Burgess, 1975, p. 206).

In the first half of 1893 the MFGB was at its strongest. Its member unions had grown during the economic boom and the Durham and Northumberland unions had briefly joined it. However the bulk of the unionised Scottish miners as well as those of South Wales were to join the MFGB later. Nevertheless the MFGB represented 253,000 of 310,600 trade unionists working in the British coal industry. Figure 5.1 indicates where the MFGB's strength lay in July 1893, shortly before the lock-out began. By this time coal was a relatively highly unionised industry, with a union density of about 60 per cent compared to a British average for males of around 14 per cent.

The MFGB rejected sliding scales for wages. Sam Woods, the vice president, commented at the Federation's annual conference in January 1892:

We hold it as a matter of life and death that any condition of trade ought to render the working

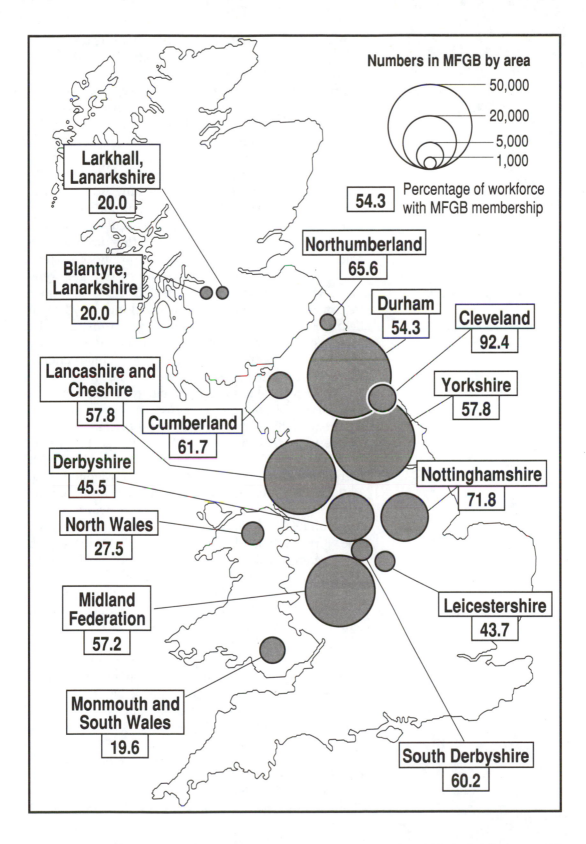

Numbers in MFGB by area

50,000
20,000
5,000
1,000

54.3 Percentage of workforce with MFGB membership

Larkhall, Lanarkshire
20.0

Blantyre, Lanarkshire
20.0

Northumberland
65.6

Durham
54.3

Cleveland
92.4

Yorkshire
57.8

Lancashire and Cheshire
57.8

Cumberland
61.7

Nottinghamshire
71.8

Derbyshire
45.5

North Wales
27.5

Leicestershire
43.7

Midland Federation
57.2

Monmouth and South Wales
19.6

South Derbyshire
60.2

man a living . . . notwithstanding all the teachings of political economists, all the doctrines taught by way of supply and demand, we say there is a greater doctrine overriding all those, and that is the doctrine of humanity. We believe that the working man is worthy of hire, and hold at the present moment that wages are as low as they ever ought to be. (Page Arnot, 1949, p. 205)

The Great Lock-out did have the effect of dramatically cutting the supply of coal and pushing up the price. Many areas of the MFGB had earlier supported the idea of a one or two week general holiday to cut back output, a procedure which often pleased both sides: the men gaining a break and the owners disposing of surplus stocks at higher prices. The price rise encouraged some owners to keep their pits working at the 1890 wage rates. In turn working MFGB men paid a shilling a day levy to help those locked-out, thereby enabling the dispute to be prolonged. The prospect of the dispute continuing further into the winter brought about government intervention. Moreover the November settlement which maintained existing wage rates until a conciliation board met in February 1894 was one that owners were willing to accept given the temporary high coal prices.

The impact of the 1893 lock-out varied across the MFGB's areas. The matter was complicated by the fact that some areas had been forced to accept wage cuts since 1891. In these areas the MFGB policy required that the area demand a pay increase to restore wages to the common 1890 level, backed by the threat of strike action. The Northumberland union balloted its members, with 7,994 against strike action and 6,943 for. In Durham, 20,782 were willing to take strike action but 19,704 were not. There was, however, clear support in the area for arbitration. So both Northumberland and Durham withdrew from the MFGB. In September the MFGB Executive balloted its districts as to whether their members would accept '25 per cent reduction in wages or any part thereof' or the employers' offer of arbitration. The results were unequivocal on these points, only 221 being willing to accept the wage cut and 383 arbitration with 143,695 and 139,587 respectively against. However on the third question of whether men should resume work if they could do so at the old wage rates, the vote was 61,923 for with 91,369 against.

In mid-September 3,000 men were at work in Cumberland where all collieries were paying the old rate, 11,000 men were working in North Staffordshire and others were working in others parts of the Midland Federation. By late September in all areas except Derbyshire there seemed to be a majority feeling in favour of a return to work where the 1890 wages were on offer. Consequently, faced with a drift back to work in these mines, the MFGB Conference agreed subject to a collective return to work and to those returning paying a shilling a day levy. Figure 15.2 illustrates the position a fortnight after this decision. The levy did help at a time when many mining families were suffering, with their savings gone. From August many families were reliant on soup kitchens and other relief. As in 1912, 1921, 1926, 1972, 1974 and 1984–5 support committees played a crucial role in enabling the miners to stay out.

W. E. Gladstone, the Prime Minister, intervened when it became clear in mid-November that other attempts at conciliation had failed. The dispute was threatening to cause major disruption to other industries, was jeopardising domestic fuel supplies for the winter and was becoming bitter in many places (most notably on 7 September at Featherstone, West Yorkshire, where the military shot two men after the Riot Act was read). Lord Rosebery, then Foreign Secretary, chaired a conference at the Foreign Office on 17 November and secured agreement. That night he noted in his diary, 'One of the most anxious and happiest days of my life . . . it would have been a good day to die on' (Marquess of Crewe, 1931, p. 433).

The resulting settlement involved the MFGB accepting arbitration from February 1894 through the conciliation board. This continued the explicit link between wages and coal prices. In the short term the dispute did alter the market price of coal, prevent immediate wage cuts in the MFGB area and end the call for 25 per cent wage cuts. However with effect from August 1894, the conciliation board cut wages by ten per cent. This reduction was only recovered in three stages in 1898–9, the last being early in the Boer War. The miners' income was also adversely affected by short-time working. The MFGB's membership dropped, only to return to its 1893 level after the turn of the century.

Sources and further reading
The miners' national organisation is covered by Robin Page Arnot, *The Miners: A History of the Miners' Federation of Great Britain 1889–1910*, 1949. Histories of the individual

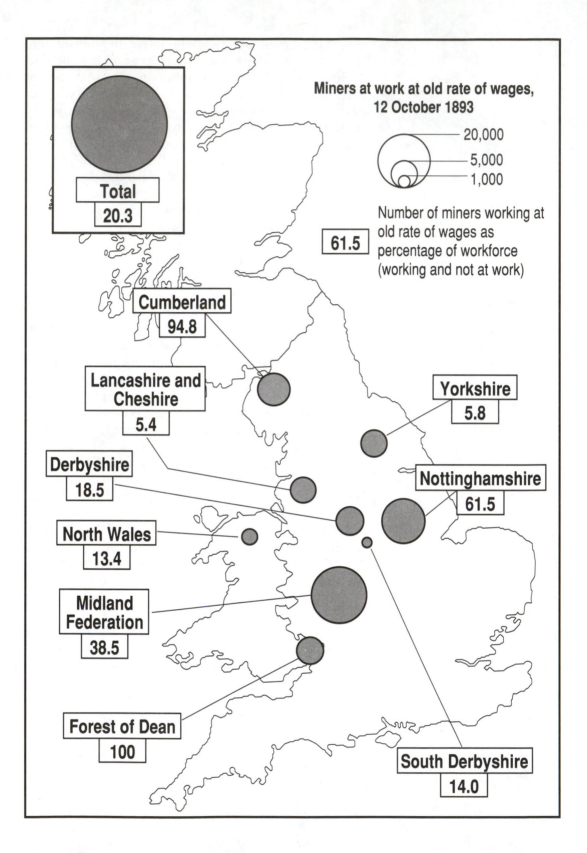

Miners at work at old rate of wages,
12 October 1893

20,000
5,000
1,000

61.5   Number of miners working at
old rate of wages as
percentage of workforce
(working and not at work)

Total
20.3

Cumberland
94.8

**Lancashire and
Cheshire**
5.4

Yorkshire
5.8

Derbyshire
18.5

Nottinghamshire
61.5

North Wales
13.4

**Midland
Federation**
38.5

Forest of Dean
100

South Derbyshire
14.0

Figure 15.2
Figure 15.2 is based mostly on reports given to a MFGB conference held in Birmingham on 12 and 13 October 1893 and printed in Page Arnot, 1949, p. 244. This shows that work was available at the old wage in Nottinghamshire and the Midland Federation as well as the smaller Cumbria and the Forest of Dean areas. The hub of the dispute with the employers was in Yorkshire, Lancashire and Cheshire and Derbyshire. As the return to work at the old wages was official MFGB policy, the proportion of MFGB members among those working was broadly in line with union density. The proportions ranged from 54.6 per cent members in Yorkshire to 58 per cent in Lancashire and Cheshire and Derbyshire, 59.5 per cent in Cumberland, 66.2 per cent in the Midland Federation, 71.4 per cent in South Derbyshire and 73 per cent in Nottinghamshire.

coalfield unions are: C. Griffin, *The Leicestershire and South Derbyshire Miners, Vol. 1 1840–1914* (Coalville, 1983); J. E. Williams, *The Derbyshire Miners*, 1962; John Wilson, *A History of the Durham Miners' Association 1870–1914*, Durham, 1907. For the history of the industry as a whole, see Roy Church, *The History of the British Coal Industry, Vol. 3, 1830–1913 Victorian Pre-Eminence* (Oxford, 1986). Studies of industrial relations in the industry include John Benson 'Coalmining' in C. Wrigley (ed.), *A History of British Industrial Relations 1875–1914*, Hassocks, 1982, and Keith Burgess, *The Origins of British Industrial Relations*, 1975, ch. 3. The case study also draws on The Marquess of Crewe, *Lord Rosebery*, 2 vols, 1931, and on A. F. Thompson, *1910* (Oxford, 1964).

Section C: 1900–39 *by David Gilbert*

Industrial protest: 1900–39

Any attempt to divide the history of British industrial protest and industrial relations into convenient periods will be questionable and somewhat arbitrary. The turn of the century is a convenient date and also nearly coincides with the start of systematic collection of strike statistics by the state, but industrial protest and conflict in the early part of the twentieth century can only be fully understood in the context of developments in progress at the end of the nineteenth century.

The growth in trade union membership in the second half of the nineteenth century had helped to form what Alan Fox has described as 'an emergent system of industrial relations' (Fox, 1985, p. 174). Despite the gains made in the 'new-unionism' of the late 1880s, by the early years of the twentieth century this system was by no means comprehensive, excluding many unorganised or poorly organised male workers and the great majority of women. The system was marked by increased recognition of organised labour on the part of employers and state and a general acceptance of the principle of collective bargaining. While everyday strikes were regarded as a problem (and as a serious problem which threatened Britain's international competitiveness when compared with emerging industrial powers such as Germany and the U.S.A.), the growing commitment to collective bargaining meant a move towards a greater acceptance of minor, ordinary strikes as part and parcel of industrial society. This was to some extent reflected in the official collection and publication of strike statistics. This emergent system of industrial relations

was associated with a stabilisation of the geography of routine industrial conflict associated with the patterning of organised union power in the late-Victorian and Edwardian economy. The partial institutionalisation of the strike also provided a delimitation of its legitimate character, making it narrowly economic and setting it apart from forms of social protest.

A second influence, again a development of the late nineteenth century, was the growing importance of explicitly working-class political movements. The rise of the Labour Party and the growing influence of socialism in the labour movement had complicated consequences for industrial protest. In many ways the emergent position of Labour politicians in the political establishment assisted in the institutionalisation of industrial relations in general and strikes in particular. For example, Lib-Lab MPs played a significant part in reversing the legal challenge to the unions' role in collective bargaining posed by the Taff Vale judgement of 1901. By the 1920s, when the Labour Party was either in power as a minority government, or else in opposition with serious expectations of government, senior Labour politicians and moderate union leaders were often as anxious as any Conservative to criticise strikes. At other times, and never with greater effect than during the General Strike of 1926, they were concerned that strikes should be normal 'trade disputes' and not means to wider political ends.

While the rise of the Labour Party and the growing political influence of union leaders helped to define and limit the form of the strike, the growth of an explicit politics of class conflict, albeit outside the mainstream of British working-class politics, did threaten to give new form and meaning to industrial protest. When a period of relative peace in British industrial relations in the period 1898 to 1907 was followed by a sustained period of industrial conflict, which was to continue unabated until the General Strike in 1926, there was considerable fear on the part of the establishment that industrial protest would become overtly political, threatening both the industrial order and the more general stability of British society. There were a number of moments when these fears were especially heightened, particularly in the period 1911–3, during the First World War, and in the strike wave of the years immediately after the war.

After the 1917 Bolshevik Revolution, British Communism provided the main focus to establishment fears, but before and during the First World War the threat to social and industrial order seemed to come from syndicalism. The syndicalists envisaged that the trade unions, albeit in a radically democratised form, could be the instruments of revolutionary social change. They also emphasised the role of direct action, combining industrial militancy with civil disorder. The perceived seriousness of the threat can be judged by the reaction in Parliament and the press to the publication of *The Miners' Next Step,* a syndicalist tract in South Wales in 1911, and the consternation caused by a combination of strikes in munitions factories and rent protests in Glasgow during the First World War. However, while there were undoubtedly places and moments where syndicalists had some influence, their overall impact was very limited. Even in cases like so-called 'Red Clydeside', most workers involved in strikes had a clear concern with their immediate interests rather than insurrection. In wartime Glasgow, the main issue in the munitions strikes was the defence of the privilege of skilled unionised engineering workers against the dilution of their position by the introduction of new workers.

Similarly, while the post-war strike wave certainly seemed threatening in an international context of revolution and serious industrial and social conflict and while there were some important outbreaks of violence, the chief aims of most strikes were to improve pay and conditions when an up-turn in the economy improved the bargaining position of organised labour. Radicalism was often fused with rank-and-file restlessness about the responsiveness and accountability of union leaderships, but this was often more a reaction to the growth of national unions and the centralisation of bargaining procedures than a clear expression of political exceptionalism.

It was only in distinctive economic, political and cultural circumstances that there was a clear fusion of social protest and industrial conflict in early twentieth-century Britain. The Tonypandy riots of 1910 were a clear case in point. An industrial dispute was the occasion for the conflict, but the riots were also an expression of a rejection of a particular way of life by a majority of inhabitants of the South Wales township. David Smith has described Tonypandy as a social struggle over the 'definition of community'. While events elsewhere were not always as violent or dramatic as at Tonypandy, the close relationship between village and pit in many British coalfields did produce distinctive forms of industrial protest. This was most apparent in the miners' lockout of 1926, the largest strike in British history, but also in smaller struggles. The Harworth dispute of 1936–7 combined an industrial and political struggle about trade union recognition with social conflict about the nature of local society.

The General Strike of 1926 was a unique

moment in the history of British industrial relations which can only be fully understood as a composite of many different histories and geographies of the event. The geography of support for the strike needs to be considered alongside the geographies of the state's response and of the reaction to the strike on the part of many who were bitterly opposed to it. The General Strike was not a revolutionary moment in British history for the legitimacy of the established order was not fundamentally questioned by the overwhelming majority of participants. However, neither was it a simple trade dispute nor just a show of solidarity in support of the miners. No other event shows quite so well both the divisions in the class society of Britain in the early twentieth century, or the geographic complexity of those divisions. There is no single history of the strike: the political negotiations in London must be balanced by hundreds of local studies. In some places where local 'Councils of Action' were formed the strike did seem to provide the potential for radical social protest, at least to local activists. In other places, the strike passed in almost carnival mood, not a conventional strike, but a break from the stresses and rhythms of industrial society. Elsewhere the strike saw open conflict between strikers and strike-breakers, often over alternative transport services run by volunteers. And in some places the strike was no more than a distant rumble which did little more than disrupt the local train services.

The end of the General Strike, and the subsequent defeat of the miners, marked a turning point in industrial relations and industrial protest in the inter-war period. This is certainly clear from the statistical record of strikes, which show a dramatic decline from 1927 onwards in both the number of strikes and in the number of working days lost. There were various reasons for this. Although its effects can be over-emphasised, the defeat of the miners did prove to be a psychological blow to the union movement and strengthened moves on the part of union moderates towards greater conciliation in industrial relations. A series of conferences between industrialists and some prominent union leaders took place in the aftermath of the 1926 strikes (although the conferences had been first mooted in 1925, and conciliation was an established feature of the British industrial relations system.) These are normally referred to as the Mond–Turner talks, after Sir Alfred Mond, a director of the newly formed ICI, and Ben Turner, a union leader in the woollen industry. The talks were relatively unsuccessful in their avowed aims of creating new structures of conciliation, co-operation and even limited joint control in British industry, but were indicative of changes in the prevailing climate of industrial relations. There were also increased legal limitations on industrial action in the 1927 Trade Disputes and Trade Union Act, which limited sympathy strikes and placed legal restrictions on picketing.

However, the most important influence on the nature of industrial conflict and protest in the late 1920s and early 1930s was the economic slump, and in particular the growth of mass unemployment, which severely weakened the bargaining position of the trade unions. There were fewer strikes in the early 1930s than for any other recorded period until the late 1980s. Industrial protest took other forms during this period, most notably direct protests about mass unemployment. The early 1930s saw substantial demonstrations, organised mostly by the National Unemployed Workers' Movement (NUWM), and several violent confrontations took place between demonstrators and the police. The most distinctive form of protest against mass unemployment was undoubtedly the hunger march. Between 1921 and 1936 there were six national hunger marches organised by the NUWM, and several others in Scotland, Wales, and the English regions, as well as the famous Jarrow crusade of 1936. The hunger march was a particularly appropriate form of protest in a society characterised by uneven development and massive regional disparities in wealth and employment opportunities. While it was difficult to identify specific gains made as a direct result of the marches, they succeeded in bringing the hardships of the depression across the border between what contemporaries knew as 'outer' and 'inner' Britain.

That border was also crossed by many in search of work, either spontaneously or as a part of government industrial transference schemes. As the regional geography of British industry changed, so did the pattern of its industrial relations. The restructuring of the economy during the inter-war years was a contributory factor both in the major strikes of the early 1920s, which were about profits, wages, conditions and employment in the context of the decline of staple heavy industries, and in the relative industrial peace of the 1930s. Regional changes in the structure of the economy contributed towards the decline in strike activity by weakening the unions and breaking established industrial communities in 'outer' Britain, and by providing scope for new forms of production and working order in 'inner' Britain.

The new industries were located predominantly in the South East and Midlands, and for the most part produced consumer goods for the expanding markets in those parts of the country. They were based in places without long traditions of union organisation and employed local workers with backgrounds in agricultural or craft work alongside migrants from 'outer' Britain. There was also a significant increase in the number of women working in industry. The new industries often used semi-skilled or unskilled workers in assembly line work. There was likewise a continuing move into employment in services rather than manufacturing. None of these factors precluded union organisation or industrial disputes. In the post-war period, some of these new industries became the most strike-prone, altering the geography of strikes, and by the 1970s and 1980s there were major disputes involving service-sector workers, many of whom were women. However, the union movement, which in the 1930s remained dominated by skilled male workers in traditional industries had great problems in adapting rapidly to these new circumstances, particularly in a period of relative weakness.

Sources and further reading

There are very many surveys of industrial relations and industrial conflict in this period. This account draws upon: A. Fox, *History and Heritage. The Social Origins of the British Industrial Relations System* (London, 1985); C. J. Wrigley (ed.), *A History of British Industrial Relations 1875–1914* (Brighton, 1982), and *Volume II: 1914–1939*. (Brighton, 1987); and J. E. Cronin, *Industrial Conflict in Modern Britain* (London, 1979). The Tonypandy riots are discussed in D. Smith, 'Tonypandy 1910: definitions of community' *Past and Present* 87 (1980), pp. 158–84.

16. The geography of strikes, 1900–39

Most of the essays in this book are case studies, concentrating either on a single event or on a particular movement. This essay attempts to give a more general picture of the geography of strike activity in Britain between 1900 and 1939. Although there were a few earlier attempts to collect comparative strike statistics, modern British strike statistics date from the late 1880s, when the Board of Trade started to collect information on strikes. From 1888 to 1913 detailed summaries were published in the *Annual Report on Strikes and Lock-outs*, and monthly reports of strike activity appeared in the *Labour Gazette*. These published analyses were based upon strikes recorded in the trades dispute record books, or strike registers kept by the Board of Trade, and subsequently by the Ministry of Labour.

These registers form the basis of the following analysis of the geography of strike activity in Britain. An entry was made in the register for each strike of which the government was notified. The information recorded included the number of firms and workers involved, the number of working days lost, the dates of the strike, some indication of the result of the strike, the industry or industries affected, and the location of the strike. There is obviously a great amount of information in the strike registers; between 1900 and 1939 there were over 28,000 separate strikes recorded. The maps in this chapter are based on a sample consisting of all strikes in every fifth year, starting in 1903 and continuing until 1938.

Great care is needed in the interpretation of any set of strike statistics and it is important to appreciate the scope and limitations of the records in the strike registers. The most important problems arise because the statistics were based on employers' answers to questionnaires. Estimates of the number of workers involved and the number of working days lost were likely to be imprecise or even deliberately false. A number of specific difficulties are also worth pointing out. From 1897 onwards it was decided that small or short strikes involving less than ten workers or lasting less than a day should be excluded, except where the total number of working days lost was more than 100. This remains the basis of modern British strike statistics. While some lower cut-off point is necessary and the criteria chosen were applied

All the figures in this section are based upon the record of strikes in the official strike registers held in the Public Record Office at Kew in class LAB 34. The time series shown in the graphs are extracted from the annual *Abstract of Labour Statistics,* and include figures for Ireland before 1913 and Northern Ireland after. For the maps in this section strikes recorded in the registers were allocated to a particular county (or sub-region in Scotland and Wales) where possible. Most larger strikes could be allocated to one of the standard regions shown in the figures. (The standard regions used are Clive Lee's historical county near-equivalents of modern standard regions. The sub-regions used in Scotland and Wales are also taken from this source. See C. H. Lee *British regional employment statistics 1841–1971*, (Cambridge, 1979) Those strikes which could not be allocated to either a county or a region were excluded from the analysis.

consistently, this does mean that one dimension of strike activity, particularly of unofficial strike activity, is not covered by the registers. In the 1940s the Ministry of Labour published statistics of strikes lasting less than a day, which suggested that over a third of all strikes were that short. Another important and unfortunate limitation of the data is that no figures for the numbers of men and women involved in strikes are available for the period.

One problem which faces anyone attempting a study of the geographic characteristics of strike activity is the assignment of strikes to particular places. In the period in question, however, national or cross-regional strikes were very much the exceptions to a rule of localised disputes. In most years, over 95 per cent of strikes took place within a single county. Even in 1913, one of the peak strike years of the period and a year which was marked by a number of major disputes, 83 per cent of all recorded working days lost were in strikes which took place within one county. This says something both about the strikes and the way that they were recorded in the registers. Because of the way in which bargaining took place and the number of employers involved, it was often difficult to distinguish between a single large dispute and a series of smaller disputes sharing common grievances. It was easier to record such events as a series of separate strikes. This skews the strike statistics towards smaller, localised disputes, but also makes it easier to produce maps of British strike activity.

It is difficult to produce one measure or statistic of overall strike activity. This is because of the wide range of disputes which have to be included. Social scientists, historians and economists looking at strike activity have used three statistics, each of which has strengths and weaknesses. The most straightforward is a simple measure of the number of strikes taking place (in the first figure, the statistic given is weighted by the size of each region's workforce.) The obvious weakness of this statistic is that it gives the same weight to a major national dispute lasting several weeks as to a small local dispute. For example in 1926, the year of the national nine-month lockout, there were far fewer strikes in British mining than in any other year on record. An alternative is to count the number of workers involved in disputes. The strike registers include estimates of both the number of workers involved directly and the total number of workers not at work because of a strike. This gives a better picture of the relative importance of large and

Figure 16.1
Number of strikes per hundred thousand workers 1903–38. The small maps show the regional pattern of strikes for every fifth year between 1903 and 1938. The larger map shows the average number of strikes each year per hundred thousand workers for these eight years; the geographic units are old administrative counties for England, and sub-regions for Scotland and Wales. The graph shows the total number of strikes in each year from 1900 to 1939.

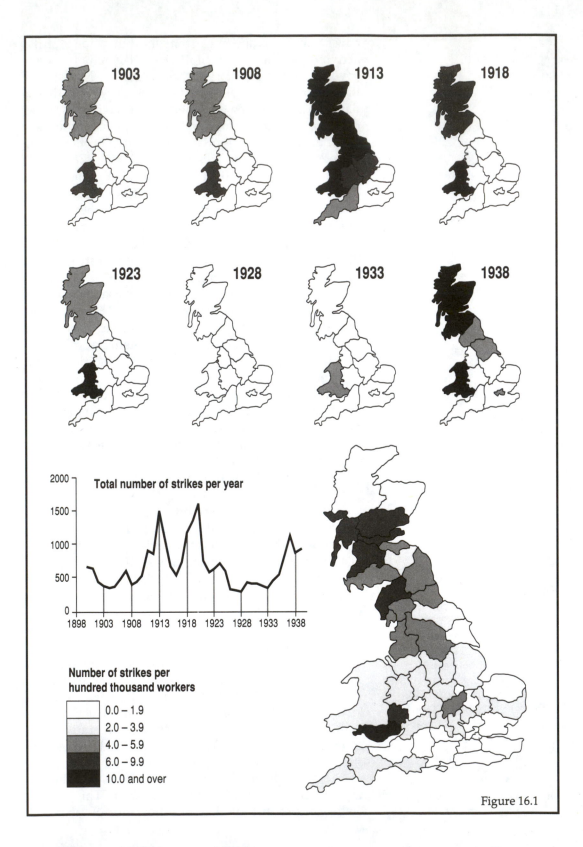

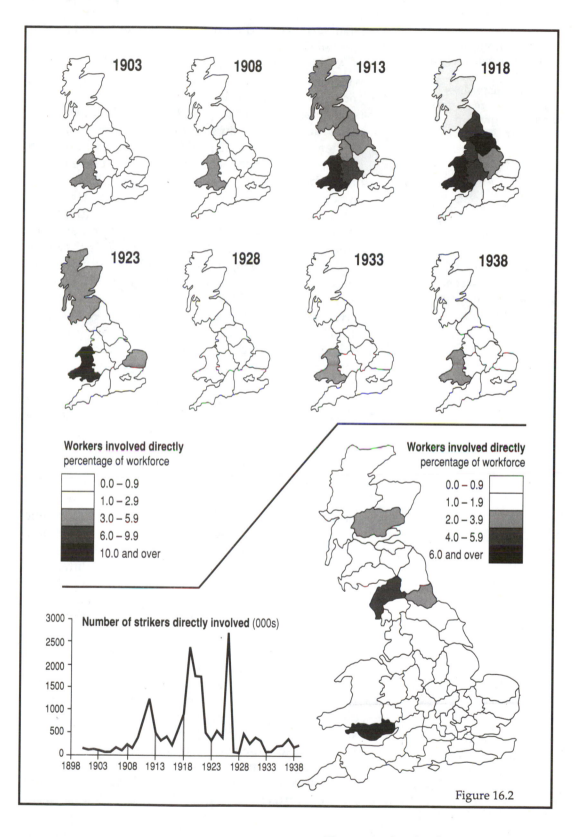

1903 **1908** **1913** **1918**

1923 **1928** **1933** **1938**

Workers involved directly
percentage of workforce

	0.0 – 0.9
	1.0 – 2.9
	3.0 – 5.9
	6.0 – 9.9
	10.0 and over

Workers involved directly
percentage of workforce

0.0 – 0.9	
1.0 – 1.9	
2.0 – 3.9	
4.0 – 5.9	
6.0 and over	

Number of strikers directly involved (000s)

Figure 16.2

Figure 16.2
Workers directly involved in
strikes (percentage of workforce)
1903–38.
The small maps show the
regional pattern of workers
directly involved in strikes for
every fifth year between 1903
and 1938. The larger map shows
the average number of workers
directly involved each year (as a
percentage of the workforce) for
these eight years; the geographic
units are old administrative
counties for England, and sub-
regions for Scotland and Wales.
The graph shows the total
number of workers involved
directly in strikes for each year
from 1900 to 1939.

Figure 16.3
Working days lost per hundred
workers 1903–38.
The small maps show the
regional pattern of working days
lost for every fifth year between
1903 and 1938. The larger map
shows the average number of
working days lost each year per
hundred workers for these eight
years; the geographic units are
old administrative counties for
England, and sub-regions for
Scotland and Wales. The graph
shows the total working days
lost in each year from 1900 to
1939.

small strikes, but does not discriminate between short
and long ones.

A third measure is the number of working days lost,
which is sensitive both to the number of workers involved
and to the length of strike. Unfortunately, if this measure
is taken as the indication of strike activity, then a few
major disputes will swamp large number of smaller,
shorter disputes. The General Strike and miners' lockout
of 1926 are the obvious examples of this, but there are
others. In East Anglia, in April and May 1923, there were
two disputes of six weeks duration recorded in the strike
registers, one involving 8,000 farmworkers (the 'great
strike' of Norfolk agricultural labourers), the other 10,000
building workers. These stoppages resulted in the loss of
half a million working days: in no other year in the five-
yearly sample did the annual total of working days lost
in East Anglia exceed 80,000.

It is difficult to choose between these three measures
of strike activity, especially when comparing regions
and counties with different industrial structures. Each
captures a different dimension of strike activity, with the
number of strikes picking out smaller strikes, the number
of workers involved giving some general measure of
strike activity, and the number of working days lost
showing both the patterning of major disputes and giving
some indication of the overall economic cost of strikes.

The history and geography of each of these indicators
is examined in detail in the first three figures in this
section. Each diagram has a series of maps showing the
regional distribution of strikes in each of the sample
years, a graph showing annual totals for Britain as a
whole, and a county map showing the average of the
eight sample years. There are some important differences
between these three statistical series. For example, the
strike waves in the years before and after the First World
War were of similar magnitude in terms of the number of
strikes, but the strike wave of 1918 to 1921 involved far
more workers. The number of working days lost is
dominated by the two major mining disputes in 1921 and
1926. These years are not included in the sample years,
and because of this the county map in diagram three is
probably the least representative of these maps. Despite
these differences, certain generalisations can be made
about the geography of strikes, the most marked feature
being the concentration of strikes, strikers and working
days lost in South Wales, central industrial Scotland, and
parts of Northern England.

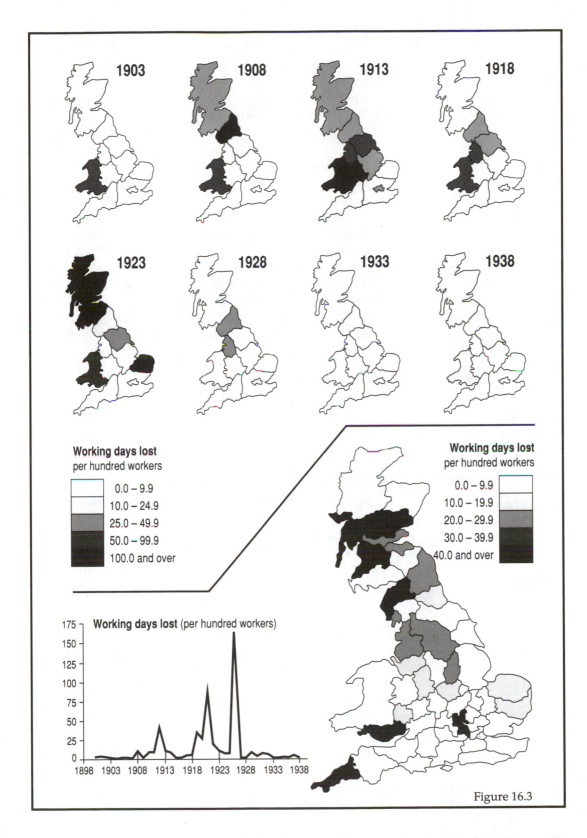

Working days lost
per hundred workers

	0.0 – 9.9
	10.0 – 24.9
	25.0 – 49.9
	50.0 – 99.9
	100.0 and over

Working days lost
per hundred workers

	0.0 – 9.9
	10.0 – 19.9
	20.0 – 29.9
	30.0 – 39.9
	40.0 and over

Working days lost (per hundred workers)

Figure 16.3

This pattern accords with contemporary impressions of the geography of strike activity and with the assessment made by K. G. J. C. Knowles in his detailed study of strikes in Britain between 1911 and 1947. Knowles concluded that 'regional influences on striking are to a large extent industrial causes in disguise' and that 'regional differences, on analysis, prove much slighter than industrial.' (Knowles, 1952, p. 208). The maps in the first three diagrams here do reflect differences in the industrial structure of the regions and counties. The patterning of strikes between 1900 and 1939 is dominated by the geography of a few industries, particularly coal mining. Between the turn of the century and the outbreak of the Second World War over one quarter of all strikes and over 60 per cent of working days lost were in mining; during the 1920s nearly three-quarters of days lost were in mining. Other relatively strike-prone industries such as engineering, shipbuilding and textile manufacture accounted for much of the remaining strike activity, and these industries, like mining, were concentrated in particular regions of the country.

However, within industries there were significant regional differences in the level and character of strike activity. The clearest expression of these differences came in the largest strike of the period, the miners' lock-out of 1926 (see section on the lock-out), but evidence of regional differences can also be found in the overall record of strike activity. Figures 16.4 and 16.5 shows two series of maps which are adjusted for industrial structure, in an attempt to highlight a regional component in strike propensity. The method used follows the same form as that used by Smith *et al.* in their study of British strikes in the 1960s and 1970s (see section on the Geography of Strikes 1940–93). Each of the measures of strike activity was weighted by a ratio to take account of the regional industrial structure. For example, if a region had proportionately four times as many miners as the national workforce, then each of the indices would be divided by four for strikes involving miners in that region. Even after this adjustment substantial regional differences do remain, although obviously not as pronounced as in the first three figures. Wales, Scotland and parts of Northern England remain significant centres of strike activity in the first forty years of the twentieth century, even when an allowance is made for differences in industrial structure.

Contemporary qualitative discussions such as Lord

In figures 16.4 and 16.5 adjustment for industrial structure was made on the basis of the breakdown of the decennial census into 27 occupational categories in C. H. Lee *British regional employment statistics 1841–1971* (Cambridge, 1979) The adjustment procedure is explained in more detail in the text.

Figure 16.4
Number of workers involved in strikes per thousand workers 1903–38.
Figures adjusted for industrial structure.
The small maps show the regional pattern of workers involved, adjusted for industrial structure, for every fifth year between 1903 and 1938. The larger map shows the average number of workers involved each year per thousand workers for these eight years, also adjusted for industrial structure.

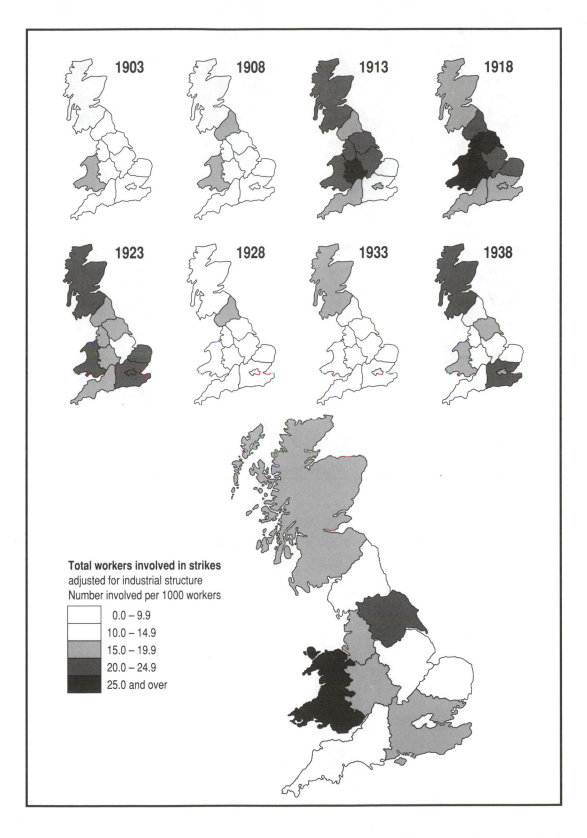

Total workers involved in strikes
adjusted for industrial structure
Number involved per 1000 workers

	0.0 – 9.9
	10.0 – 14.9
	15.0 – 19.9
	20.0 – 24.9
	25.0 and over

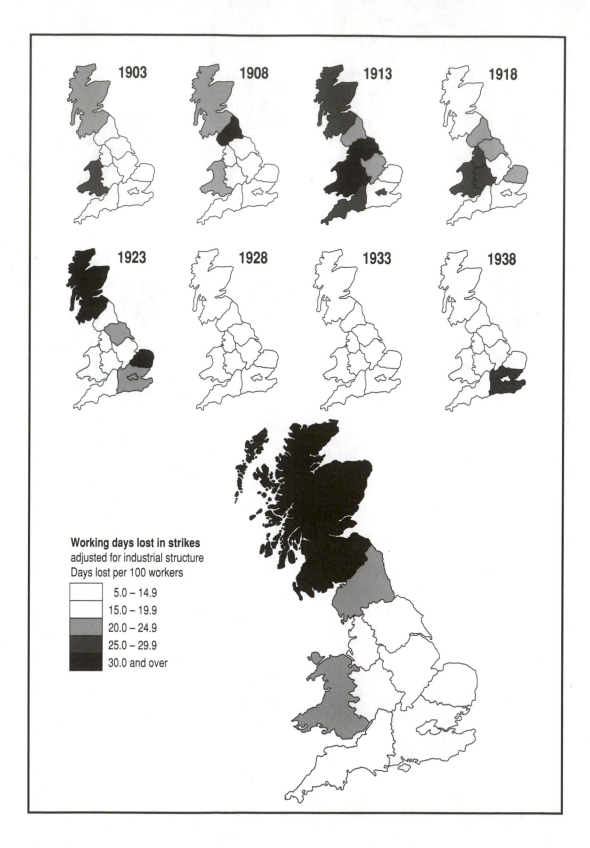

Working days lost in strikes
adjusted for industrial structure
Days lost per 100 workers

	5.0 – 14.9
	15.0 – 19.9
	20.0 – 24.9
	25.0 – 29.9
	30.0 and over

Figure 16.5
Working days lost per hundred
workers 1903–38.
Figures adjusted for industrial
structure.
The small maps show the
regional pattern of working days
lost, adjusted for industrial
structure, for every fifth year
between 1903 and 1938. The
larger map shows the average
number of working days lost
each year per hundred workers
for these eight years, also
adjusted for industrial structure.

Askwith's *Industrial Problems and Disputes* (1920) explicitly recognised regional differences in strike behaviour, and it is significant that the 1917 Commission of Inquiry into Industrial Unrest, the most comprehensive government survey of strikes and industrial militancy during the period, was organised geographically rather than on an industrial basis. The Commission was a response to the militancy of the pre-war years and the continuance of strikes in certain parts of Britain during the war itself, but its reports went beyond assessment of the immediate causes of recent disputes. The reports can be read as searches for more general social and cultural explanations of long term historical differences in industrial protest between British regions.

This emphasis is clearest in the report on Wales (Cd. 8668), which is the first in a long tradition of studies attempting to explain the exceptional record of unrest and militancy in South Wales. Small scale disputes about wages, conditions, dirty coal allowances and other grievances were endemic in the South Wales pits. There had also been a number of major regional disputes, most notably the Cambrian Combine Strike of 1910–11, and South Wales miners had been prominent in the national coal dispute of 1912. They were to be prominent again in 1921 and 1926. The Commission attempted both to explain why labour relations in the South Wales coalfield were worse than those in other coalfields (so that changes could be made in South Wales and to prevent other coalfields following the Welsh example), and to ascertain whether the social, economic and cultural characteristics of South Wales had a more general influence on behaviour in industries other than mining.

The report looked at a wide range of factors, including what now seems a rather embarrassing discussion of typical Welsh 'racial' characteristics. The report is more convincing where it discusses such issues as the geology of the coalfield and the ease and safety of mining, the structure of ownership and organisation of the coal industry, the influence of physical geography on the urban structure of the region and the consequences of rapid immigration into the Valleys. The report sensibly makes no clear argument for a single, simple explanation of industrial militancy in South Wales, but it is clear that by the time of the report South Wales was a strongly distinctive region with established traditions of political culture and social organisation which encouraged militancy both within the coal mining industry and in other industries, such as shipbuilding and transport.

In most other regions of Britain, with the possible exception of central Scotland, it is less easy to recognise certain common regional characteristics which would have influenced strike propensity. The other reports of the 1917 Inquiry reflect this, as they concentrate more closely on the characteristics of individual industries. Differences between regions were seen as being due to differences in economic organisation, with factors such as plant size, rates of female employment and organisation of the labour process important, rather than clear differences in specifically regional characteristics or political cultures. Outside of South Wales, distinctively militant or strike-prone political cultures were more commonly identified at a sub-regional level, ranging in scale from 'Red Clydeside' and the dockland areas of London and Liverpool, to the localised radical communities of the 'Little Moscows' (see section on Little Moscows and radical localities).

Sources and further reading

The most detailed study of the history and geography of strikes in this period remains K. G. J. C. Knowles, *Strikes – a study in industrial conflict.* (Oxford, 1952). The early history of British strike statistics is discussed in Creigh, S. W., 'The origins of British Strike Statistics', *Business History* XXIV, 1 1982, 95–106. Consideration of the exceptionalism of South Wales is made in P. Cooke, 'Class practices as regional markers: a contribution to labour geography' in D. Gregory and J. Urry (eds.), *Social Relations and Spatial Structures* (Basingstoke, 1985), and D. M. Gilbert, *Class, Community and Collective Action. Social Change in Two British Coalfields, 1850–1926* (Oxford, 1992).

17. The General Strike of 1926

The General Strike of 1926, and the miners' lock-out which followed it, were the culmination of a crisis in the coal industry which had been developing since the end of the First World War. Long-established export markets for British coal were under threat both from the coal industries of other countries and from the development of alternative sources of power. The coalowners' response to a crisis of profitability in the industry was to attempt to reduce miners' wages. In 1921 proposals for wage cuts and a return to independent district (or coalfield) wage-rates had resulted in a three-month national coal strike. The French occupation of the Ruhr in 1923 brought some temporary relief to the industry, but Britain's return to the pre-war gold standard in April 1925 was a severe blow to competitiveness at a time when export markets were already shrinking.

On 30 June 1925, the coalowners issued an ultimatum giving a month's notice of severe cuts in wages. The Miners' Federation of Great Britain (MFGB), a confederation of the various coalfield unions, turned for support to the TUC, particularly to the railway unions and the Transport and General Workers' Union (TGWU), the MFGB's partners in the so-called 'Triple Alliance'. These unions placed an embargo on the movement of coal and this, combined with the threat of a national coal strike, forced the government to intervene. On 31 July the government agreed to subsidise the coal industry until 1 May 1926, and instituted the Samuel Commission to enquire into the condition of British mining. This partial victory after the concerted action of the unions was known as 'Red Friday', in contrast to 'Black Friday' (15 April 1921) when the railway and transport workers in the 'Triple Alliance' had let the miners down, leaving them to fight the 1921 dispute alone.

Red Friday proved to be only a temporary halt on the road to industrial conflict and, when the Samuel Report came down clearly against the continuation of the subsidy beyond the end of April 1926 (while also calling for the long-term reorganisation and modernisation of the industry), a major clash between the unions and the government was all but inevitable. The final offer by the mine owners was of a 13 per cent reduction in wages and a lengthening of the working day from seven to eight hours, terms which were even worse than those recommended in the Samuel Report. On 1 May 1926, when the government had already enforced an Emergency Powers Act, a Conference of Union Executives approved a proposal for a National Strike and placed the conduct of the strike in the hands of the General Council of the TUC. Last minute negotiations between the General Council and the Cabinet were broken off by the Prime Minister, Stanley Baldwin, on the pretext that the strike had already started and the freedom of the press threatened when print workers refused to print an anti-strike editorial in the *Daily Mail*. The General Strike began at midnight on 3 May 1926.

The strike lasted nine days and, in terms of response if not of outcome, was remarkably successful. It is difficult to give a quantitative assessment of the geography of the General Strike for the simple reason that there was a partial breakdown both of transport and communications during the period of the strike lasted. At the time, neither the government nor the TUC at their headquarters in Eccleston Square in London had a very clear idea of what was happening across the country. There are certainly no central systematic records giving details of the numbers who did or who did not support the strike in particular places, although most accounts written after the event stress that most of those who were called out did answer the call. In all, between one and a half and two million workers came out on strike, in addition to the million miners who had been locked out. The written history of the General Strike is characterised by a large number of local studies, most of which draw upon the recollections of strikers, volunteers, and others caught up in the events of the nine days. This reflects the way in which the strike touched the lives of ordinary people, becoming a reference point in the memories of those who experienced it.

The geography of the strike can be seen as an amalgam of three elements: the response by workers to the strike call, the government's policing and control of the strike, and the reaction of opponents of the strike, notably the volunteers in the 'Organization for the Maintenance of Supplies' (OMS). The first of these was conditioned by the ambivalence of the General Council of the TUC towards the strike. The moderate leadership of the TUC found itself in an uneasy position, continually stressing that what was clearly a political strike was no more than a extension of an industrial dispute about the hours of work and pay of miners. Almost above all else, the

Figure 17.1
The response of strikers in the General Strike, 1926.
This map shows the assessment of the strike made by the Plebs League during the strike. It is a partial assessment of the strike, but does show the that the main areas of concern for the supporters of the strike were in small towns away from the main industrial areas and some southern cities.
Source: R. W. Postgate, E. Wilkinson, and J. F. Horrabin *A Workers' History of the General Strike* (London, 1927).

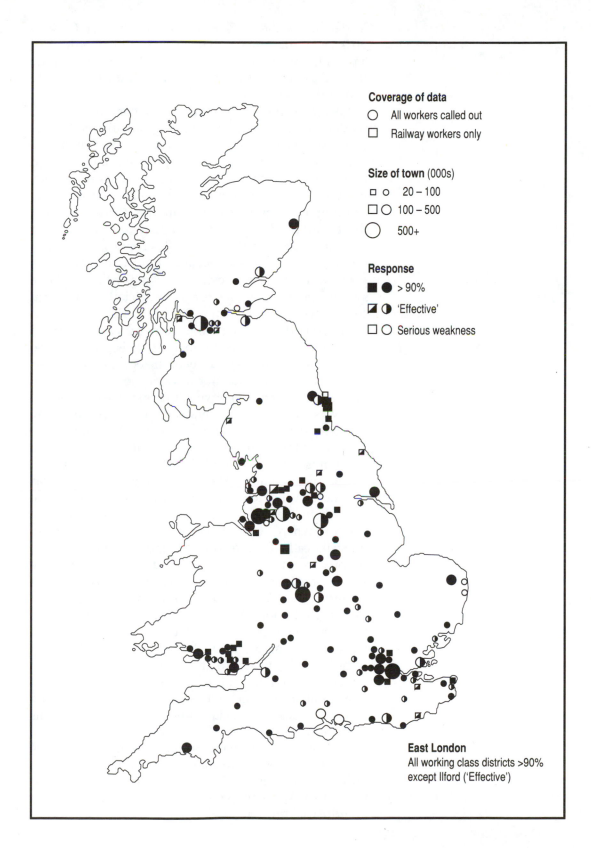

Coverage of data

○ All workers called out

□ Railway workers only

Size of town (000s)

□ ○ 20 – 100

□ ○ 100 – 500

○ 500+

Response

■ ● > 90%

◨ ◑ 'Effective'

□ ○ Serious weakness

East London
All working class districts >90%
except Ilford ('Effective')

leadership of the TUC was adamant that the General Strike was not a breakdown of constitutional order, nor a potentially revolutionary moment. It was this attitude that led directly to the abandonment of the strike at the end of the nine days.

One reflection of this desire for containment and moderation was the decision not to call all workers out on strike. The plans drawn up by the Strike Committee of the TUC divided workers into a first line and a second line of strikers. In the first-line were all transport workers, most workers in heavy industry, all workers in the printing trades and the press, building workers (except those employed on housing and hospital work). Power workers were asked to stop all supplies, except for lighting. Among those not called out by the TUC were postal workers, including those working on the telephone system, and most engineers and electricians. Workers in certain occupations, such as health workers and those involved in distributing food, were expressly excluded from the strike call. To some extent the geography of the strike reflected the geography of the occupations called out, although this was not always the case. In many places the distinction between the first line and second line was not clearly understood: for example, many workers in the cotton towns of Lancashire joined the strike, even though these were places with weak traditions of unionisation and not officially part of the first line.

The most comprehensive survey of the strike was produced by the Plebs League, which placed the response in particular areas into one of three categories: solid support, where over 90 per cent of strikers responded to the strike call; 'effective' support; and those places where serious weaknesses were reported. The Plebs League survey was based on a questionnaire sent to the Trades Councils and Councils of Action which provided the local organisation of the strike, and cannot be seen as more than a partial and one-sided view of the response. However, the map of the Plebs League survey does give some limited indication of the geography of the response which was solid in London, in most coalfield towns and in a number of other centres. The response was more patchy in most provincial cities, and in smaller towns away from the coalfields. The General Strike was unique in the history of British industrial relations for being the one moment when formal cross-union, locally co-ordinated organisations like the Trades Councils and Councils of Action played a major role in the organisation of industrial protest.

One of the most famous incidents of the General Strike was the football match played between strikers and police in Plymouth on 8th May. It was reported by the government in its strike newspaper, the *British Gazette*, and has entered the mythology of the General Strike.

However, this example of peaceful co-operation has had a disproportionate influence on popular images of the strike. There were also many confrontations involving strikers, police and strike-breakers, and the government took the possibility of a violent breakdown of social order very seriously. Police reinforcements were moved to areas of likely conflict and the Emergency Powers Act of 1920 was used to detain hundreds of strikers. There were important geographic patterns to the use of these powers. The areas with the most arrests under the act were London and the mining areas of the North East and Yorkshire. Well over half of the arrests made were for offences concerning the obstruction of vehicles. One notable feature of the geography of arrests was that relatively few were made in South Wales, which reflected both the power of local union branches in the valleys and the problems that the authorities had in recruiting Special Constables.

The second map gives details of the mobilisation of the armed forces during the strike. Although the army and navy were not used to police the strike directly, the second map gives some idea both of the Government's assessment of the geography of potential insurrection during the strike and its commitment to keeping the major ports open. A number of the places with reputations as radical localities or regions (see the section on 'Little Moscows and radical localities' for further details) were picked out as areas of particular threat. The largest concentration of troops was in the Docklands of East London, where armoured cars were used to escort supply convoys, and machine guns were mounted at the dock gates, while battleships were moored in the lower Thames. Battleships and troop re-inforcements were also sent to South Wales and to Clydeside.

The third element of the geography of the General Strike was that of conservative and mostly middle-class reaction. The strike was the only occasion in the history of British industrial relations when there was significant organisation of large numbers of ordinary people *against* a strike. The most visible and well-reported manifestation of this was the OMS, although there were probably as many volunteers helping to break the strike who were organised locally by Chambers of Commerce or on an *ad*

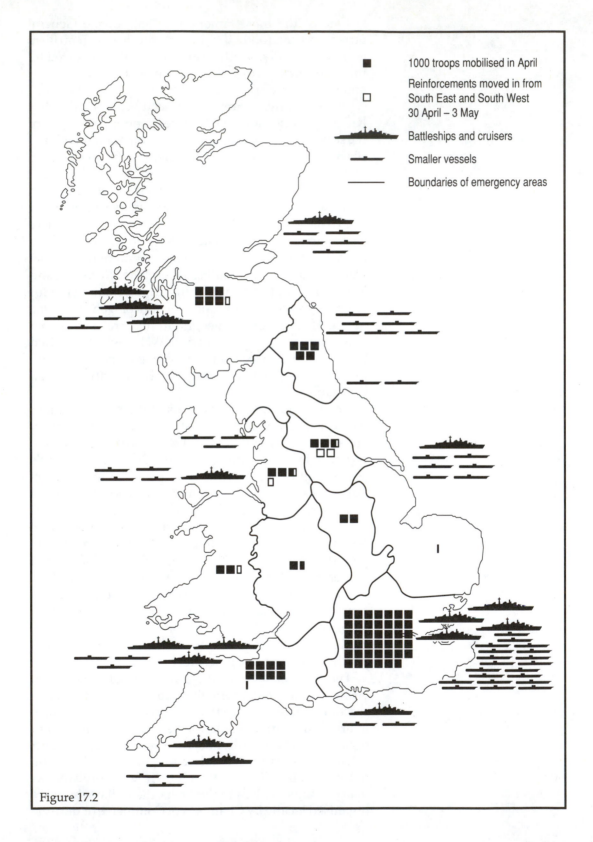

Figure 17.2

Figure 17.2
The response of the state to the General Strike, 1926.
This map shows regional military dispositions in May 1926. Note the correspondence between the military concentrations and areas with established radical reputations.
Source: J. Foster 'British Imperialism and the Labour Aristocracy' pp 3–57 in J. Skelley (ed.) *The General Strike, 1926* (London, 1976)

hoc basis. Student volunteers also came from the older universities, notably Oxford, Cambridge and University College London. Volunteers were used to help run transport services or else enroled as Special Constables. The majority of the volunteers were middle class, and this was reflected in the geography of opposition to the strike. While most towns and cities with large middle-class populations saw significant recruitment of volunteers, there was also substantial recruitment in the Home Counties and other southern counties. Most of the violent incidents during the General Strike were clashes between volunteers and strikers and were concentrated in city centres where the two were most likely to meet. Volunteer-driven buses and lorries were especially likely to be attacked.

Information about the strike and its progress was also unevenly distributed across the country. The distributions of *The British Gazette* and the TUC's newspaper, *The*

Figure 17.3
The response of volunteer workers to the General Strike, 1926.
As with most information about the General Strike, this map gives only a partial picture of the national response to the call for volunteers. It does show how the volunteers were often concentrated in areas away from the main support for the strike.
Source: C. Wrigley 'The General Strike, 1926 in Local History. Part One: The Government's Volunteers' *Local Historian* Vol. 16 (1984), 36–48. This is an analysis of the figures in the Public Record Office files HO 45/12336/2130.

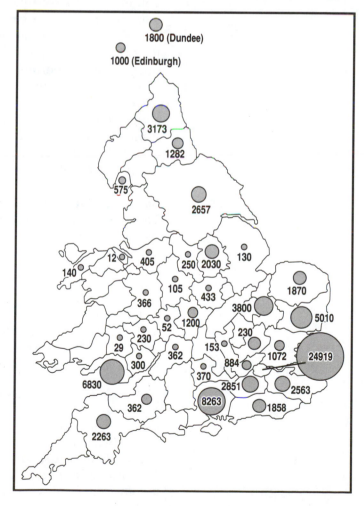

British Worker, were concentrated in areas of strong support for the two sides in the strike. Even the spread of information about the strike through the radio reports of the fledgling BBC was extremely uneven. The geography of this new mass medium, supposedly serving the whole nation, was in fact very concentrated. While in the London suburbs people crowded round radio receivers in high street electrical shops for the latest news of the progress of the strike, in many South Wales valleys there was not a single radio set.

The different geographies of the General Strike reflected the class divisions of the period and the government's perceptions of possible insurrection. There were areas of solid support for the strike, especially in most of the coalfields, where effective local control of trade and transport passed to the strike committees and Councils of Action, and areas like the Home Counties where opposition to the strike was strong and many volunteers were recruited. Between these two extremes were most of the urban areas of Britain which were contested terrain during the strike. When the TUC ended the strike on May 12, leaving the miners to fight on their own, many supporters of the strike were completely incredulous given the evidence of their local areas, and felt deeply betrayed. There is little evidence that the support for strike was waning, especially in its heartlands. It was not worry that the strike was disintegrating which caused the TUC to call it off as much as fear that it would escape their control.

Sources and further reading
There are very many books on the General Strike. The most recent general account is K. Laybourn, *The General Strike of 1926* (Manchester, 1993), which includes detailed case studies of the strike in particular regions. M. Morris, *The General Strike* (Harmondsworth, 1976) is one of the best social histories of the events of May 1926. A good conventional history of the strike which mixes political and social history is G. Phillips, *The General Strike* (London, 1976). Details of the state's response to the strike can be found in J. Morgan, *Conflict and Order. The Police and Labour Disputes in England and Wales 1900–1939* (Oxford, 1987). The local organisation and geography of the OMS is discussed in C. Wrigley, 'The General Strike, 1926 in Local History. Part One: The Government's Volunteers' *Local Historian* Vol. 16 (1984), 36–48. Two of the maps for this section are based on those in S. V. Ward, *The Geography of Interwar Britain: The State and Uneven Development* (London, 1988), for which grateful acknowledgement is made.

18. The miners' lock-out of 1926

At the end of the General Strike, the miners were left to fight on alone in a lock-out which lasted for a further seven months before their eventual defeat. When measured in terms of working days lost, this was the largest dispute in the history of British industrial relations, directly involving over a million miners. The geography of the lock-out is central to any understanding of its history, particularly the way in which support for the strike weakened during the autumn of 1926. The chronology of the strike in different coalfields is shown in figure 18.1. This map is drawn using figures from government reports, specifically those of the Divisional Inspectors of Mines (PRO CAB 27 333/334). The returns from the Inspectors represent only one view of the support for the strike and the MFGB consistently claimed that fewer miners were returning to work than the numbers claimed by the government. However, the Divisional Inspectors' returns provide the only consistent quantitative record of the regional support for the strike and, while the absolute number of miners returning to work may have been contested, the pattern of support and desertion of the strike given accords with qualitative assessments of the progress of the strike given by both sides.

The first significant returns to work came in the pits of the South Midlands Division in Warwickshire, Shropshire and Staffordshire. By early August, both the government and the leadership of the MFGB saw this area as the weak link in the dispute. The 30 July edition of *The Miner* described Warwickshire as 'the cockpit of the entire struggle'. Arthur Cook, the charismatic Secretary of the MFGB, and other members of its leadership set about an intensive campaign of meetings and speeches in the Midlands in an attempt to prevent men from returning to work. This set the pattern for the rest of the strike. Cook's impassioned campaigning had an immediate effect on the return to local pits, but this effect was only temporary, and the drift back to work resumed three or four days after his appearance. As the return to work increased in pace, Cook devoted more and more time to addressing local meetings and there are reports of him speaking at over twenty-five meetings in a single weekend.

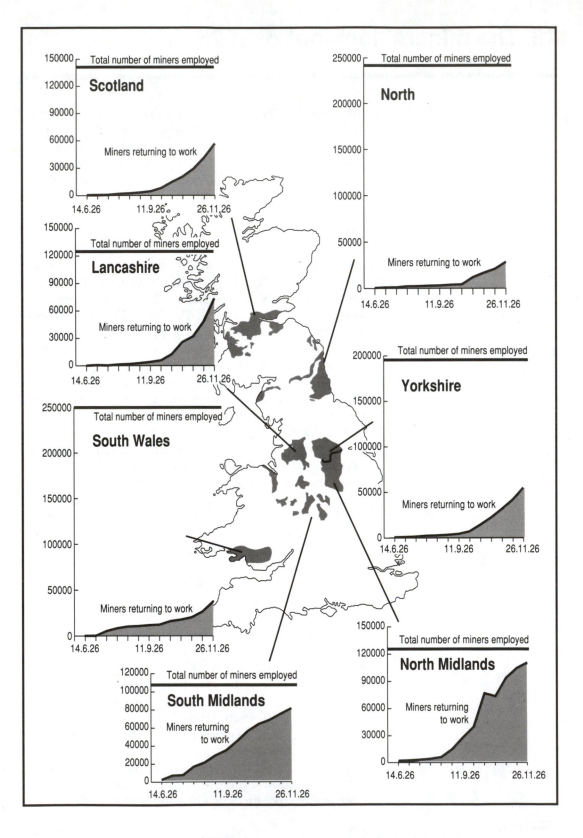

Scotland

Total number of miners employed

Miners returning to work

150000
120000
90000
60000
30000
0

14.6.26　11.9.26　26.11.26

North

Total number of miners employed

Miners returning to work

250000
200000
150000
100000
50000

14.6.26　11.9.26　26.11.26

Lancashire

Total number of miners employed

Miners returning to work

150000
120000
90000
60000
30000
0

14.6.26　11.9.26　26.11.26

Yorkshire

Total number of miners employed

Miners returning to work

200000
150000
100000
50000
0

14.6.26　11.9.26　26.11.26

South Wales

Total number of miners employed

Miners returning to work

250000
200000
150000
100000
50000
0

14.6.26　11.9.26　26.11.26

South Midlands

Total number of miners employed

Miners returning to work

120000
100000
80000
60000
40000
20000
0

14.6.26　11.9.26　26.11.26

North Midlands

Total number of miners employed

Miners returning to work

150000
120000
90000
60000
30000
0

14.6.26　11.9.26　26.11.26

Figure 18.1
The geography of the return to work in the miners' lock-out of 1926.
The figures for returns to work are compiled from the reports of the Divisional Inspector of Mines, in the Public Record Office, reference CAB 27 333/334. These are government figures which may overstate the scale of the return. The patterning of the return to work does co-incide with qualitative assessments from both sides in the dispute.

The geography of the return to work changed rapidly from the end of August, although the return to work continued unabated in the South Midlands. The dispute was broken by the North Midlands, and the Nottinghamshire coalfield in particular. Throughout September and October, Nottinghamshire miners returned to work at a rate of over 500 men each week, and large numbers of miners were also abandoning the strike in Derbyshire and Leicestershire. By mid-October, three-quarters of Nottinghamshire's 54,000 miners were back at work. The fate of the strike in Nottinghamshire was sealed by the formation of a right-wing breakaway union, led by the rebel Labour M.P. George Spencer, which was committed to negotiating an independent settlement with the Nottinghamshire owners. By the time the national dispute ended at the end of November, the Spencer Union (officially the 'Nottinghamshire and District Miners' Industrial Union') had branches at almost all pits in the county. Mining unionism in Nottinghamshire remained divided until the Harworth dispute of 1936–7 (see section on the Harworth dispute).

In contrast to the Midlands Districts, in other coalfields the strike remained very solid almost to the end of the dispute. In mid-November, when over 80 per cent of Midlands miners had returned to work, only about 30 per cent of Scottish miners, 20 per cent of Yorkshire miners and 10 per cent of Northern miners had gone back. Support for the strike was strongest in South Wales, where the South Wales Miners' Federation (SWMF) estimated that only three per cent of miners had returned to work by early November.

At the end of the dispute, the miners were forced to capitulate completely, leaving Cook's earlier rallying cry of 'not a penny off the pay, not a second on the day' sounding hollow. Most miners returned to longer hours and lower wages, and a significant number of miners were prevented from returning to work at all. Unemployment among miners for the rest of the inter-war period kept wages depressed and kept the mining unions on the defensive. The MFGB itself had been greatly weakened by the concession of district agreements, and the abandonment of national bargaining.

Just as the geography of the General Strike revealed some of the fault lines of early twentieth-century British society, so the pattern of support for the miners' dispute was also evidence of regional differences in political culture and working organisation. There is no single, simple reason why the strike remained so solid in the North East and South Wales and was so weak in the Midlands. At a superficial level, there were differences in the immediate interests of miners in the dispute. Many pits in the Midlands coalfields were relatively profitable: geological conditions were often easier to work, and much Midland coal went to the relatively stable domestic market. The generous district settlement offered to the Spencer Union in Nottinghamshire in part reflected this. But the differences between the coalfields went much deeper.

Differences in the politics of the area unions were important. In South Wales there was an established and developing tradition of radical politics, whether in the form of the Communist Party or, more usually, the Labour Party. Between 1910 and 1920 there was a generational change in the leadership of the SWMF, bringing in men with an education in left-wing, even revolutionary, politics. In the Midlands mining unions there was much more continuity between the leaderships of the 1920s and early generations of Lib-Lab and Liberal union leaders, and there was an established tradition of conciliatory industrial politics.

Differences in union politics were reinforced by more general differences in regional political cultures. The strike was strongest in those areas where support for the Labour Party (or even for the Communist Party) was strongest. Politics in the Midlands coalfields were more complicated. Liberalism retained an appeal to a section of the working class and mining populations and there was also significant support for Conservatism. In the Midlands, more miners lived in close proximity to sizeable middle-class districts. As well as more general influences on attitudes towards the strike, there were also quite specific influences which were different in the Midlands. The local press tended to be much less sympathetic and often openly hostile towards the miners' cause. Local Poor Laws Boards of Guardians were also less sympathetic towards strikers and their families and often either refused assistance completely, or gave very low rates of relief. The Guardians at Lichfield were notoriously harsh, reflecting the antipathy between the ratepayers of the Cathedral city and the striking miners of the surrounding industrial areas. In South Wales, by contrast, although the rate burden was often nearly impossible to bear and staggering debts were built up which took many years to pay off, Poor Law Boards like those at Pontypridd, Bedwellty and Merthyr attempted to maintain high scales of relief payment.

Contrasts in political culture were strengthened by differences in working order. The 'butty' system of subcontracting lasted longest in the Midlands coalfields, and, although by the time of the 1926 lock-out this system was less important than it had been in the nineteenth century, the butties still formed a distinctive stratum of the workforce, often forming a distinctive, intermediate social group in mining towns and villages. In Nottinghamshire, butties were associated with Conservative and other forms of right-wing politics and formed the organisational backbone of the Spencer Union.

The urban and social geography of different coalfields also influenced the pattern of solidarity. The strike in the North East, South Wales and certain parts of the Scottish and Yorkshire coalfields was marked by intense community organisation. In many towns and villages in these coalfields, the pit was virtually the only source of male employment. In some such villages, the colliery company maintained close control over the lives of miners and their families, but in many more places the local union branch had become an important focus to local life beyond the pit. The importance of the union in local life, and the close-knittedness of many mining villages, had direct implications for the conduct of the strike. Institutions like soup kitchens, cheap food stalls and boot repair workshops helped to stretch financial resources during the dispute and increased the sense of local solidarity. In such tightly-knit and often relatively isolated villages it was easy to take action against strike-breakers who were sometimes violently attacked and who were almost always ostracised by their local communities.

In the Midlands coalfields, the relationship between pit and place was rather different. There were many places in the Midlands coalfields where the colliery company was still the dominant force in local life. Nowhere was this more the case than in the new pits of the Dukeries in Nottinghamshire, where company villages had been built with social control as an explicit consideration in their design (see section on the Harworth dispute). The first returns to work in Nottinghamshire took place in the Dukeries pits during the summer of 1926. In other parts of the Midlands, miners lived in more complicated towns than the single industry townships and villages of South Wales or the North East. Many miners lived in the suburbs of Birmingham or Nottingham or lived in smaller towns where there were a number of other industries. Many Midlands miners commuted to their place of work, rather than living in the local pit village. In such circumstances it was difficult to provide the same intensity of communal support for the strike, and it was more difficult for tactics of intimidation and ostracism to maintain the discipline of the strike.

These differences in political culture, working order and social geography, which lay behind the geography of the 1926 lock-out, were long-term features, with their origins in the nineteenth century and before. They were also to be enduring features in the geography of conflict in the British coal industry. Both sides in the 1984–5 strike clearly acknowledged the similarities to and continuities with the 1926 dispute, in the weakness of the strike in the Midlands pits, the formation of a breakaway union in Nottinghamshire or, in the rediscovery of the importance of community in industrial conflict in South Wales, the North East, Scotland and Yorkshire.

Sources and further reading

Regional differences in the support for the lock-out are discussed explicitly in David Gilbert, *Class, Community, and Collective Action* (Oxford, 1992) and Peter Sunley, 'Striking parallels: A comparison of the geographies of the 1926 and 1984–85 coalmining disputes.', *Environment and Planning D Society and Space* 8 (1990) 35–52. Many regional studies of the miners and mining included detailed studies of the events of the lock-out. These include H. Beynon and T. Austrin, *Masters and Servants: class and patronage in the making of a Labour organisation: the Durham miners and the English political tradition* (London, 1994), H. Francis and D. Smith, *The Fed: A History of the South Wales Miners in the Twentieth Century* (London, 1980) and A. R. Griffin, *The Miners of Nottinghamshire: A History of the Nottinghamshire Miners' Association, Volume 2* (London, 1962). There are a number of good thematic studies of the lock-out in M. Morris, *The General Strike* (Harmondsworth, 1976). G. Noel, *The Great Lockout of 1926* (London, 1976), and R. P. Arnot, *The Miners: Years of Struggle* (London, 1953) provide contrasting narratives of the lock-out.

19. Little Moscows and radical localities

Strikes and industrial protest in interwar Britain were very rarely associated with explicitly rejectionist politics. Communists and members of associated organisations, such as the Minority Movement and the National Unemployed Workers Movement, played an important local organising role in the General Strike and in protests about mass unemployment. However, their influence on the political attitudes of most of those they led was very limited. For the vast majority of those taking part in the General Strike, and even for most of the hunger marchers, the struggle was for specific measures and for fairness and social justice within the existing order, rather than for a wholesale and dramatic re-ordering of British society. In most urban and industrial communities, the local Communist was a committed outsider, often detached from and slightly despairing of the routines and rhythms of everyday life and associational culture.

There were, however, a few places where industrial militancy was fused with a political ideology which rejected the established order and where local Communists did gain some local control over popular politics. These places gained fame and notoriety for the character of local politics, for their records of industrial militancy, and for their leading role in major disputes such as the miners' lockout of 1926. It is hard to be systematic about this geography of exceptional places for there was often very little difference in social or industrial conditions between a radicalised community and surrounding places. The geography of the 'Little Moscows' owed much to circumstance and to the creation and promotion of local traditions of militancy and political extremism.

The three best-known Little Moscows were all mining villages: Chopwell near Blaydon in the North East coalfield, Mardy (or Maerdy) at the head of the Rhondda Fach in the South Wales coalfield, and Lumphinnans in the Fife coalfield. However, the terminology was not restricted to mining settlements. The Vale of Leven, an area of Dumbartonshire where most of the working population was employed in textile dyeing and printing, was known as 'Little Russia'. The Little Moscows were mostly small, relatively isolated villages reliant on a

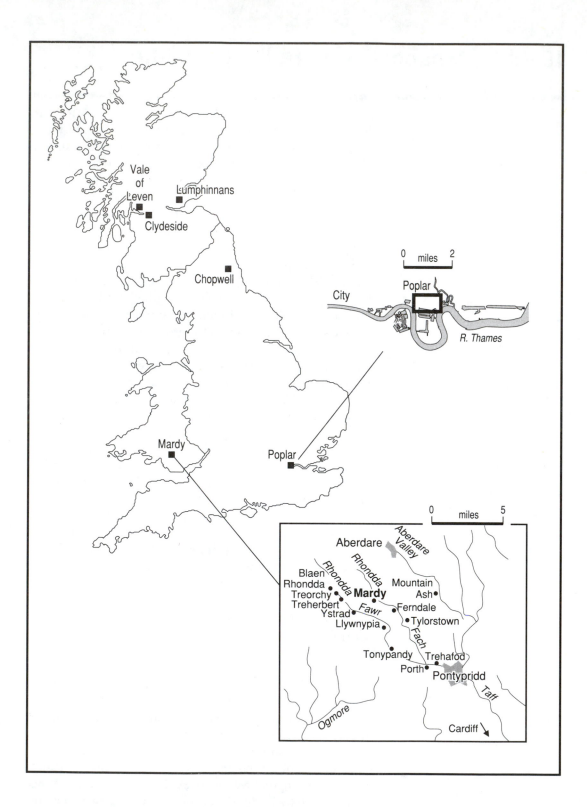

Figure 19.1
Little Moscows and radical
localities 1900–39.
This map shows places
mentioned in the text. The insets
show Mardy's isolated position
as the last village in the Rhondda
Fach, and Poplar's position in
London.

single industry which was in decline, with consequent unemployment. This, of course, did not make them stand out from a large number of other places in similar predicaments. What made the Little Moscows distinctive was the engagement of Communists in local politics and associational culture and the importance of a rhetoric and iconography which drew upon the vocabulary of Communism and class conflict and the example of the Soviet Union. This local culture was expressed in banners, murals and even street names, like Marx Terrace in Chopwell. The construction of these local identities was aided by the hostility of the local and regional press. Very often terms such as 'Red village' or 'Little Moscow' were used both disparagingly by the press and with reactive pride by many inhabitants. For the headline writers, there was only room for one Little Moscow in any given region or coalfield, even if Communists or other radicals were important in a number of places.

The relative isolation, small size and tight-knittedness of the Little Moscows created situations where there was the potential for a politically committed group to gain local political control. Mardy was the last village in the Rhondda Valley (see inset map), at the end of the main road and railway, and somewhat detached even from the society of the Valleys. Many of the villages at the heads of other Welsh Valleys also had reputations for militancy. During the General Strike, intrepid reporters from the main regional papers, *The Western Mail* and *South Wales Daily News* , travelled up the Rhondda to the village, sending back reports as if from behind enemy lines. In a small local society, particular individuals could have great influence on local politics. The histories of Mardy and Lumphinnans are inextricably tied to the early careers of Arthur Horner and the Moffat brothers, Abe and Alex, all committed Communists who later became important national figures.

In single-industry communities, it was possible for there to be a fusion of workplace politics and local politics. In many mining villages, the local union lodge became a kind of unofficial local government and, in the Little Moscows, Communists were relatively successful because they used their position in the union to influence local social life more generally. In Mardy, Communists were involved in all manner of local activities and institutions, from football teams to discussion groups to soup kitchens during the great strikes. They were to some extent the inheritors of a rich tradition of

Figure 19.2
Red Clydeside 1915–19.
This map shows both the
distribution of ASE members in
Clydeside and the main centres
of the rent strikes. ASE rank-and-
file members were prominent in
the unrest over the dilution issue
in Clydeside, and active in the
Clyde Workers' Committee. The
first strike broke out at Weir's of
Cathcart in February 1915. David
Kirkwood was chief shop
steward at the Parkhead Forge.
Govan and Partick were the
main centres of the rent strike.
Sources: The figures for ASE
membership are taken from ASE
Monthly Report for January 1912.
Figures shown are for groups of
branches in particular areas of
Glasgow and Clydeside. For
example, the figure for Partick
also includes members in the
Finnieston, Glasgow West,
Partick, Temple and Whiteinch
branches.
Areas of secondary support for
the rent strike are taken from S.
Damer 'State, Class and
Housing: Glasgow 1885–1919' in
J. Melling (ed.) *Housing , Social
Policy and the State* (London,
1980).

associational life which had earlier been directed by the
Nonconformist chapels. In this active engagement in
everyday life lay both the strengths and limitations of the
Little Moscows. Communists gained popular legitimacy,
but were also diverted from radical rejectionist politics
towards community politics, and the defence of the
immediate interests of the local population. Mardy,
Chopwell, and Lumphinnans were exceptional in the
form and ideology of politics, but in terms of the content
of practical politics, they were merely at one extreme of
a scale which included other places with similar social,
industrial and geographic characteristics.

Other places with rather different characteristics were
associated with radicalism and were given the epithet
'Red', notably Red Poplar and Red Clydeside, which
Lenin described as the 'Petrograd of the West'. If the
politics and culture of the Little Moscows could be
thought of as industrial protest in the sense that there
was a close link between working order, union
organisation and community politics, the activities of
these radical localities are perhaps best thought of as
social movements. In both cases, radical politics took
place in an urban context and reputations for militancy
were forged in protests which were not exclusively
industrial. Clydeside's red reputation came about
through a combination of protest by well-organised
skilled workers in the munitions factories and shipyards,
and protest by tenants about the nature of the urban
environment. The two events which started the 'legend
of Red Clydeside' were the strike of 10,000 engineering
workers in February 1915, and the rent strike which took
place later in the same year. The industrial strike was for
a higher rate of pay, but also represented a rank-and-file
revolt against the moderate central leadership of the ASE
which had recommended acceptance of a modest increase
before the strike. The strike was co-ordinated by a
committee of shop-stewards, in defiance of the union.
Several of the most important of these shop stewards
were committed members of Marxist political parties
such as the Socialist Labour Party and the British Socialist
Party, which were forerunners of the Communist Party,
while others were active members of the Independent
Labour Party. After the 1915 strike, the shop stewards
movement formed the Clyde Workers' Committee with
William Gallacher of the BSP as president.

However, although the industrial agitation in
Glasgow's factories during the First World War was co-

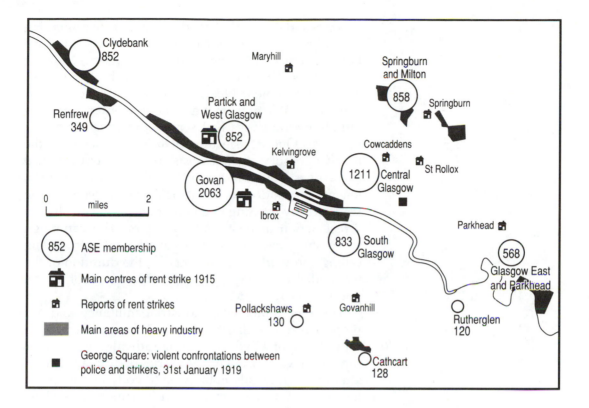

Clydebank 852

Maryhill

Springburn and Milton 858

Springburn

Renfrew 349

Partick and West Glasgow 852

Kelvingrove

Cowcaddens

St Rollox

Govan 2063

Ibrox

1211 Central Glasgow

0 miles 2

833 South Glasgow

Parkhead

568 Glasgow East and Parkhead

852 ASE membership

Main centres of rent strike 1915

Reports of rent strikes

Main areas of heavy industry

George Square: violent confrontations between police and strikers, 31st January 1919

Pollackshaws 130

Govanhill

Rutherglen 120

Cathcart 128

ordinated by a radical left-wing organisation and clearly worried the government, the central issues were always the immediate defence of the interests of a skilled workforce, and action was directed against the imposition of the Munitions of War Act of 1915. This Act had provisions for the dilution of work in the factories through the introduction of unskilled men and women workers and was used by the shipbuilding companies of the Clyde to break-up the pre-war working order and to erode the wartime bargaining position of the unions. The government agreed to demands for a gradual process of dilution, but a second major strike broke out in Glasgow in April 1916, when David Kirkwood, one of the leaders of the CWC, was prevented from inspecting the conditions of new workers at Parkhead Forge. The government responded severely to this strike, possibly because resistance to the Munitions Act was spreading to other industrial areas, and there was also industrial strife in the South Wales coalfield. Several of the leading members of the CWC, including Kirkwood, were arrested and removed from the Glasgow area.

The rent strike in the autumn of 1915 was not directly connected to the industrial action in the munitions factories and shipyards. It marked the start of a continuing campaign by the working class of Glasgow to improve housing conditions, which led eventually to the Housing Act of 1924. The city was characterised by large, over-crowded tenement blocks close to the factories and shipyards. Wartime movement of workers into the munitions industries had served to increase housing pressures. One of the features of the rent protests was the involvement of women activists, such as Helen Crawfurd and Agnes Dollan of the ILP. In the autumn of 1915, tenants responded to threatened rises in rents by the landlords by refusing to pay rent and, occasionally, by direct action against rent collectors. The campaign successfully resulted in the government introducing ceilings on working class rents for the duration of the war and also widened the scope and support of radical politics on Clydeside.

The rent campaigns, industrial militancy and the prominence of socialist activists all contributed to the reputation of Clydeside as a radical region. This reputation was sustained by a series of dramatic events after the war, mostly notably on 'Bloody Friday' on 31 January 1919, when a demonstration of unofficial strikers in George Square in central Glasgow was violently dispersed by police and tanks were subsequently moved onto the streets of the city.

The borough of Poplar in London's East End came to prominence in 1921 when a number of councillors, including the leader of the Labour council, George Lansbury, were gaoled for refusing to pay rates to the London-wide bodies which were legally entitled to them. The council had argued that the burden of local taxation on London's poorest borough was too great and that money should be redistributed to Poplar from richer parts of the city. The council chose to spend its rates revenues on the relief of the local poor. Poplar council was also committed to a minimum wage policy and ambitious slum clearance plans, and the term 'Poplarism' became a shorthand for a certain type of engaged municipal socialism. Protest in Polar had more of a basis in traditions of popular culture, community organisation, gender relations, suffrage politics and street life than in the organisation of waged labour. Lansbury consciously directed the party away from the influence of the local unions, which for the most part represented skilled-male workers in steady employment, who formed a very small proportion of the population of the East End.

Sources and further reading
The best overall discussion of the Little Moscows is to be found in S. MacIntyre, *Little Moscows* (London, 1980). Contrasting histories of radicalism on Clydeside can be found in J. Hinton, *The First Shop Stewards' Movement.* (London, 1973), and I. McLean The Legend of Red *Clydeside* (Edinburgh, 1983); a discussion and synthesis of these can be found in J. Melling, 'Work, culture, and politics on "Red Clydeside": the ILP during the First World War', in A. McKinlay and R. J. Morris, *The ILP on Clydeside, 1893–1932: from foundation to disintegration.* (Manchester, 1990). The most comprehensive account of Poplarism is Noreen Branson, *Poplarism 1919–1925. George Lansbury and the Councillors' Revolt* (London, 1979). The relationships between place, labour organisation and forms of practical politics are discussed in M. Savage, *The dynamics of working class politics: the labour movement in Preston 1880–1949* (Cambridge, 1987) and D. Gilbert, *Class, Community and Collective Action. Social Change in Two British Coalfields, 1850–1926* (Oxford, 1992).

20. The national hunger marches 1921–36

Some of the most familiar and emotive images of the inter-war period are of hunger marchers on the road to London. The hunger marches have assumed great symbolic importance, not only in the history of working-class protest, but also in the history of regional divisions in Britain. The hunger marches were deliberate attempts to cross the 'north-south' divide, bringing home the reality of mass unemployment to parts of the country which were relatively untouched by the depression. A correspondent for the *Hertfordshire Mercury* (13 November 1936) reporting on the last national hunger march in 1936, commented that 'what the eye does not see the heart does not grieve,' and that the march had been 'good for the souls' of that prosperous England unaffected by the suffering of the depressed areas.

Although even the South East was suffering significantly in the early 1930s, there was great regional and local unevenness in the impact and experience of unemployment throughout the 1920s and 1930s. The first map in this section shows regional disparities in unemployment in 1933, but it should be remembered that particular towns within the depressed regions experienced much higher rates of unemployment than these average figures. In some towns, particularly those dependent on shipbuilding or coal-mining, there were periods in the 1930s when over three-quarters of the adult male workforce was out of work.

The hunger march with the firmest place in the public memory of inter-war Britain was the Jarrow crusade of 1936, yet the crusade was in many ways an exceptional event. The attention which the media gave to the Jarrow crusade at the time, and its subsequent romanticisation in popular culture and historical writing, has to some extent usurped the place of the national hunger marches organised by the National Unemployed Workers' Movement (NUWM).

Between 1921 and 1936 there were six national hunger marches organised by the NUWM. There were also several important marches in Scotland, Wales and the English regions and a march to London by Welsh miners in 1927. The NUWM was formed in 1921, in the first downturn of the economy after the post-war boom. It

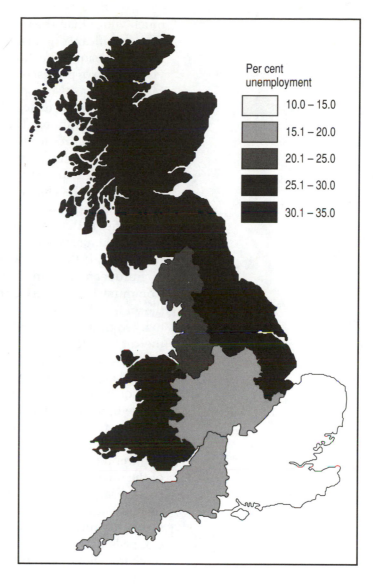

Figure 20.1
Insured unemployment by
administrative division in Great
Britain 1933.
Source: Ministry of Labour Gazette.

was a militant organisation, with close connections to the
newly-formed Communist Party of Great Britain (CPGB).
Wal Hannington, the most important leader and
spokesman of the NUWM, was a founding member of
the party, and many other activists within the Movement
were also party members. The NUWM claimed a
membership of 100,000 between 1933 and 1935, but it is
probable that its membership was never greater than
about half that number and was under 20,000 for most of
its history. Although this membership represented only
a tiny fraction of the unemployed (unemployment in the
early 1930s probably directly affected between 8 and 10
million people), the NUWM had an influence which was

much wider than the Communist Party and it was the most significant organisation of the unemployed during the depression. The hunger marches were the most visible form of protest organised by the NUWM, but the Movement was also responsible for concerted campaigns against government legislation and for national and local demonstrations. The Movement also ran shelters and advice centres for the unemployed.

The relationship between the Communist Party and the rest of the Labour movement in Britain was a crucial influence on the character of the hunger marches. To some extent this also conditioned the attitude of the authorities to the marches and the coverage given in the press and on news-reels. Until the adoption of a united front policy in the mid-1930s, in the context of the growth of European fascism and the Spanish civil war the Communist Party was extremely antagonistic towards the wider labour movement. This antagonism was most marked in the early 1930s when the CPGB came under the direct influence of Moscow and adopted a 'class against class' policy which had as its chief target the 'social fascists' in the Labour Party and the trade unions. Most of the marches were ignored or officially condemned by the Labour Party and the TUC and were treated by both the authorities and the press as the work of a small extremist and communist-dominated organisation and as unrepresentative of the plight or views of the majority of the unemployed. The national march of 1936, which was the largest and in some ways most successful of the marches, was the only time when the organisers actively set out to gain the support of local Labour parties, Trades Councils and union branches, although many of the other marches did rely on the unofficial support of such organisations for food and shelter on the road.

The first national hunger march took place at the end of 1922, following an earlier NUWM march from London to Brighton to lobby the Labour Party conference. The idea for the march also drew upon the example of local deputations to the workhouse or local Poor Law Guardians' board rooms, which had long been a feature of the protests of the poor and unemployed. The first march was a rather chaotic affair, with small groups of marchers from around the country arriving at different times during November and December. In all around 2,000 unemployed marched and there were large demonstrations in London on 23 November 1922 and on 7 January 1923.

Although all of the marches were general protests against the waste and degradation of mass unemployment, most of them were responses to changes or threatened changes in the treatment of the unemployed by the government. The second march in 1929 was a direct response to the 1927 Unemployed Insurance Act. Nearly 1,000 men marched on London from various parts of the country to protest at the tightening of the 'Not Genuinely Seeking Work' clause in the act, and the new requirement of 30 weeks' contribution in a two year period to qualify for unemployment benefit. Partly as a result of the march, the 30 stamps requirement was suspended.

The 1930 march was the smallest of the marches, with only about 350 marchers. This march was relatively unsuccessful both because it came at a time when the NUWM was most isolated from the general labour movement, which meant that the marchers were almost completely dependent on the casual wards of Poor Law institutions for accommodation, and because the immediate *raison d'etre* of the march had been removed when the Labour Government abolished the 'Not Genuinely Seeking Work' clause just before the start of the march. The main innovation of the 1930 march was a small separate contingent of women marchers. Although only about 25 women marched in 1930, this set a precedent and all the later marches included a women's march.

Major changes in the system of unemployment relief which were introduced in the early 1930s shifted the focus of discontent to the means-testing of unemployment pay. After 1931, the household resources of the long-term unemployed were taken into account when the amount of relief payable was calculated. This provoked great resentment, both because of the financial penalties on families with unemployed members and because of the increasing intrusion of the state into the lives of the unemployed, which brought with it overtones of the surveillance and scrutiny of paupers under the hated Poor Law. The fourth national hunger march of 1932 took place in the aftermath of a series of major demonstrations and violent incidents in British cities, most notably in Manchester, Belfast and on Merseyside. The NUWM styled the 1932 march as the 'Great National March against the Means Test', and its stated aim was to deliver a petition with a million signatures to Parliament. In all, over 2,000 marched to London in eighteen contingents, including a contingent of 25 women who left Burnley on 9 October.

Unlike the earlier marches, there were outbreaks of violence on the way to London. The most serious trouble was at Stratford-upon-Avon on 20 October 1932 where there were clashes between the Lancashire contingent and the police. When the contingents arrived in London there was further violence. On 27 October the marchers were joined by many thousands of demonstrators (Hannington estimated the crowd at 100,000, while the police estimated 25,000) for a meeting in Hyde Park which ended in fighting close to Marble Arch. A large demonstration on 30 October in Trafalgar Square was relatively peaceful, but there was further trouble on 1 November. Hannington was arrested in the morning on a charge of 'attempting to cause disaffection among members of the Metropolitan Police'; he was taken directly to Brixton gaol and was later sentenced to three months' imprisonment. In the evening, an unsuccessful attempt was made to present the petition by the NUWM. The marchers were prevented from entering Whitehall from Trafalgar Square and, after fighting in the Square, the police confiscated the petition from a cloakroom at Charing Cross station. The petition was returned the NUWM some days later when the marchers were preparing to leave London by train. It was never presented to Parliament. In the week in which the marchers were in London nearly 200 people were injured, and many of the leaders of the NUWM were arrested.

The fifth national march took place in 1934 and passed off much more peacefully. In part this was a reflection of the changing attitude of the TUC, which had previously organised its only official demonstration against unemployment during the 1930s, and the NUWM leadership's new policy of seeking a united front. Although the TUC did not endorse the NUWM march of 1934, local Labour parties and trade union branches gave much greater support than had been the case in 1932 when the marchers had been forced to use workhouse casual wards for shelter. This was one of the smaller marches with only about 700 marching.

The final national march took place in November 1936 and, although it was somewhat overshadowed in the London press by coverage of the Jarrow crusade, it was both well-supported and well-organised. Will Paynter described it as

'the most successful of the hunger marches . . . made possible by united front and popular front movements.'

(Paynter's introduction to Kingsford, 1982, p. 11).

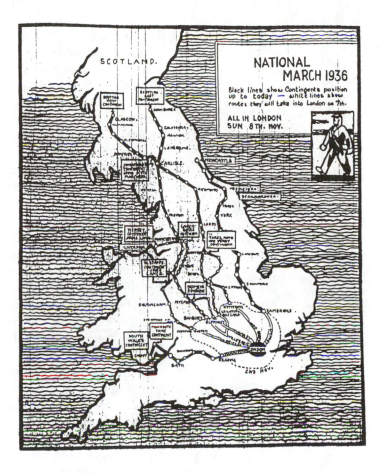

Figure 20.2
The 1936 National Hunger
March.
Reproduction of map published
in the *Daily Worker* 2 November
1936.

Reception committees representing the labour movement met the marchers in many towns and there was very little harassment by the police. The second map (published in the *Daily Worker* on 2 November 1936) shows that support for the march was rather less geographically widespread than in 1932. Unemployment had fallen by nearly a million from its peak in 1932 and many areas in the South and the Midlands were experiencing employment growth as new industries producing consumer-goods expanded. The 1936 NUWM march and the Jarrow crusade were reminders that there remained deep pockets of unemployment elsewhere in the country.

It is hard to judge how successful the national hunger marches were as protests against mass unemployment. Concessions were made by the government after several, although it is uncertain whether these were the direct result of the marches. The marches were not great mobilisations of the unemployed. None of the national marches had more than 2,000 participants and, despite the violence of 1932, the militancy of the leadership of the NUWM and the fears of the press and the authorities, the marches often seemed more concerned with respectability than revolution. Perhaps the most important effect of the hunger marches was on public opinion. It became increasingly difficult for the press to sustain the charge that the contingents of unemployed marching on London were the vanguard of a revolutionary army when many thousands of people had direct experience of marches passing through their towns and villages.

As well as being a response to the uneven effects of capitalism in inter-war Britain, the hunger marches also drew upon pre-modern traditions of collective action in which the physical petitioning of monarch or government and the march on the capital played an important role. By the final march, the rhetoric used to describe the marchers in many papers had changed from sensational reports of Moscow-backed revolutionaries to respectful, sympathetic, even ennobling portraits of the marchers. *The Economist* (15 March 1934) commented that the 1934 march and demonstration had 'made an impression on public opinion', and that 'the hunger marchers themselves appeared anything but revolutionary. Their ranks were orderly; the slogans inscribed on their banners were cogent, but in the main uninspiring; and the marchers probably secured most sympathy by their discipline, their confident humour, and their pinched and hungry faces.'

Along with social surveys like the Pilgrim Trust report of 1938, journalistic features like the influential *Times* articles of March 1934, and literary treatments of unemployment like Orwell's *The Road to Wigan Pier* and Greenwood's *Love on the Dole*, the hunger marches played a significant role in changing the climate of opinion about the unemployed and unemployment. All of these influences, while failing to produce dramatic changes in government policies at the time, helped to build a growing consensus favouring reflationary intervention in the economy, the development of a more coherent regional policy, and the introduction of systematic welfare provision without means-testing.

Sources and further reading
There are a number of recent discussions of the hunger marches which have attempted to place the Jarrow Crusade in the broader context of inter-war protest about mass unemployment. These include P. Kingsford,

The Hunger Marchers in Britain 1920–1939 (London, 1982); I. MacDougall, *Voices from the Hunger Marches Vol. 1* (Edinburgh, 1990); R. Croucher, *We Refuse to Starve in Silence. A History of the National Unemployed Workers' Movement* (London, 1987); and J. Stevenson and C. Cook, *The Slump. Society and Politics during the Depression* (London, 1977). A committed contemporary account of the hunger marches and the history of the NUWM is given in W. Hannington, *Unemployed Struggles 1919–36* (London, 1973).

21. The Jarrow Crusade of 1936

Although the Jarrow Crusade involved only 200 marchers from a single town, it achieved a much greater impact on public opinion than any of the national marches organised by the NUWM. The national press gave far more publicity to the Jarrow march than to the NUWM hunger march taking place at the same time and regional papers like the *North Mail and Newcastle Chronicle*, all but ignored the local contingent in the national march, while giving detailed daily coverage of the 'Jarrowsaders' progress. The Crusade has passed into the mythology of the North East, of the labour movement and into the popular imagination. Many people have no knowledge that there were other, larger marches in the depression.

It is hard to be sure why Jarrow took such a firm hold on popular imagination, but two factors certainly contributed. Firstly, the Jarrow march brought public attention to the plight of a town and a community, rather than just unemployed individuals or families. It was difficult to take the line that the unemployed were work shy or scroungers when a whole town was being 'murdered' by unemployment. Unemployment rates were high throughout the North East in the depression but, because of its complete dependence on shipbuilding and steel-making, Jarrow suffered more than most places. As Ellen Wilkinson, the left-wing Labour MP for the town, put it in her account of the town and the march, by 1933 the town

> was utterly stagnant. There was no work. No one had a job, except a few railwaymen, officials, the workers in the co-operative stores, and the few clerks and craftsmen who went out of the town to their jobs each day. The unemployment rate was over 80 per cent.

The local medical officer estimated that 6,000 were unemployed and 23,000 were dependent on relief out of a population of 35,000. When Palmers' shipyard, which employed the majority of men in the town, was closed in 1936 it seemed to end all hope.

A second reason for Jarrow's fame was the character of the response to this disaster. Although Wilkinson was the moving force behind the Jarrow march, it set out to be non-political and to encompass the whole of the local

community. Wal Hannington of the NUWM gave advice and wanted the Jarrow march to join with the national march, but it was decided to keep the Jarrow protest separate. This had a number of consequences. It made the Jarrow march distinctive and forced attention towards the particular severity of the situation in the town. It also meant that the march could be supported by a broad cross-section of local organisations. The plan for the march was endorsed by practically the whole of the local Council, and appeals for financial contributions were sent out bearing the signature of the Mayor. The Council was not a Labour monopoly, and the local Conservative Party came to play an important role in the organisation of the march. Arrangements for food and shelter on the march were made by an advance party consisting of the two party agents for the local parliamentary division, the Conservative agent, Councillor Suddick and the Labour agent, Harry Stoddart. In the later stages of the march, when it had left the Labour heartlands of the industrial North and was passing through more prosperous Southern towns, the reception and accommodation was often provided by local Conservative Associations.

The departing march was blessed by the Suffragan Bishop of Jarrow and the church gave great support to the march along its route. The marchers were guests of the Bishop of Ripon on their first weekend on the road and, when Ellen Wilkinson fainted at Loughborough she was invited to rest at the home of the Bishop of Leicester. The march quickly became known as the Crusade. The *North Mail and Newcastle Chronicle* (6 October 1936) described it as 'Jarrow's great work pilgrimage'. Wilkinson was keen on this symbolism, and this type of rhetoric further distanced the Jarrow Crusade from the NUWM marches, which often styled themselves as armies of the unemployed. However, like the 1932 national march, the Jarrow March also attempted to legitimise itself by drawing upon secular democratic traditions: at the head of the procession was carried an oaken box containing a bound-leather book with the 12,000 signatures of the town's petition to Parliament. The petition was ostentatiously presented for safe-keeping to the Chief Magistrate of each town where a night was spent .

The march left Jarrow on 4 October 1936. Although a large number of men had volunteered, a deputation of 200 was selected and each man was inspected by the borough medical officer. The route of the 300 mile march

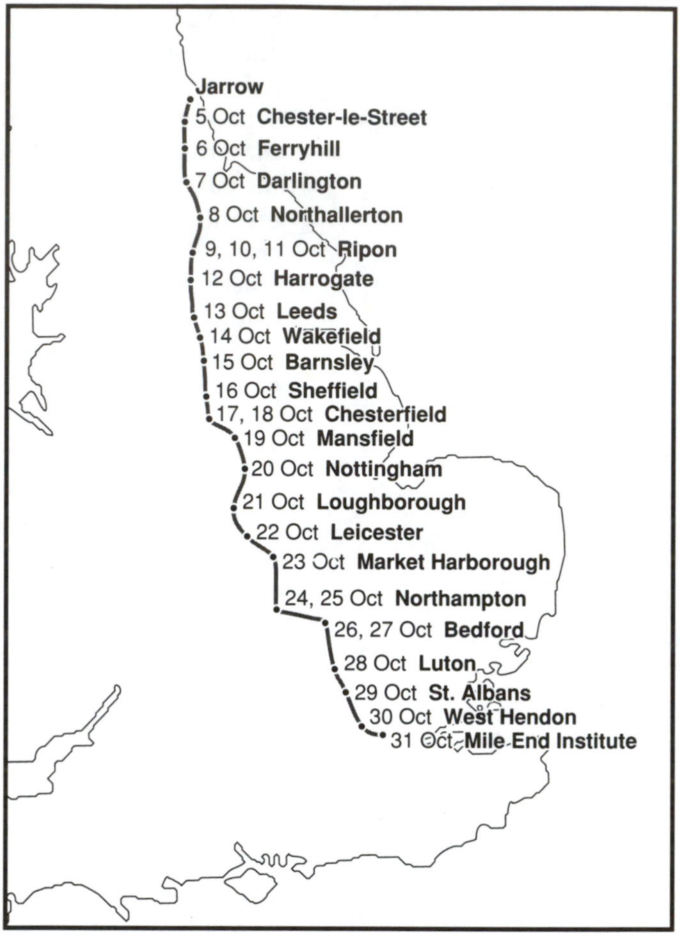

Figure 21.1
The route of the Jarrow march
1936.
The route of the march can be
followed in the daily reports by
S. E. Sterck for the *North Mail and
Newcastle Chronicle* between 4
October and 6 November 1936.

to London is shown in the map. As can be seen, there were some rest days along the way, at Ripon, Chesterfield, Northampton and Bedford, but on most days the marchers covered between fifteen and twenty miles. The two best accounts of the march are in Ellen Wilkinson's *The Town that was Murdered* and the daily reports of S. E. Sterck in the *North Mail and Newcastle Chronicle*.

Some days were better than others. Wilkinson's account highlights 'the twenty mile stretch from Bedford to Luton when it rained solidly all day and the wind drove the rain in our teeth.' The reception at 'cheerless' Mansfield was particularly poor, and at Market Harborough the marchers spent the night on stone slabs in the Poor Law casual ward. By contrast, there was 'wealthy Harrogate where the Territorial officers looked after us (and) Leeds where the chief newspaper proprietor gave us a meal the men still talk of — with free beer!' At Barnsley the men were treated to hot baths while Wilkinson enjoyed the 'muscle-easing luxury of the women's municipal foam bath' and later Sterck reported that Nottingham managed to save 'the Midland's reputation for hospitality' as the 'Crusaders walked on money' thrown to them in the streets. The arrival in London was something of an anti-climax on a wet and grey late-October day and many of the men were deeply disappointed when the petition was presented by Wilkinson while they were on a sight-seeing trip down the river. The marchers returned to Jarrow by train on 4 November.

Like the NUWM marches, the Jarrow Crusade achieved relatively little in the way of improving the situation for the unemployed in Jarrow. Ellen Wilkinson's continuing lobbying of the Board of Trade after the march helped to bring a small steelworks to the town, but unemployment remained chronic in Jarrow until the war. The Jarrow Crusade's lasting success was to focus attention on those places which were being left behind in the recovery of the late 1930s and, in the longer term, to become a symbol of the suffering caused by unemployment. Some on the left have criticised what Wilkinson described as a 'quiet and constitutional march' for the way it unashamedly courted favourable publicity from the national press, for the way it brought the Conservative Party and Church into the protest and for the way the organisers carefully avoided any association with the NUWM or the Communist Party. Certainly, the Jarrow march has taken attention away from the NUWM marches and the Jarrowsaders did not encounter the same hostility and hardship experienced by other hunger marchers. But in seeing the full range of institutions in its local community as resources to be drawn upon, and by exploiting sympathetic elements of the mass media and establishment, the Crusade probably came closer to fulfilling the potential of the hunger march as a practical form of protest than the more militant and ideologically-exclusive marches of the NUWM.

Sources and further reading

The best single contemporary account of the Jarrow march is E. Wilkinson, *The Town that was Murdered. The Life-Story of Jarrow* (London, 1939), but it is also well worth following the march in the reports of S. E. Sterck in the *North Mail and Newcastle Chronicle* (4 October–6 November 1936). The march is set in its context in J. Stevenson and C. Cook, *The Slump. Society and Politics during the Depression* (London, 1977).

22. The Harworth dispute of 1936–7

Peter Wyncoll, the historian of the Nottinghamshire labour movement, described the Harworth dispute of 1936–7 as 'one of the classic battles in the history of Trade Unionism' and contemporary reports in the left-wing press made comparisons with Tolpuddle. The dispute was fought over the issue of company unionism. In Nottinghamshire during the 1926 miners' strike, the rebel Labour M.P. George Spencer had formed a break-away union – the Nottinghamshire and District Miners' Industrial Union – which had negotiated with the owners before the end of the stoppage. This new union, sometimes known as the Spencer Union, was supported by the Nottinghamshire Owners' Federation, both financially and through the owners' refusal to negotiate with the existing union, the Nottinghamshire Miners' Association (NMA), which was affiliated to the MFGB. The Harworth strike was the pivotal moment in a struggle to rid Nottinghamshire of the Spencer union and an important part of a wider campaign against 'non-political unionism' in inter-war Britain.

Harworth also has significance as an episode in social history, for the dispute marked in the most dramatic fashion the failure of a particular type of social control. Robert Waller has described Harworth and the other new post-First World War mining villages of the Dukeries as attempts on the part of colliery companies to create new communities and to shape the lives and character of their workforces. The Harworth strike was a violent reaction to these local social regimes. Although the strike was primarily about the issue of company unionism, the violence, particularly in its micro-geography, showed that the strike was equally a rejection of a certain form of community by a considerable proportion of the local population. During the strike the *Daily Worker* reported that 'men and women alike comment that they are not only against the tyranny of the pit, but also against the tyranny which exists in the village.'

The rural village of Harworth was transformed in the early 1920s by the sinking of a pit about half-a-mile to south-east by the Barber-Walker Company. In common with other colliery developments in Nottinghamshire in the 1920s, there was particular emphasis on the provision

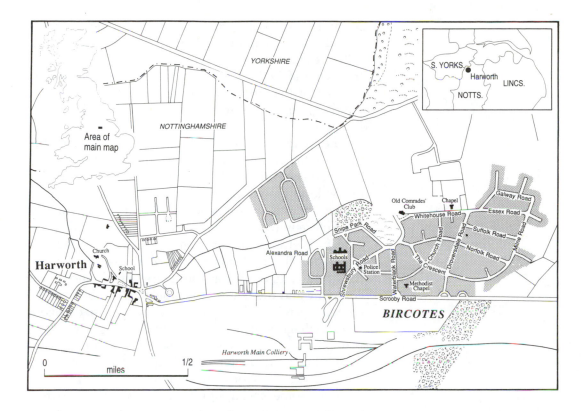

Figure 22.1
Harworth in 1936.
The new planned village of
Bircotes was situated some way
from the older village of
Harworth. There was some
segregation in the new village
with better housing on Scrooby
road. Scrooby Road, strategically
placed between the village and
the pit gates was also the front
line in the riots of December 1936
and April 1937.

The inset map shows
Harworth's position on the
county border. Geologically
Harworth was part of the
Yorkshire coalfield, but it was
politically contested terrain.

of housing for the miners. In some places in the Dukeries
this meant the construction of a completely new village,
as at Edwinstowe. This was practically the case at
Harworth where nearly 1,000 houses were built to the
east of the old village in a new development called
Bircotes. These new houses were of a standard far above
those in most contemporary colliery settlements and the
village was built with the architectural and town planning
values of the garden city movement very much in mind.
The village map shows the low density of housing and
the curved roads typical of this type of development.

However, although material conditions in Bircotes
were clearly better than those in most colliery villages,
there was another side to what the company described as
a 'new model village'. Shortly after the 1926 strike, the
New Statesman described the new colliery villages of the
Nottinghamshire coalfield as 'a new feudalism'. The
most obvious way in which the company extended its
power into everyday life came through its ownership of
all the housing in Bircotes. The company used its position
as landlord to influence behaviour in Bircotes and used
the threat of eviction as a sanction against trouble-makers
at the pit. This relationship between control of everyday

life and of the labour process also worked the other way round. Miners complained that they were threatened with redundancy or with poorer places underground if their wives failed to keep control of unruly children. By the end of the strike in May, 172 eviction cases were pending, about one in six of the company houses in Bircotes.

The company also owned most of the social facilities in the village, in particular the Institute building. In many other coalfields, the Institute was under the control of the local branch of the trade union, and the union movement was strengthened by its extension from the workplace into day-to-day social life. This was not the case in Nottinghamshire, and in Harworth the Old Comrade's club came to be an alternative social centre. In the dispute, this club was the centre of resistance to the company and the Institute was seen as symbolic of the company's role in the village. There were also divisions in the village which reflected divisions in the labour process. The best houses, in Scrooby Road between Shrewsbury and Waterslack Roads were reserved for butties, subcontractors in the Nottinghamshire pits, who retained some social significance even though their economic role had been eroded by developments in professional colliery management.

As Richie Calder, writing for the *Daily Herald* (30 April 1937) put it,

'had Harworth been a mile and a half further north the dispute would never have arisen.... Harworth lies in a tiny pocket of Nottingham which juts into Yorkshire. An accident of geography made it the centre of a desperate industrial struggle.' (See inset map.)

Geologically, Harworth was a part of the South Yorkshire coalfield and the closest pits were Maltby and Dinnington in South Yorkshire. Almost half the miners who came to the village between 1925 and 1931 came from Yorkshire, bringing with them quite different experiences of union affiliation, community organisation and collective action in the lockouts of 1921 and 1926. Harworth was also reckoned to be the first pit with work available for North East miners travelling south on the Great North Road. North East miners played a significant role in the re-emergence of the NMA in the village.

During the early 1930s there was little friction at the pit and the membership of the NMA was very low. However, partly because of the poor agreements that the

Spencer Union had negotiated with the company, by mid-1936 the NMA branch had increased its membership to over 300 out of a workforce of around 2,300 and was seeking recognition from the company. The local branch leader by this time was Mick Kane, who had come to Harworth from Scotland in the early thirties. Kane was a Communist Party activist who was to play a leading role throughout the strike with the direct support of the CPGB. A strike started in November 1936, after a series of confrontations over dirty coal allowances and the length of 'snap-time' (meal breaks). Kane clearly felt that the increased support for the NMA in the village suggested that there was underlying support for a test of strength on the union issue. The central issue of the dispute rapidly became that of union recognition. The dispute had been in progress for a month when the MFGB Executive gave full backing to the strike on 11 December, calling on the men to strike over recognition of the NMA at Harworth. Over 1,000 men followed the official strike call, leaving between 600 and 1,100 miners working each day. It is probable that a clear majority of local miners were on strike as a considerable number of working miners were brought into Harworth by bus.

On 16 December 1936, a crowd of about 200 confronted the police protecting working miners at the colliery gates. Stones were thrown, a police car was wrecked, and the police drew staves to force the crowd back. Several women were among those arrested: at the trial of Frances Cowell the prosecution suggested that 'women seemed to be the chief agents in provoking exitement and getting everybody worked up, so that anything serious might happen' (as reported in *Nottingham Guardian* 16 January 1937.) Two days before the December disturbances, between 500 and 600 women had paraded through the streets appealing to those still employed to join the strike.

Around 900 miners remained at work throughout the strike. Twice a day the police assembled working miners outside of the village, in what the strikers described as 'the chain gang'. The working miners were then processed into the village. As soon as the procession had turned into Scrooby Road, a police cordon was thrown across the road further on past the entrance to the colliery. Scrooby Road became the front line, not only when the chain gang went to work but also during the day when movement around the village was controlled. Much of the evidence given to Ronald Kidd and set out in his report on the dispute for the National Council for Civil Liberties (NCCL) concerns the limitation of inhabitants' movement in the village by the police.

The newly-formed NCCL was particularly concerned by events in Harworth because the dispute saw some of the first uses of the Public Order Act of 1936. Many of those arrested at Harworth were charged with vague and potentially far-reaching public order offences such as the use of 'insulting language' or 'threatening behaviour'. The Act gave the police great potential for control and intervention in local life, and there are direct continuites between the policing of Harworth in 1937 and the 1984–5 strike where public order offences under the 1936 Act and related common law offences made up over half of 10,000 charges brought against miners in England and Wales.

In April 1937, as the MFGB moved towards a national stoppage to support the NMA at Harworth, serious rioting broke out again. As in December, the riots centred on the procession of the chain gang and the arrival of buses of working miners from outside of the village. On Friday 23 April a crowd attacked the buses with stones and staves. The police temporarily lost control and the pickets moved down Scrooby Road to the Institute where they ransacked the building and beseiged the club officials who had to be rescued by police. Another section of the crowd set off into Bircotes and smashed windows at the houses of men who were out at work.

The following evening there was further serious rioting. Just before midnight the police raided a dance at the hall in the middle of the old village. This dance had been organised in aid of the children's relief fund. The police were expecting trouble and had already locked in the audience at the cinema, just down the Scrooby Road. The police entered the dance hall to arrest several miners including Mick Kane on charges of 'besetting' arising from the previous night's events. There are a number of different accounts of what followed, but a large and probably organised crowd left the Old Comrades' Hall armed with railings torn from fences and confronted the police at the Hall in Harworth, and then again outside the Institute building at about quarter to one. At one o'clock the police made several baton charges, leaving around twenty strikers injured. One police car was turned over in Scrooby Road and another was wrecked. The Institute was ransacked for the second time in two days. After the baton charges, the situation quietened and the streets were clear by about two o'clock. Thirty-five men and one woman were arrested and significantly all those charged came from Harworth and Bircotes. Kane was sentenced to two years' imprisonment and hard labour. Eleven others were given sentences ranging from four to fifteen months. Further police reinforcements were brought into the village after the violence of the weekend and saturation policing maintained an uneasy calm during the following week.

The Harworth dispute is sometimes presented as a victory for the labour movement, but the settlement of the strike was effectively a compromise enforced on the two unions and the Nottinghamshire employers by the government. The two unions were fused into the new Nottinghamshire and District Federated Union, with George Spencer as its President. The violence of the events and the threat of a national strike ensured the intervention of the government, and showed that it was as committed to the established structure of industrial relations as the trade union movement. In one of his last parliamentary speeches as Prime Minister, Stanley Baldwin pleaded for peace at Harworth and for the importance of a stable industrial relations system:

> 'What is the alternative to collective bargaining? There is none except anarchy... another alternative is force, but we may rule out force in this country, and I would lay it down that as long as the industrial system remains as it is, collective bargaining is the right thing. I have no doubt about that.'

Sources and further reading

The most recent and most detailed account of the Harworth dispute is in N. Fishman, *The British Communist Party And the Trade Unions* (London, 1995); this account concentrates on the role played by the Mick Kane and the Communist Party in the dispute. Baldwin's plea for industrial harmony at the end of the dispute is quoted in R. Page Arnot, *The Miners in Crisis and War: A History of the Miners' Federation of Great Britain (from 1930 onwards)* (London, 1961), where another account of the dispute can be found. The dispute is also considered in P. Wyncoll, *The Nottinghamshire Labour Movement 1880–1939* (London, 1985) and A. R. Griffin, *The Miners of Nottinghamshire: A History of the Nottinghamshire Miners' Association, Volume 2* (London, 1962). The social history of Harworth is discussed in R. J. Waller, *The Dukeries Transformed: The*

Social and Political Transformation of a Twentieth Century Coalfield (Oxford, 1983); a good contemporary account of early conditions in Harworth can be found in *New Statesman* 24 December 1927. The civil liberties isses raised by the strike are discussed in R. Kidd, *The Harworth Colliery Strike. A report to the executive committee of the National Council for Civil Liberties* (London, 1937); a commentary on this can be found in J. Morgan, *Conflict and Order. The Police and Labour Disputes in England and Wales, 1900–1939* (Oxford, 1987).

Section D: 1940–90 *by Chris Wrigley*

Industrial protest: 1940–90

Industrial protest was usually at the forefront of popular unrest in the four decades from the Second World War. Yet strikes and trade union mass rallies were not the only form of dissent in these years. In the 1980s and early 1990s there were youth riots in many parts of the country, in market towns of the south as well as in northern industrial towns such as Newcastle-upon-Tyne. These disturbances were strongly associated with unemployment. There were others, where unemployment and social deprivation were mixed with racial tension, as at Bristol, St Paul's, in 1980, Southall and Brixton, London and Toxteth, Liverpool, in 1981, as well as a few instances which were primarily racial as at Nottingham Hill, London and at Nottingham in 1958 and in Tottenham, London in 1985. There were also huge demonstrations on political issues, ranging from opposition from 1968 onwards to Britain's support of American intervention in Vietnam to anti-poll tax protests in 1990. May Day rallies could also provide focal points for political and social as well as industrial grievances, large turn-outs often occurring when such links were made.

Yet it was usually the big industrial issues which mobilised large numbers of people into protest. This was so in such cases as the campaigns against Edward Heath's Industrial Relations Act, 1971, cuts in the National Health Service in the early 1980s and John Major's plans of autumn 1992 to close down a huge part of the British coal industry.

Strikes remained prominent features of post-war British industrial society. Regardless of comparative statistics of other industrial nations, strikes were often depicted as 'the British disease'. They not only exercised the minds of Conservative politicians and monetarist economists but, together with the cliche of the rule-book-minded, obstructive trade unionist, were a feature of many British books, plays, films and television series since the Second World War. A notable example is Anthony Burgess's *1985* (London, 1978) in which Britain was depicted as 'TUCland', one large closed shop. The lead figure Bev ('it could stand for three things, Beveridge, Bevin or Bevan') struggles to survive after he tears up his union card when his wife dies because striking firemen do not save her from arson. Written by its author in tax-exile in Monaco, it was an anti-trade union (and anti-Arab investment) riposte to George Orwell's *1984* (London, 1949). Strike-happy workforces and hide-bound trade unionists were memorably portrayed in such British films as *Chance of a Lifetime* (1950), with its theme of the need for both sides of industry to work together, *I'm All Right Jack* (1960), which satirised both sides of industry, and the more chilling *The Angry Silence* (1960), about a worker who was sent to Coventry. These stereotypes also featured in a range of comedies, from the 1960s television series *The Rag Trade* to such films in the 'Carry On' series' as *Carry On Cabby* (1963) and *Carry On At Your Convenience* (1971).

Middle class opinion and that of much of the press had always been anti-trade union. After the Second World War criticism increased with high levels of industrial unrest nationally (as in 1957) or well publicised strife in particular industries (such as the car industry from the late 1950s) and with rising inflation. In 1963 opinion polls conducted for British Election Study research teams found 63.5 per cent of all respondents felt trade unions had too much power, yet 70.0 per cent also felt business had too much power. The 1963 data, when presented by class, revealed that the unions were felt to have too much power by 78.5 per cent of the professional and managerial class, 76.1 per cent of those who deemed themselves middle class and 52.8 per cent of the manual working class. By 1970, 73.1 per cent of all respondents overall saw the unions as having too much power (against 54.7 per cent on business) and by 1979 this had reached 81.1 per cent (against 60.3 per cent on business). In the later years, the percentage critical of union power among the manual working class rose to 66.4 and then 75.2, before falling to 40.9 in 1987 (when the overall figure of those critical had dropped to 45.4).

Often strikes have been depicted in the media and in the Parliament as the work of a few individuals. If for many people — including some historians — explanations for the Russian revolution of October 1917 can be reduced to the work of a handful of determined Bolsheviks, then, equally for some, the leaders of strikes can appear to be the main explanation for the strikes occurring. For much of the British press, men such as Jack Dash (London dockers), Derek Robinson ('Red Robbo' of British Leyland) and Arthur Scargill (National Union of Mineworkers) have fulfilled this role. In the case of the 1966 national seamen's strike, Harold Wilson, the Labour Prime Minister, gave added currency to such conspiracy views when he declared that the dispute was continuing because of the influence of 'a tightly-knit group of politically motivated men' (i.e. communists). Yet putative strike leaders, including Dash, Robinson and Scargill, were only able to lead in a direction that the workforce was willing to go.

Was Britain especially strike prone? Attempts to answer this have given rise to all manner of statistical problems associated with international comparisons. Different countries vary in what they record for strikes: some excluding 'small disputes',

Table 1
Working days lost per 1,000 workers employed in mining, manufacturing, construction and transport and communication (with fourth column giving all industries and services).

	average 1961–69 (rank order)		average 1970–79 (rank order)		average 1980–89 (rank order)		all industries average 1980–89 (rank order)	
Australia	424	(5)	1298	(3)	770	(2)	350	(4)
Canada	1026	(3)	1840	(1)	960	(1)	470	(2)
France		(80)	321	(6)	312	(7)		(150)
Germany (West)	24		92		50		50	
Ireland	1114	(2)	1163	(5)	530	(4)	380	(3)
Italy	1438	(1)	1778	(2)	290	(7)	620	(1)
Japan	239		215		20		10	
Sweden	18		42		330	(5=)	180	(6)
United Kingdom	274	(7)	1088	(6)	740	(3)	330	(5)
United States	1001	(4)	1211	(4)	330	(5=)	120	(7)

Source: *Employment Gazette*, December 1971, October 1973, January 1981 and December 1991
(From the mid 1980s the French figures have a significantly different coverage. Note also that the 1961–9 figures for France are artificially low as the French statistics omit 1968.)

which are classified differently in various countries; some including, some excluding 'political' strikes; and taking different approaches to lay-offs of workers in associated industries to that experiencing the strike. Moreover, labour force statistics can result in like and unlike being compared between, say, a country with large agricultural units and one with smaller units which often employ family labour. All these problems make it wisest to handle international comparisons with considerable caution. However, with that reservation in mind, it can be noted that comparisons of strike proneness which have been made for 1963–9 suggested that Britain came sixth or seventh of fifteen industrial nations, with Ireland, Italy, Canada, United States and Australia repeatedly appearing in a worse light, while West Germany, Japan and others had notably better records. Table 1 provides details of the seven most strike prone countries and also West Germany, Japan and Sweden. While there is a consistency of place among the worst affected, it is notable that in the 1970s the problem became markedly worse in Britain and Australia. The fourth column draws on the figures available only for the 1980s which cover all industries, thereby lessening the impact of such a dispute as the British coal strike of 1984–5 on the overall picture of the decade.

Table 2 provides an indication of the increasing propensity to strike in the period from 1969–72, again with the significant point being the degree to which the United Kingdom's position with regard to days lost worsened markedly.

It is possible that one part of the explanation for the upturn in overall British strike statistics may be the politicisation of industrial relations. The Conservative's loss of office in 1964 led to the immediate setting up of a party policy group 'to review the position of the trade unions in our society today and to consider what changes if any

Table 2

Working days lost per 1,000 workers employed in mining, manufacturing, construction and transport and communication.

	average 1964–7	average 1969–72
Australia	393	1010
Belgium	175	460
Canada	1030	1738
Denmark	120	80
Finland	165	1082
France	263	278
Germany (West)	8	93
Ireland	1320	978
Italy	1025	2158
Japan	205	245
Netherlands	15	68
New Zealand	190	365
Sweden	30	78
United Kingdom	195	1118
United States	1005	1520

Source: *Employment Gazette*, December 1971, October 1973 and January 1981.

in the law relating to unions were required'. The resulting policy, Fair Deal at Work (1968), was intended not only to strengthen trade unions in relationship to unofficial action but also to regulate them and to make the breaking of collective agreements, inter-union disputes, strikes to enforce closed shops or solidarity strikes costly in the courts. Robert Carr declared, 'Responsible, accountable but also strong unions — that is the purpose' (Taylor, 1993, p. 183). However, the Industrial Relations Act, 1971, was seen by the unions as a hostile measure and led to vigorous opposition.

The Wilson government's proposed industrial relations reform, *In Place of Strife*, had led to some 80–90,000 workers striking in protest on 1 May 1969. When the Conservatives published their proposed legislation some 350,000 workers struck on 8 December 1970, 170–180,000 on 12 January 1971, and 1,250,000 on each of 1 and 18 March 1971. Thereafter, when the measure had become law, there were a series of strikes following the imposition of fines by the Industrial Relations Court: some were 170,000 involved in July 1972 over the imprisonment of five dockers, 55,000 and 160,000 on 18 and 20 December 1972 respectively over fines on the AUEW, 323,000 on 5 and 12 November and 12,000 on 19 and 23 following further fines on that union. 'Political strikes' are not included in the British statistics yet the high profile given to the 'right to strike' in a period of increasing inflation may have added to the propensity to strike generally.

The issue of the role of the unions became politicised further during the premiership of Margaret Thatcher. The unions were 'the enemy within', emphatically not 'one of us'. Hostile legislation and hostile words built not only on concern about the economy but also on the electorate's disenchantment with the unions, and had the bonus effect of damaging the main Opposition party. Moreover, if the unions had helped restrain wage levels during the Attlee government and during Wilson and Callaghan's 'Social Contract', such support was even less forthcoming for Margaret Thatcher's proposals than those of Edward Heath. The ability to strike within the law was made increasingly difficult and in many instances striking had political connotations as a consequence. Nevertheless, as Table 1 illustrates, Britain under Mrs Thatcher did not become a strike-free zone, far from it.

Indeed in terms of working days lost per thousand workers employed, Britain's position relative to other industrialised countries barely changed.

Sources and further reading

The best background accounts are H. Clegg, *A History of British Trade Unionism Since 1989: Vol. 3: 1934–1951* (Oxford, 1994), Robert Taylor, *The Trade Union Question in British Politics: Government and Unions Since 1945* (Oxford, 1993) and Robert Taylor, *Workers and the New Depression* (London, 1982). For a short survey see C. Wrigley, 'Trade Unions, the Government and the Economy' in T. R. Gourvish and A. O'Day (eds), *Britain Since 1945* (London, 1991). For the British Election Study opinion poll data see Ivor Crewe, Neil Day and Anthony Fox, *The British Electorate 1963–1987: A Compendium of Data from the British Election Studies* (Cambridge, 1991). For the issue of unions and economic decline see the recent surveys by M. Dintenfass, *The Decline of Industrial Britain 1870–1980* (London, 1992) and D. Coates, *The Question of UK Decline: The Economy, State and Society* (Hemel Hempstead, 1994). See the section on strikes 1940–85 for literature on strikes. For a brief survey of riots, see Neil Evans, 'Voices of the Unheard: Contemporary British Urban Riots in Historical Perspective' in I. G. Jones and G. Williams (eds), *Social Policy, Crime and Punishment: Essays in Memory of Jane Morgan* (Cardiff, 1994).

23. The geography of strikes, 1940–90

by David Gilbert

To a considerable extent the geography of strike activity reflects changes in the nature of industrial relations in particular industries and changes in the geography of industrial structure. There are marked continuities in the geography of strike activity throughout the twentieth century, with the most strike-prone regions being those associated with particular industries, most notably coal mining. However, since the 1960s other industries and activities have increased in influence because of a decline in the number of stoppages in mining, due to both the overall decline of the coal industry and changes in the structure of its industrial relations. During the 1960s and 1970s a significant proportion of strikes were in the motor vehicle construction industry and, since the late 1970s, strikes among public sector workers have become much more common. Both of these developments have influenced the geography of strike activity.

As the earlier section on the geography of strikes in the first part of the twentieth century made clear, different measures of strike activity give different emphases to any discussion of its history and geography. There is a fairly clear pattern if we examine the aggregate number of officially recorded strikes per year. There was a fairly steady increase in the number of strikes each year from the Second World War until the 1970s, followed by a marked decline in the 1980s. During the 1940s there were on average 1686 strikes each year, with a marked peak at the end of the war. This was a considerable increase when compared with the depression, when the annual number of strikes reported had fallen as low as 302 in 1928 and only exceeded 1,000 in 1938. However, in terms of number of workers involved and working days lost, the 1940s were marked by relatively low levels of strike activity. There were, on average, 2,119 strikes in each year during the 1950s, 2,446 during the 1960s, and 2,601 during the 1970s. The highest number of strikes recorded in any one year was 3,906 in 1970. The 1970s were also marked by very high numbers of working days lost. In 1972 nearly 24 million working days were lost and over 29 million in 1979, which was the worst disruption since 1926.

During the 1980s there were a number of major strikes, notably the miners' strike of 1984–5 (which alone accounted for 26 million working days), but the decade saw a marked reduction in the number of disputes. On average there were only 1,129 strikes each year during the 1980s, and in 1992 there were only 240 strikes, the lowest number in a hundred years of official strike records. The factors which influenced this history of the rise and decline of post-war strike activity were geographically uneven in their timing and their scope. While it remains to be seen if the current low level of strike activity is more than a temporary phase in the history of British industrial relations, it is clear that changes in the geography of Britain's industrial structure, particularly the significant de-industrialisation which has taken place in parts of the country, mean that the geography of strike activity will never be the same again.

The single most important influence on the changing geography of strike activity in late-twentieth century Britain has been decline in the number of strikes in the coal industry, both because of the dramatic decline in the numbers of miners employed, particularly from the late 1970s onwards, but also because of earlier changes in industrial relations and collective bargaining in the industry. In most years from the end of the Second World War to the early 1960s, over half of all British strikes involved coal miners. Indeed, in 1956 and 1957 four out of five disputes were in the coal industry. However, most of these disputes were local in scale (usually limited to miners in a single pit), relatively brief and had very limited effects on production. For example, in 1957, while there were more strikes in coal mining than any other year (2,224 in all), only 0.5 million working days were lost, which was only about 6% of the national total.

Prior to 1966, many of these disputes involved the piecework component of faceworkers' pay, and there was a dramatic reduction in such disputes when the National Power Loading Agreement was introduced which abolished piecework in most British pits. Such small disputes were found in all British coalfields, although they were most common in the Yorkshire coalfield. Differences in industrial and political cultures meant that in some coalfields these small disputes were much more likely to escalate into strikes which lasted for more than a day or two, or which involved sympathetic action on the part of miners in other pits. Durcan, McCarthy and Redman examined strikes where over

Figure 23.1
Net major strikes by region 1946–1973.
Figures show the number of stoppages of more than 5,000 working days lost each year per million workers. Stoppages which could not be allocated to an individual region have been excluded.
Source: W. Durcan, W. E. J. McCarthy and G. P. Redman *Strikes in Post-War Britain. A study of stoppages of work due to industrial disputes, 1946–73* (London, 1983).

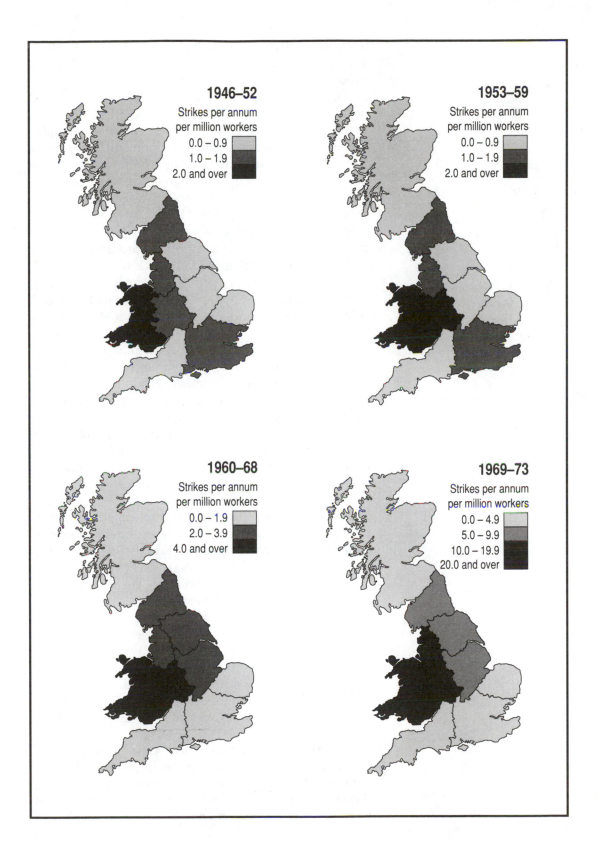

5,000 working days were lost for the period from 1946 to 1973 and found that the Yorkshire, South Wales and Scottish coalfields consistently had a greater share of strike activity than other coalfields. During their period of study, 41 per cent of these larger strikes (78 of 186) took place in the Yorkshire pits. Since the late 1960s, mining disputes have become far less common and have ceased to be the dominant feature of any map of day-to-day strike activity in Britain, although of course the national disputes of 1972, 1974 and 1984/5 were major events with their own geographies of industrial conflict. Before renewed industrial protest about British Coal's pit closure programme in the autumn of 1993, the annual number of strikes in British mining had fallen as low as 5 (for the 12 month period ending in April 1993) and it is very unlikely that any one industry will ever again have such a central role in the history and geography of British industrial relations.

As the number of strikes in the coal industry declined, other industries increased their significance in the geography of industrial conflict. While employing far fewer workers than the coal industry and contributing far less to the aggregate of strike activity, until the 1980s the docks were the most strike-prone sector of British industry. Liverpool and Hull were the most strike-prone of British ports, and also the ports where reputations for militancy lasted longest. The number of strikes in the Port of London declined from the late 1960s onwards and in other ports after the national dispute of 1972, although the formal decasualisation of dock labour in 1967 was not as unambiguously successful in reducing industrial conflict as the Nation Power Loading Agreement had been in coalmining. The decline of the dock strike in the 1980s and early 1990s is in part due to changes in technology and working practices, in part due to the overall decline in the number of dockers, and in part due to changes in the geography of the industry. Work has moved away from ports like London, Liverpool and Hull, with their long-established traditions of industrial militancy, to other ports without such traditions, particularly Dover and the East Coast bulk-container ports.

The car assembly industry has also had a considerable effect on the geography of strikes in post-war Britain. Strikes in the industry were relatively rare before the Second World War but, by the 1960s and 1970s, strikes were extremely common and there were a number of major disputes costing more than half a million working days. The shop-floor movement and wildcat strikes, although also important in engineering more generally, came to be particularly associated with the car industry. Strikes in the car industry were seen as central to the 'British strike problem'. The vehicle industry along with much light engineering had been established in the inter-war period and was concentrated away from the traditional heartlands of heavy industry. The increasing number of disputes in these industries shifted the geography of strikes in Britain in the 1960s and 1970s towards parts of the Midlands and the South East. There were no major disputes in the car industry during the 1980s and there has also been a dramatic reduction in the number of small disputes, both official and unofficial. Although the geography of the industry has changed in the late 1980s and early 1990s, with new green field factories associated with Japanese manufacturers situated or planned for the North East, East Midlands, Wiltshire and South Wales, this has had as yet very little influence on the geography of strikes.

Two major studies of strikes before the mid-1970s gave explicit consideration to the geography of strikes. Durcan, McCarthy and Redman's *Strikes in Post-War Britain* (1983) examined the details of the strike record between 1946 and 1973 focussing particularly on major disputes, which they defined as those where more than 5,000 working days were lost. Durcan *et al.* provide a regional analysis of these disputes for four periods. The first figure shows the regional distribution of major strikes in all industries except coalmining in each of these periods. Even these major stoppages were relatively localised, with only 7.5 per cent extending beyond the boundaries of the standard regions. The maps show a number of features of the strike record in this period. It shows the dramatic increase in the strike rate between 1946 and 1973 in all regions of Britain. The two Midlands regions saw the greatest growth in strike activity and the West Midlands became firmly established as the English region most affected by major strikes. While the major strike rate in Scotland was relatively low, particularly when compared with the relative propensity of the region in earlier periods, Wales remained the most strike-prone region of Great Britain, even in an analysis excluding mining strikes.

Smith, Clifton, Makeham, Creigh and Burn's study of *Strikes in Britain* (1978) looks in more detail at the period from 1968 to 1973. This study provides a rather more sophisticated analysis of the geography of strikes, both because it considers sub-regional units and because it makes an adjustment for industrial structure. The second figure shows working days lost per 1,000 workers for 1968–73 in each subdivision of Great Britain, after the standardisation for industrial structure expressed as a ratio to the national average. Thus a sub-region with a ratio score of two had twice as many working days lost as the national average after standardisation, while one with a score of 0.5 had half as many. The standardisation procedure involved weighting the figures for days lost to give the expected number days lost if the subregion had the same industrial structure as Great Britain as a whole (the exercise excluded strikes in Northern Ireland.) Thus, if, for example, a sub-region had proportionately five times as many dockers as the national workforce, then each of the indices would be divided by five for strikes involving dockers in that region.

Smith *et al.* concluded that differences in industrial structure only partly explained geographical variations in strike-proneness. They undertook a regression analysis of their adjusted strike activity ratios, seeking to explain statistically differences between sub-regions by such variables as rate of earnings growth, average plant size, activity rates, female employment rate, population density and inter-subregional migration rates. These socio-economic variables provided only a very limited explanation of the pattern of adjusted strike-proneness and Smith *et al.* suggested that more research was required on the wider range of socio-cultural factors not included in their analysis. What their analysis and the second figure point to is continuities of strike-prone localities and their association with areas of long-established traditional industries. On this basis, Merseyside was the most strike-prone locality, with 2.43 times the national average of working days lost. Merseyside has long had a reputation for confrontational industrial relations, particularly in the docks. This reputation extended to other industries in the period, and since Smith *et al's* study there have been further major disputes in the area, notably in the car industry later in the 1970s and in local government and other parts of the public sector in the 1980s. While even within Merseyside strikes are and have been relatively rare events, affecting only a minority of workplaces and involving a minority of workers, it provides a good example of the way in which local

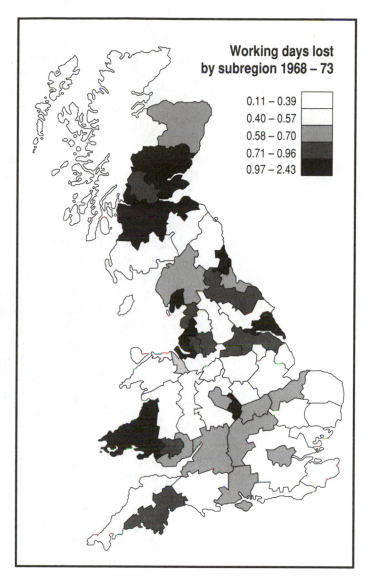

Working days lost by subregion 1968 – 73

☐	0.11 – 0.39
☐	0.40 – 0.57
▨	0.58 – 0.70
▨	0.71 – 0.96
■	0.97 – 2.43

Figure 23.2
Working days lost by subregion
1968–73.
Industry adjusted Great Britain
ratios of working days lost in
subdivisions of standard regions:
annual averages of all stoppages
recorded 1968–73.
A ratio score of unity indicates
that the subdivision had the
same strike propensity as Great
Britain as a whole after
adjustment for industrial
structure.
Source: C. B. Smith, R Clifton, P.
Makeham, S. W. Creigh and R.
Burn *Strikes in Britain*
Department of Employment
Manpower Paper No. 15 (HMSO
London, 1978), table 15.

political culture can have a long-term influence on
industrial relations even in the context of fundamental
changes in the pattern of employment.

A number of other areas with reputations for
radicalism and militancy established before the Second
World War also exhibit relatively high levels of industrial
conflict. The second most strike-prone sub-region by this
measure was Glasgow (1.74 times national average),
followed by Furness (1.43) and the Western Valleys of
industrial South Wales (1.27). The only the only other
sub-region with a score for working days lost significantly
above the national average was the Coventry area (1.28),

a reflection of the number of strikes in vehicle manufacture and light engineering at the time.

There were significant changes in both the character and scale of industrial conflict in the 1980s which influenced its geography. The first half of the decade was marked by several very large strikes, particularly those in the steel and coal industries. These two strikes can be seen as unsuccessful responses by workers in publicly-controlled heavy industries to the economic and political processes of de-industrialisation and regional restructuring. These were two of the largest strikes in post-war history and dominate the statistical strike record for the period when assessed in terms of working days lost. Over a third of all working days lost in industrial stoppages between 1980 and 1989 were in these two disputes. 16 million days were lost in the miners' strike of 1984–5, and 8.8 million in the steel strike of 1980, from a total of 72 million in the whole of the 1980s. In the early 1980s, simply because of these major disputes, strikes were concentrated in the traditional areas of heavy industry, particularly South Wales, South Yorkshire, the North East and central Scotland. The failure of these strikes, and the subsequent decline of employment in these industries, means that this geographic patterning of major industrial conflict is unlikely to be repeated.

A second feature of the strike record in the 1980s and early 1990s has been a decline in the number and severity of strikes in the private sector and an increase in strikes in the public sector. While the steel and miners' strikes involved industrial workers, a central feature of this shift in strike activity to the public sector has been a growth in disputes involving service workers. In the 1980s, major strikes of over half a million working days lost took place in local government, the civil service, the NHS and in the education sector, as well as many smaller stoppages. When combined with the reduction in private sector strikes, this trend has significantly altered the geography of industrial conflict, moving it away from the old heartlands of heavy and manufacturing industry.

The causes of these changes are complicated and contested. The Conservative governments of the period have claimed credit for the overall reduction in strike activity, claiming that the power of militant unions has been broken, while at the same time direct conflict between the state and it employees has become the dominant form of industrial conflict. Government reforms, particularly in the legal position of strikes, have

Figure 23.3
Working days lost per 1,000 employees by region 1976–1990. Annual average number of working days lost over each five year period divided by the corresponding average number of employees in thousands.
Source: Regional Trends.

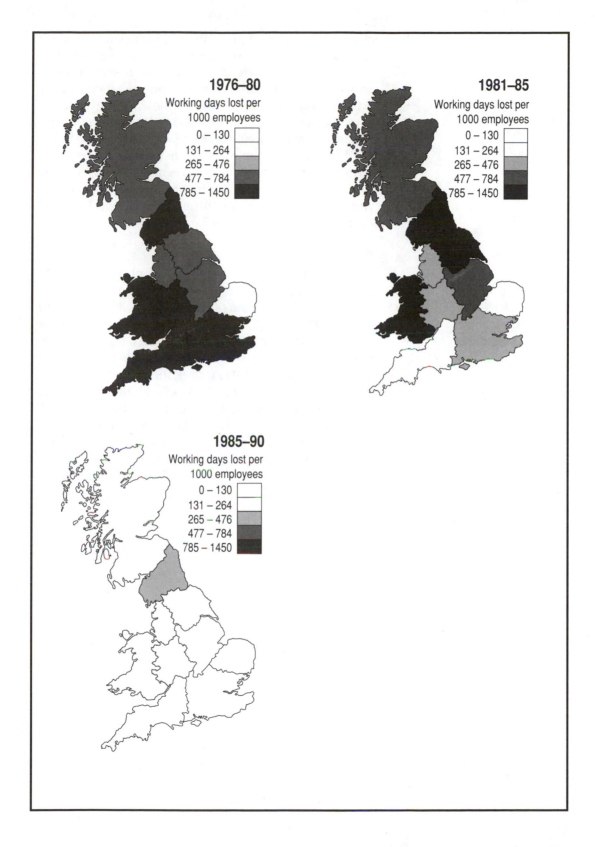

clearly played some part in altering the balance between employers and organised labour, but changes in British industrial relations clearly need to be understood in a wider context of changes in working practices, in the organisational structure of British industry, the influence of the two most severe recessions in post-war history and continuing mass unemployment. The three maps in the third figure show the regional distribution of working days lost for the period after 1976, highlighting both the decline in strike activity in the late 1980s and the weakening of regional contrasts. The second map is overwhelmed by the 1984–5 miners' strike.

Sources and further reading
The two detailed studies of strikes mentioned are: J. W. Durcan, W. E. J. McCarthy and G. P. Redman, *Strikes in Post-War Britain. A study of stoppages of work due to industrial disputes, 1946–73* (London, 1983); and C. B. Smith, R Clifton, P. Makeham, S. W. Creigh and R. Burn, *Strikes in Britain* Department of Employment Manpower Paper No. 15 (London, 1978). Figures for later disputes are taken from *Regional Trends*. A review of the post-war history and geography of strikes can be found in M. P. Jackson, *Strikes. Industrial conflict in Britain, U.S.A. and Australia* (Brighton, 1986); recent changes in British industrial relations are reviewed in S. Kessler and F. Bayliss, *Contemporary British Industrial Relations* (Basingstoke, 1992).

24. Coal disputes, 1940–45

Coal in the Second World War, as in the First World War, was a crucial war industry. Between 1939 and 1942 the average numbers employed in it fell from 766,000 to 709,000, a net loss of 7.4 per cent compared to 16 per cent in the first year of the First World War. Thereafter the number employed stabilised between 708 and 710,000 for the remainder of the war. The combination of strong demand and a reduced labour force with accumulated grievances and resentments from the pre-war period made coal an industry likely to experience wartime industrial strife.

The scale of industrial unrest in coal was exceptional during the Second World War. The industry accounted for 46.6. per cent of all stoppages in 1940–4 (against 13.4 per cent in 1915–8), cost 55.7 per cent of days lost (against the earlier war's 25.3 per cent) and involved 58.5 per cent of all workers directly or indirectly involved in stoppages (as opposed to the earlier period's 36.9 per cent). In September 1944 a report published by an American Coal Mission included the observation: 'we are compelled to point out that the centre of the problem of increased production is the bad feeling and antagonism which pervades the industry and which manifests itself in low morale, non-co-operation and indifference' (Court, 1951, p. 220). A major part of this was to do with pay, both pre-war and during the war.

Miners' pay had fallen relative to other workers between 1921 and the outbreak of war. In spite of the wartime favourable conditions the miners had not caught up with other comparable groups of workers. Indeed, in June 1942 Ernest Bevin, speaking of efforts to get former miners to return to the coal industry, stated in the House of Commons that 'in the last six months I have transferred, at a great loss of wages to themselves, over 36,000 men from munitions factories to the mines' (Page Arnot, 1961, p. 345).

In 1940 stoppages in the coal industry accounted for just over half of all days lost through industrial conflict in Britain. Most came about from small disputes. One of two large disputes was in Yorkshire in February and March, involving 20,000 workers and losing 1,300,000 days work over wages; the other was in January in Scotland, where a dispute in a Lanarkshire colliery led to

26,000 miners striking in sympathy across the county and beyond.

The year 1941 was relatively peaceful on the coal fields, though Lanarkshire was marked by numerous local disputes. Overall coal mining accounted for just under a third of all days lost through the stoppages of that year. One of the most notable strikes of the war began in late November 1941 in Kent. At the Betteshanger colliery there was a dispute over two abnormally difficult coal-faces. The miners concerned refused to accept special allowances negotiated by local union officials or to accept an arbitration award. After the men at one coal face continued a go-slow policy, management and the local branch of the union came into conflict and all work stopped at the pit on 9 January 1942. The Ministry of Mines arranged for summonses to be taken out against all 1,050 underground workers. When the case came before the magistrates' court in Canterbury on 23 January, the chairman of the local branch of the union was sentenced to two month's imprisonment, the secretary and one of the committee to one month, all the men who had been working on the coal-face where the recent go-slow had been in operation were each fined £3 (with a month in prison if the fine were not paid within two months) and the other miners £1 (with a fortnight in prison if not paid). The dispute was settled. The Home Secretary remitted the remainder of the union officials' prison sentences in early February but not the fines. By May only nine miners had paid their fines and warrants for arrest of the remainder were issued. However, the Ministry of Labour advised the Home Office to recommend the magistrates not to act on the warrants. This advice was taken, thereby avoiding any attempt to imprison over a thousand miners but showing, just as the South Wales miners had done in July 1915, the practical limits to legislating against industrial stoppages if there was a determined collective disregard for such laws.

Unrest in the coal mines became more serious in 1942, with coal mining accounting for over half the days lost in British industry and services through disputes. Up to 1942 miners' wages had risen in line with average male earnings, but they had not recovered any of the financial ground that they had lost relative to comparable groups of workers since 1921. In June 1942, faced with a serious shortfall in coal production and growing unrest over pay, the government established a Ministry of Fuel and

Figure 24.1
The aggregate loss of working days in the Lancashire, Staffordshire, Yorkshire, Durham areas and Scotland was 300,000. The loss in South Wales and Monmouthshire was 550,000 while that in Yorkshire was 1,000,000. The Welsh and Yorkshire stoppages led to cuts in electricity and gas supplies to some less essential industries. *Sources*: R. Page Arnot, *The Miners In Crisis and War* (London, 1961), p.396. Also B. Supple, *The History of the British Coal Industry, Vol. 4: 1913–1946* (Oxford, Clarendon Press, 1987) and H. Clegg, *A History of British Trade Unions Since 1889, Vol. 3: 1934–51* (Oxford, 1994).

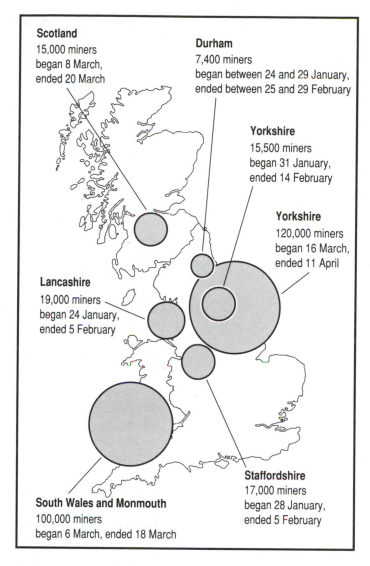

Scotland
15,000 miners
began 8 March,
ended 20 March

Durham
7,400 miners
began between 24 and 29 January,
ended between 25 and 29 February

Yorkshire
15,500 miners
began 31 January,
ended 14 February

Yorkshire
120,000 miners
began 16 March,
ended 11 April

Lancashire
19,000 miners
began 24 January,
ended 5 February

South Wales and Monmouth
100,000 miners
began 6 March, ended 18 March

Staffordshire
17,000 miners
began 28 January,
ended 5 February

Power to control the coal industry. It also set up an independent board of inquiry under Lord Greene, the Master of the Rolls, to look into wage levels and also longer term procedures for settling wages and working conditions in coal. This rapidly recommended the first wartime substantial pay increase for miners and brought in an output bonus paid on a district (not individual pit) basis. The Greene award led to fewer coal disputes in the second half of the year.

New negotiating machinery was set up at national, district and pit level. At the top tier was the National Reference Tribunal, chaired by Lord Porter. In October 1943 the Miners' Federation put in a claim for a national minimum of £6 a week underground and £5.50 on the surface (in June 1942 the miners had received £4.15 and £3.90 respectively). The resulting award of £5 and £4.50 by Porter and his colleagues in January 1944 led to the greatest loss of working days in any wartime dispute. See figure 24.1.

The scale of the unrest, as well as its location, stemmed largely from the award failing to improve either actual wage rates or the earnings of piece workers who were earning more than minimum rates. In low pay areas — South Wales, Scotland and the North East — piece-workers' differentials had been or were being eradicated. District negotiations which were under way to try to rectify this were undermined when the Minister of Fuel and Power made clear that the government (as controller of the industry) would not pay for any major adjustments arising from such talks. Hence the spread of industrial action shown in figure 24.1. These strikes led to negotiations between the Ministry, the Miners Federation and the owners which resulted in an agreement on 20 April 1944 which gave piece-workers the benefits of earlier agreements and higher payments for increased output. This ended this wave of strikes. In 1943 stoppages in the coal industry accounted for just under half of all days lost in industrial disputes in British industry, whereas in 1944 they reached a remarkable two-thirds.

The last major dispute of the war was in March 1945. It concerned the erosion of craftsmen's differentials, a matter not dealt with in 1944. The dispute involved 16,000 workers and lost 180,000 working days.

Sources and further reading
Two volumes in the History of the Second World War, Civil Series: W. H. B. Court, *Coal* and H. M. D. Parker, *Manpower* (London, 1951 and 1957 respectively). R. Page Arnot, H. Clegg and B. Supple (as cited, figure 24.1). M. W. Kirby, *The British Coalmining Industry 1870–1946* (London, 1977).

25. Unofficial dock strikes and the 1945–51 Labour governments *by Jim Phillips*

For the British labour movement, the 1945–51 period was ostensibly one of unprecedented triumph and unshakeable unity. Backed by the whole-hearted support of its trade union allies, the first ever majority Labour government executed a programme of social reconstruction and economic recovery. But at a time of great economic emergency, the alliance between Labour and the unions was subjected to considerable private strain due to a series of unofficial strikes in the strategically vital docks industry.

Given the government's central task, the trade-based programme of economic recovery, the ports were of obvious importance and ministers were consequently alarmed by the frequency of unofficial dock strikes. In the seven calendar years 1945–51, 14.27 million working days were lost in all industries. Of these, 2.89 million were lost in the docks, where only about 80,000 people were actually employed. By way of comparison, during the same period 3.97 million days were lost in the traditionally unruly coal mining industry, where 700,000 men were employed. In crude terms, the average docker was on strike six times more often than the average coal miner (for all statistics relating to the strikes, see PRO: LAB 34/60-67). 'Join the army and see Smithfield', went one Cockney barb, for, as indicated below, in order to safeguard economic recovery and to protect cargoes of rationed food, the government sent large numbers of troops to work in the docks on several occasions:

Table 25.1 Troops used in strikes.

Dispute	Numbers
October 1945 (All ports)	21,000
July 1946 (Southampton)	40
April 1947 (Glasgow)	700
June 1948 (London)	2,000
May–June 1949 (Avonmouth/Bristol)	1,200
June–July 1949 (London)	12,792
April 1950 (London)	3,000

Source: Steve Peak, *Troops in Strikes*, (London, 1984).

By definition, these unofficial strikes also defied one of the government's closest allies, the Transport and General Workers' Union, and occurred during an important period of reform in the docks. Building upon Ernest Bevin's wartime achievements as Minister of Labour, the Labour government established the Dock Labour Scheme in 1947. This sought to replace the harsh system of casual employment by offering the workforce increased economic security. Local dock labour boards compiled lists of registered men, who reported for work twice a day (once on Saturdays) and, in return, received a guaranteed weekly maintenance. The TGWU had long campaigned for the Scheme and was additionally rewarded with a joint share — both on the National Board responsible for the Scheme's overall management and the various local boards — in its administration. With the Scheme being devised in a spirit of both social justice and economic efficiency — the supply of labour in such a vital industry could not go unregulated — the recurrence of unofficial strikes was as embarrassing for the union as it was irritating for the government.

Labour's political and industrial leaders were unwilling to accept that work-place problems had survived the introduction of dock labour reform, and portrayed the strikes not as symptoms of industrial unrest but as acts of political subversion. In July 1949, for instance, the Home Secretary, Chuter Ede, stated that the 'only reason' for a London dock strike was the Communists' determination to disrupt trade, economic recovery, 'and with it the whole process of Marshall Aid on which the recovery of Europe depends'.

As government ministers and union leaders privately realised, however, the strikes actually had nothing to do with political subversion. In the closed world of the docks, the workforce had never fully submitted to the TGWU's authority, maintaining a tradition of local rather than national loyalties. Ironically, given the references which the union's leader, Arthur Deakin, frequently made to communist involvement, the Communist Party was also unable to penetrate this tradition and in most ports its influence in the unofficial movement was negligible. On the Mersey, the second largest docks system in Britain, the vast majority of dockers were hostile to communism. Partly reflecting the Roman Catholic Church's influence in Liverpool, this also denoted the survival of the unusually strong syndicalist tradition which had been implanted on the Mersey prior to the First World War. In London a significant number of communist activists were prominent in the unofficial movement, but here too there was a general suspicion of the Communist Party because it subordinated dock issues to political objectives. Hence the communist dockers who did assume unofficial leadership in London were loyal to other dockers rather than the Party. They were active, for instance, in the 1945 strike which the Party — initially a strong supporter of the Labour government — strongly opposed.

The difficult historical relationship between the union and the workforce was, in fact, the basic problem in the docks. After 1945 this difficulty was compounded by the union's close association with the unpopular disciplinary functions of the Dock Labour Scheme. Although dockers welcomed the Scheme, under its disciplinary code they were forced to concede valued freedoms which they had enjoyed under casualism. No longer free to decide whether or not to try for work on any given day, nor free to accept or reject any work that was offered to them, tension was inevitable as dockers passed from one of the least to one of the most disciplined industrial regimes. Moreover, while the Scheme gave the workforce greater economic security, it did little to improve working conditions. Dockers were still recruited casually and, in addition to their guaranteed maintenance, continued to be paid by the piece. As a cargo's piece-rate reflected its market price rather than the physical labour involved in shifting it, this recruitment process inevitably injured industrial relations by encouraging favouritism amongst employers and a competitive struggle for better-paid jobs.

The employers' preference for casual recruitment signified their generally unhelpful attitude towards industrial relations in the docks. Their opposition to sharing administrative power with union representatives under the Scheme was unremitting and they shamelessly exploited the strikes to argue for a restoration of their monopoly powers. This increased the pressure on the TGWU and intensified the underlying tension in the docks, but each of the main strikes was caused by a dispute which the union had with its members rather than with employers.

The geography of the strikes thus reflected the character of each particular internal union dispute. In October 1945 an unofficial committee on the Mersey connected the union's poor defence of local men in a

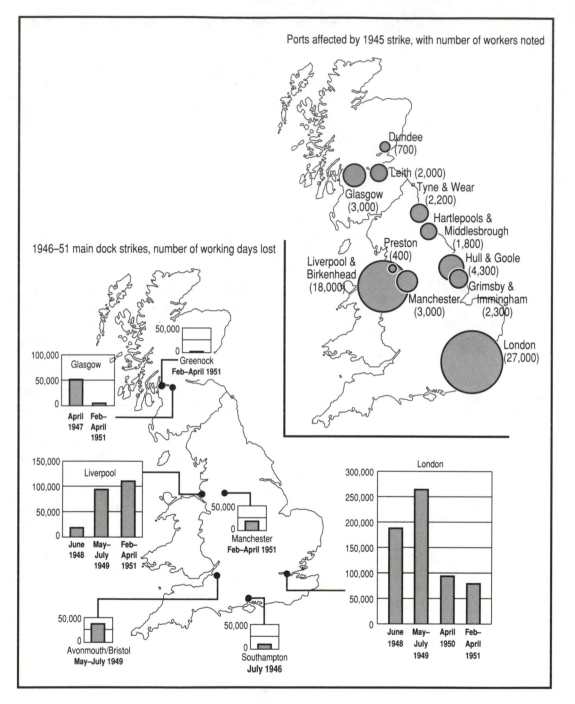

Ports affected by 1945 strike, with number of workers noted

Dundee (700)

Leith (2,000)

Glasgow (3,000)

Tyne & Wear (2,200)

Hartlepools & Middlesbrough (1,800)

Preston (400)

Hull & Goole (4,300)

Liverpool & Birkenhead (18,000)

Manchester (3,000)

Grimsby & Immingham (2,300)

London (27,000)

1946–51 main dock strikes, number of working days lost

Glasgow
April 1947 / Feb–April 1951

Greenock Feb–April 1951

Liverpool
June 1948 / May–July 1949 / Feb–April 1951

Manchester Feb–April 1951

Avonmouth/Bristol May–July 1949

Southampton July 1946

London
June 1948 / May–July 1949 / April 1950 / Feb–April 1951

recent piece-rate dispute with its alleged refusal to press upon employers a package of improved pay and conditions—nicknamed 'The Dockers' Charter'—which had been adopted as official union policy in August. Negotiations with the employers had actually begun, but union members had not been kept informed, and the

Figure 25.1
Ports affected by the main
unofficial dock strikes, 1945–51
Given that they were easily the
largest employers, strikes in the
Mersey ports and the Port of
London were particularly
significant.

Merseyside strike was supported across the country.
Work was disrupted in Dundee, Garston, Glasgow,
Grimsby and Immingham, Hull, Leith, London,
Manchester, Preston, Sunderland and Hartlepool. This
massive strike lasted for four weeks, involved 43,000
men, cost the industry more than one million working
days, and was settled only after a secret compromise
between the union and the unofficial movement. This
allowed the latter to claim that the men were resuming
work so that the union could re-open negotiations with
the Employers' Association which had refused to hold
talks while the men were on strike.

There were important local strikes in Southampton in
July 1946, where 2,000 men struck work for five days,
and in Glasgow in April 1947, where 3,500 men struck
work for two weeks. But the next major strike came in
London, in June 1948. This was also a local problem, but
because of its size — 27,000 men, one-third of the national
workforce, were employed there — and its consequent
economic importance, a strike in London naturally
assumed national significance. Again, the trouble
stemmed from the workforce's belief that the union had
failed to defend the interests of its members properly, for
TGWU representatives on the London Dock Board had
recommended that eleven TGWU members be suspended
without pay for a week after a piece-rate dispute in the
Regent's Canal Dock. A two week strike involving more
than 19,000 men in all four sectors of the London docks
followed. Supported by a two-day sympathetic strike of
9,000 dockers in Liverpool, the dispute cost 200,000
working days.

Figure 25.2
The Port of London 1945–51.
More than one-third of the Port's
workforce was concentrated in
the Royals section (a). The
unofficial movement's influence
was strongest in this, the most
important section of the Port in
economic terms, but all sectors
were involved in the various
strikes: the 1948 stoppage began
in Regent's Canal Dock (b), and
the 1949 Canadian dispute was
centred on the Surrey (c) as well
as the Royal Docks.

While the unofficial movement enjoyed a broad base
of support within London, it was particularly influential
in the Royals Group. The Royals were London's largest

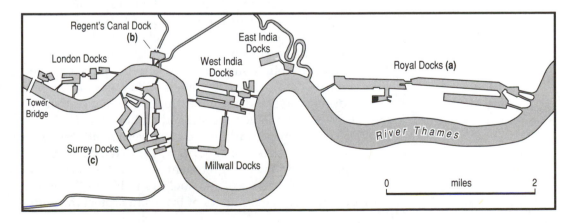

and most modern section and therefore also the most significant in economic terms. They employed 10,000 men and were the only docks that could accommodate the deep sea liners which carried the bulk of Britain's food imports from the Americas and Australasia (Fred Lindop, 'Unofficial Militancy in the Royal Group of Docks, 1945–67', *Oral History* Vol 11 No 2 [1983]). The Royals Group was one of the scenes of more protracted trouble which began in May 1949. This stemmed from a dispute between the Communist-led Canadian Seamen's Union, Canadian shipowners and the virulently anti-communist American Federation of Labour, which was bent on replacing the CSU as the monopoly organiser of Canadian shipping labour. The AFL's tactics — essentially, it offered the employers terms which undercut those which the CSU had been operating under — led to a strike on CSU-crewed ships in Britain. TGWU officials instructed their members to carry on working these vessels, but dockers at Avonmouth, Bristol, Southampton, Leith, Newport and in the Surrey and Royals Docks of London all refused to do so, arguing that this would prejudice the outcome of another union's dispute with an employer and would be tantamount to black-legging. With employers refusing to engage any labour while the Canadian vessels lay idle lengthy stoppages ensued both on the Avon and in London, while Liverpool was drawn into the affair when a ship arrived there from strike-bound Avonmouth. Collectively these various stoppages cost the industry approximately 400,000 working days and the affair ended only after the CSU abandoned its own strike on 22 July.

The period witnessed two other important strikes. In March 1950, following a TGWU Executive inquiry into the 1949 London stoppage, three leaders of the unofficial movement were expelled from the union. This was an attempt to restore the union's authority, but it backfired completely. In April a two week unofficial strike in protest at the expulsions ensued, which enjoyed particular support in the Royals Group where the three expelled men worked. This cost the industry another 93,750 working days and provided further evidence that the TGWU was unable to command authority in the docks. As such, it greatly influenced the government's response to the next strike, in February 1951, which began in opposition to a wage agreement between the TGWU and the Port Employers' Association. Hitherto, while deploying large numbers of troops to protect the wider community from the effects of the strikes, the government had been content to leave the task of restoring workplace discipline to the union. Support for the strike was unusually patchy, being confined to pockets on the Mersey and London, but — impatient with the union's inability to maintain order in the docks — the government decided on this occasion to confront the unofficial movement. Prosecutions were initiated against seven of the strike leaders under the 1940 emergency regulation, Order 1305, which was still in force and which forbade strikes and lock-outs in connection with trade disputes. However, after the men had been arrested in an East London pub, support for the strike actually increased, and the unofficial movement successfully organised a series of one-day strikes to coincide with the men's appearances at the Old Bailey. Work was disrupted at Birkenhead and Liverpool, Glasgow and Greenock, Manchester and London, with about 210,000 working days lost in all. Meanwhile, the trial itself ended in embarrassing defeat for the government, with the seven acquitted after the jury had been unable to agree that the strike had involved a 'trade dispute'. The trial also placed considerable private strain on the government's relationship with the TGWU, for Deakin resented the government's assumption of responsibility for what he believed to be an internal union matter. In addition, the trial drew fresh attention to his union's problems in the docks and revived the unofficial movement's flagging fortunes.

Historians have broadly concluded that the unity of the labour movement was an invaluable source of comfort to the 1945–51 governments, with the TGWU leading TUC support for the wage freeze and Bevin's anti-communist foreign policy. Yet this 1951 episode indicates that there was considerable private strain between the government and the TGWU. This tension — which had been slowly building up from 1945 as a result of developments in the docks — was an equally important feature of the 1945–51 labour alliance, but curiously one which historians have been slower to acknowledge.

Sources and further reading
For an account of the general 1945–51 situation, see Kenneth O. Morgan, *Labour in Power 1945–51* (Oxford 1984). For the governments' response to the strikes, see Justin Davis-Smith, *The Attlee and Churchill Administrations and Industrial Unrest 1945–55* (London, 1990).

26. Strikes in the motor car manufacturing industry

The motor car industry was one of the three most strike prone industries of the post Second World War period, along with coal mines and docks. 'They're striking again at Dagenham' (or Longbridge, Cowley or wherever) was an often heard complaint in the 1950s and 1960s, a period of relative peace in the coal industry.

Industrial unrest became markedly worse from the end of the 1950s. There are difficulties in comparing the period before 1958 with that after since the basis of the statistics changed. Before 1958 the manufacture of parts and accessories had been excluded but cycles had been included in the motor vehicles category of the Standard Industrial Classification. However, as Durcan, McCarthy and Redman have observed, in both periods the manufacture of cars, commercial vehicles, engines and vehicle bodies dominate the series. Hence one can gain a broad picture of change by using the data that they have provided.

Between 1949 and 1957 there had been on average 27.7 strikes per year involving an average of 9.5 per cent of the employees in the industry. In contrast, between 1960 and 1973 there were an average of 273.7 strikes per year involving an average of 43.9 per cent of employees. Over the whole period there were 460 major stoppages (those involving a loss of 5,000 working days or more). These constituted 14 per cent of all stoppages and accounted for 59 per cent of workers involved and 84 per cent of days lost. The causes of these major strikes were attributed in the government's statistics to wage demands (35 per cent), other wage disputes (20 per cent), trade union principle (8 per cent), redundancy (7 per cent), discipline (6 per cent), demarcation or sympathetic action (2 per cent) and miscellaneous issues (20 per cent). The major strikes often directly affected fairly small numbers of workers: 30 per cent of them involved less than 250 workers, 61 per cent less than 1,000 and 95 per cent less than 10,000. While the major strikes accounted for most days lost, the industry was prone to small strikes, the number between 1960 and 1973 varying between 83 in 1961 and 291 in 1970 (the average being 166.9).

Production of cars was concentrated in a few

companies and a few areas of Britain. In 1947 the Big Six — Nuffield (20.9), Austin (19.2), Ford (15.4), Standard (13.2), Vauxhall (11.2) and Rootes (10.9) — accounted for 90.8 per cent of British car production, with Rover (2.7), Singer (2.1) and Jaguar (1.6) supplying much of the remainder. Twenty years later, in 1967, the Big Five — BLMC (made up of BMC created from a 1952 merger of Austin and Morris, Jaguar, Leyland and Rover, 46.8), Ford (28.4), Vauxhall (12.7) and Rootes (which had taken over Singer in 1955, 11.7) — accounted for 99.6 per cent of production. However, their share of the home market became less assured as British tariffs on imported cars dropped from 30 to 15 per cent between 1962 and 1970. During the 1960s the share of imports on the home market rose from 7 to 14 per cent. This was especially serious as the rapid post-war expansion of the home market had ended by the mid-1960s and the British share of world markets continued to decline.

After the Second World War the industry was heavily concentrated in the West and Central Midlands and London and the Home Counties. See figure 26.1. The main change in the location of the industry came with the Macmillan government's strong pressure on the major companies to expand in areas of high unemployment. See figures 26.2 and 26.3. According to Durcan, McCarthy and Redman's work on strikes between 1946 and 1973, 48 per cent of those in motor car manufacturing occurred in the West Midlands, 21 per cent in the South East, 12 per cent in the North West and 7 per cent in Scotland, with the West Midlands share falling during the period while that of the North West rose.

However, geographic areas have not been deemed central to explaining the level of strikes in the vehicle assembly industry. Commentators have put more emphasis on the companies and on individual plants. Turner *et al.* observed that while some car manufacturing plants located well away from others, such as Vauxhall at Luton, had relatively tranquil industrial relations, other plants had not. Conversely, they observed of the Coventry area that

> the Rootes plants seemed unaffected by the Standard strikes of the mid 1950s, and Standard appears to have been quite uninvolved by the Rootes movement of 1959–60 — while neither of these groups, in their quite long intervals of relative quiescence, responded to the chronic militancy of Jaguar's workers. (Turner *et al.*, 1967, p. 349)

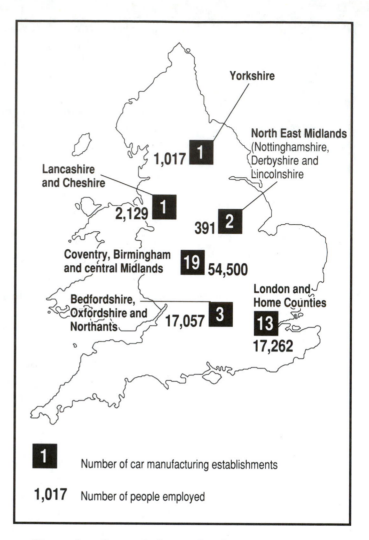

Figure 26.1
Distribution of car manufacturers, 1947.
Source: PEP (Political and Economic Planning), *Motor Vehicles: Engineering Report 2* (London, 1950), p.7.
Several of the small independent producers did not last much longer. For example, Jowett of Bradford, the Yorkshire producer on the map, ceased production in 1953 partly because Ford had bought Briggs, its body supplier, and refused to continue making these for Jowett.

Given that the car industry has been so concentrated in a few large companies, it is not surprising that company policy or even plant policy has been a major feature in strike-proneness or relative industrial peace. The expansion of the large companies by take-over has often been a substantial cause of friction. The point of the mergers has been to reorganise and rationalise use of resources, a policy which has almost inevitably involved friction with the workforce's notions of 'job rights'. In some cases, the firm taking over modified its working and industrial policies to take account of practice in its newly acquired plant. In other cases, considerable unrest was often caused by insistence on immediate uniformity with the rest of the group both in workplace practices and in pay systems. Such corporate uniformity could not only lead to unrest in the labour force but also undermine the ability of management at plant level to manage. When Michael Edwardes was Chairman of British Leyland, 1977–82, one of his early changes was to 'restore authority to the factories, rebuilding the roles of factory managers, superintendents and foremen'. He wrote of the situation when he took over:

> Great names like Rover, Austin, Morris, Jaguar and Land Rover were being subordinated to a Leyland uniformity that was stifling enthusiasm and local pride. In fact the Cars operations were split by function and geography; nowhere did the product names appear in the organisational 'family trees'. The manufacture of engines for Jaguar was carried out in the 'Radford Engines and Transmission Plant' under a separate management from Jaguar car assembly, which took place in the 'Browns Lane Plant, Large/Specialist Vehicle Operations'. The Austin factory was designated 'Longbridge Body and Assembly Plant, Small/Medium Vehicle Operations'. The Rover factory was simply known as the 'Solihull Plant', and MG works as the 'Abingdon Assembly Plant'. In addition, the engines for these vehicles were the responsibility of a separate management function. (Edwardes, *Back from the Brink*, 1983, p. 57).

The issue of managerial control became especially important because of the rapid changes in products, technology and organisation in the industry. These changes, combined with the workforce's rising expectations of living standards, boosted unionisation and the spread of the shop steward system. In 1956, according to Steven Tolliday's estimates of unionisation, the level at Morris Motors was 25 per cent, Vauxhall and Ford were well under 50 per cent and Austin fluctuated between 60 and 90 per cent during the 1950s. By 1965, according to Turner, McCarthy and Redman's estimates, the manual workforce was 100 per cent unionised at BMC, Rootes, Rover and Jaguar, 99 per cent at Ford and 85 per cent at Vauxhall. In times of rapid workplace change, relatively full employment and rising expectations workers looked to the unions generally for results and to shop stewards in particular to negotiate on their behalf over the trade-off between wages and effort as well as other areas of contention. Outside of Vauxhall, management was willing in good times to negotiate with the shop stewards. The Donovan Commission in 1968 described the motor industry as 'in general hard-working

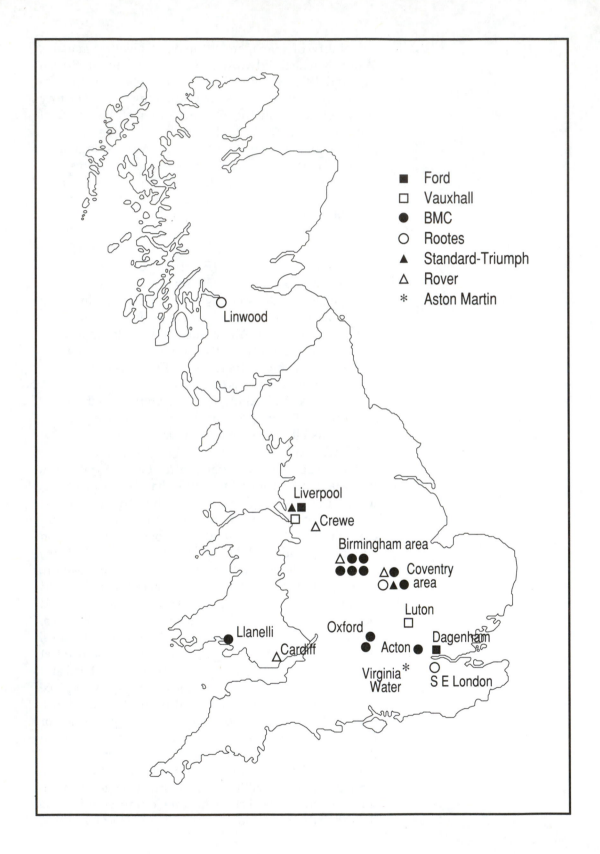

Figure 26.2
The main factories of the major car manufacturers, 1963.
This map is based on G. Turner, *Industry and People: Cars* (London, 1965), p.89 with additional information from P. W. S. Andrews and E. Brunner, *The Life of Lord Nuffield* (Oxford, 1955), H. A. Turner, G. Clack and G. Roberts, *Labour Relations In The Motor Industry* (London, 1967), G. Turner, *The Leyland Papers* (London, 1971), D. G. Rhys, *The Motor Industry: An Economic Survey* (London, 1972), P. Waymark, *The Car Industry* (Bath, 1983), S. Wilks, *Industrial Policy And The Motor Industry* (Manchester, 1984), R. Whipp and P. Clark, *Innovation and the Auto Industry* (London, 1986), K. Williams, J. Williams and C. Haslam, *The Breakdown of Austin Rover* (Leamington Spa, 1987) and M. Adeney, *The Motor Makers* (London, 1988).

In 1963 the government-induced decentralisation of the car industry was under way. Between January and September 1960 there had been announcements of the Big Five expanding in other areas: BMC in Scotland, South Wales and Liverpool, Ford at Halewood, Standard Triumph at Speke, Vauxhall at Ellesmere Port and Rootes at Linwood. Vauxhall's activities at Ellesmere Port began with a components plant in 1962 and thereafter expanded with a production building in 1964 and a substantial extension in 1966. It came to employ 10,000.

Production at Speke began fairly modestly under Standard Triumph with the manufacture and assembly of car bodies and components but in the mid 1970s saw major expansion under British Leyland, which increased employment by 2,800. Chrysler,

and responsible people' who often were 'cast in the role of mediators trying to prevent stoppages taking place while grievances can be examined.' (Donovan, 1968, p. 102). However sometimes, especially at times of economic adversity, management determined to take a tough stand, dismissing those shop stewards they deemed to be over-mighty, even if it involved sitting out a strike.

Much of the technological change and adverse working conditions in British car making plants were common to the car industries of other countries which experienced less industrial unrest. However, the British motor car industry was notable for frequent lay-offs of its labour force and substantial fluctuations in earnings. Turner *et al.* commented that 'the frequency with which managements themselves lay men off, put them on "fall-back" rates, or vary their overtime, makes it seem nothing abnormal for workers to withhold their labour'. Moreover, they observed, the high strike-incidence of the industry was in large part 'the industry's substitute for formally agreed means of dealing with recurrent labour surplus' (Turner *et al.*, 1967, p.331–2). The volatility of earnings was a major grievance in the industry. Moreover, there were repeated changes in payment systems and frequent grievances over relative pay levels. Thus, for example, the Ford workers' pay claim behind the major strike of January–March 1971 contrasted their lower pay levels to those of car workers in the Midlands at a time when Ford was the most efficient and most profitable of the car manufacturers.

Sources and further reading

The most important studies are J. W. Durcan, W. J. McCarthy and G. P. Redman, *Strikes In Post-War Britain* (London, 1983) and H. A. Turner, G. Clack and G. Roberts, *Labour Relations In The Motor Industry* (London, 1987).

For recent discussions of shop stewards see, *inter alia*, Royal Commisssion on Trade Unions and Employers Associations (Donovan), *Report* (1968), S. Tolliday, 'Government, employers and shop floor organisation in the British motor industry 1939–69' in S. Tolliday and J. Zeitlin (eds), *Shop Floor Bargaining And The State* (Cambridge, 1985), M. Terry and P. K. Edwards (eds), *Shopfloor Politics and Job Controls* (Oxford, 1988) and D. Lyddon, 'Shop Stewards and the Car Industry 1945–79' in C. J. Wrigley (ed.), *A History of British Industrial Relations 1939–79* (Aldershot, 1995). For Michael Edwardes' reflections, see his *Back From The Brink* (London, 1983).

the successor to Rootes, expanded to Linwood both on its initial site and buying from BMC the former Pressed Steel plant in 1966. At its peak in the early 1970s, 8,400 were employed at Linwood. Both Linwood and Speke were closed in 1981. Ford went to Swansea in 1965, taking over a former washing machine factory and turning it into a chassis and rear axle plant. Initially employing 1,500, it expanded in 1969, adding 1,300 additional jobs.

For the industry in addition to the items already listed, see G. Maxey and A. Silberston, *The Motor Industry* (London, 1959), P. J. S. Dunnett, *The Decline of the British Motor Industry: The Effects of Government Policy 1945–79* (London, 1980), S. Wilks, *Industrial Policy And The Motor Industry* (Manchester,, 1984) and W. Lewchuk, *American Technology And The British Vehicle Industry* (Cambridge, 1987). For the components sector, see C. Carr, *Britain's Competitiveness: The Management of the Vehicle Components Industry* (London, 1990).

For industrial relations at Ford see also J. Matthews, *Ford Strike* (London, 1972), H. Beynon, *Working For Ford* (London, 1973) and H. Friedman and S. Meredeen, *The Dynamics of Industrial Conflict* (London, 1980).

Figure 26.3
Motor car manufacturing industry 1960–73: employment by region of Great Britain.
Source: J. W. Durcan, W. E. J. McCarthy and G. P. Redman, *Strikes In Postwar Britain* (London, 1983), p.328.

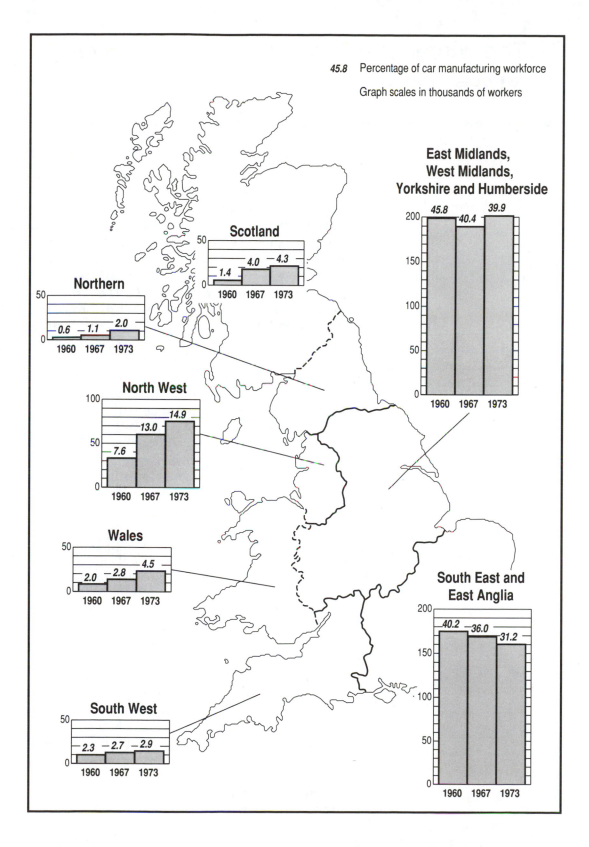

45.8 Percentage of car manufacturing workforce

Graph scales in thousands of workers

East Midlands, West Midlands, Yorkshire and Humberside

Scotland

Northern

North West

Wales

South West

South East and East Anglia

27. The winter of discontent: the lorry drivers' strike, January 1979

'The Winter of Discontent' became Conservative Party shorthand for all that was wrong with a Labour government and the Labour movement. Documentary film of rubbish piled in the streets or of news broadcasters speaking of striking grave diggers have been used as a warning in a similar way to which film of Nazi tanks sweeping across France or Russia had been used as a reminder of the consequences of appeasement. The images became as potent as the events. The 'Winter of Discontent' was conjured up again at each of the general elections of 1983, 1987 and 1992. Adding to the damage to trade union public relations was the fact that the initial talk of 'a winter of discontent' had been made by trade union leaders as warnings to the Callaghan Government.

The severity of the unrest came about because the government determined to continue with its policy of controlling incomes and set a pay limit of 5 per cent. Denis Healey later reflected that the Cabinet should have realised that this was 'provocative as well as unobtainable' (Healey, 1989, p. 462). The Labour Government's earlier stages of its policy had reduced inflation from 28 per cent in late 1974 to 7.4 per cent in June 1978. The pill of the incomes policy had been sugared by a range of accompanying measures which went well beyond the narrower limits of pre-1970 incomes policies. That the Social Contract had met so many social aspirations of the trade union movement made the talk of a 'winter of discontent' appear especially unreasonable to those who were not squeezed hard by the incomes policy. Nevertheless, many low paid workers had suffered from the combination of high inflation and an incomes policy. It was the revolt of low paid public sector workers which is best remembered from the strikes of the 'winter of discontent'.

Yet the disputes at this time which brought the government nearest to declaring a state of emergence were those concerning lorry drivers. The first was a strike of petrol tanker drivers, which began in December 1978. Tony Benn and the Cabinet were well prepared to declare an emergency and to use the army. However, an all-out strike of drivers of all the companies was very narrowly averted, though by 8 January 1979 petrol supplies were down by half as a result of strikes, as at Texaco, or picketing. That day the Shell and Esso drivers voted to accept an offer from their companies which, unlike earlier ones, had no productivity conditions attached to it. The offer was estimated at the time to be worth an increase in pay of between 13 and 15 per cent.

The second dispute was a more general road haulage one. Those involved were in the hire and reward sector, drivers of lorries owned by companies which undertook contract work (as opposed to those working for companies with their own fleets of lorries, the own account sector), though some of those working for company fleets struck in sympathy.

Like many other disputes of the period, frustration at the government's incomes policy played a central part in causing widespread and vigorous action. This was exacerbated by the prospect of EEC regulations which threatened to reduce the overtime earnings which were customary for most drivers. The drivers of larger lorries (HGV 1 drivers) were earning £53 for 40 hours, with those in most areas being guaranteed a further five hours at time and a half. For some, actual earnings were nearer £90, due to overtime worked up to the 57 hour maximum limit and to mileage bonuses for long distances. Those who drove lower grade lorries earned less, with some receiving basic pay of £48 or £49. The EEC regulations which alarmed lorry drivers would bring about a stage by stage reduction in maximum hours of work from 57 to 48. Hence the lorry drivers' pay claim was aimed not only at responding to inflation but also at offsetting such a reduction in overtime earnings.

Even so, the drivers' claim was high. The Transport and General Workers Union (TGWU) at a national conference in August 1978 had formulated a demand for a rise in the basic rate of pay to £65, an increase in overnight subsistence allowances from £6.50 to £8.50, better rates of pay for late evening and night work (these combined were estimated to be worth 23 per cent), plus a basic 35 hour week (deemed to take the total value of the claim to 49 per cent). This the TGWU intended to be achieved in regional collective bargaining, having succeeded in 1975 in moving away from the employers' favoured national pay negotiations. Moss Evans, the TGWU general secretary, was adamant that the whole claim was fully justified. He made clear that his members' pay claim, not the government's incomes policy, was his priority: 'I'm not bothered by percentages. It is not my responsibility to manage the economy. We are concerned about getting the rate for the job' (*Daily Telegraph*, 8 January 1979). The Road Haulage Association (RHA), which represented 15,500 (out of an estimated total of 46,000) operators employing some 180,000 drivers, offered a 15.25 per cent pay settlement in December 1978 and thereafter let it be known that it was under strong pressure from the government to offer no more. This government pressure was not only due to its 5 per cent pay policy but also to a Price Commission report of late 1978 which criticised the road haulage companies for not improving efficiency and absorbing some rising costs.

The lorry drivers had been increasingly impatient during the autumn of 1978. A recalled Annual Road Haulage Conference held on 19 December agreed to take strike action from 3 January 1979 if their demands were not met. The strike erupted in several regions on 2 January. See figure 27.1.

In most areas, as Paul Smith has noted, 'the dispute was characterised by lay membership control from the beginning' but 'where union organisation was weaker (e.g. Cumbria) union officers were dominant' (Wrigley, 1995). The dispute was marked by grass roots militancy. In the Birmingham area, for example, up to 1,000 drivers went on strike at midnight on 2 January, fourteen hours before a meeting of 400 shop stewards was due to take place. Speaking for these strikers, Dennis Mills, chair of the TGWU 535 branch, declared: 'We mean business. It will start biting immediately and within a matter of days it will affect shops in the High Street and industry' (*Birmingham Post*, 3 January 1979). When the shop stewards did meet, they voted overwhelmingly for a complete stoppage. Two days later, a dozen strikers occupied the TGWU office in Broad Street and from there co-ordinated the strike.

The major feature of the militancy was rigorous secondary picketing. From the outset, some major docks were picketed — notably Liverpool and Southampton. Soon afterwards, flying pickets targeted industrial estates as well as docks. The *Daily Telegraph* on 6 January reported that some 500 militant drivers from Liverpool, Hull and the Midlands had formed squads of flying pickets to paralyse lorry depots. Jack Ashwell, the national officer of the TGWU, commented two days later: 'It is a tradition among drivers that no-one crosses picket lines. A driver

Figure 27.1

Road hauliers: the start of the unofficial strike, 2 January 1979. The estimates of those on strike varied markedly. The *Daily Telegraph* suggested 15,000 strikers on 2 January and 35,000 on 4 January. The RHA and TGWU suggested lower figures as they tried to differentiate between drivers who went on strike and those who would not cross picket lines. The RHA suggested 10,000 strikers (with half in Scotland) and the TGWU 25,000 plus many more not crossing picket lines by 7 January.

The figures for Scotland were 5,000 from 2 January onwards. In Birmingham the strikers claimed 1,000 drivers in the city, Walsall, Wolverhampton, Tipton, Oldbury and Burton-on-Trent went on strike at midnight on 2 January. Two days later in the Birmingham area, after a shop stewards meeting, it was claimed 90 per cent of the 6,000 hire and reward drivers of the area supported the strike (with claims that some were working where their company had met the union's demands). In Birmingham Alan Law, the TGWU area chief negotiator, temporarily reached a settlement with the employers on 5 January whereby the drivers were promised terms equal to the best agreed anywhere else. However soon after, while 3,000 West Bromwich drivers voted not to join the strike, the Wolverhampton and south Staffordshire TGWU branch voted by 637 to 4 to strike.
Sources: Birmingham Post, Daily Telegraph and *Guardian*, 2–9 January 1979.

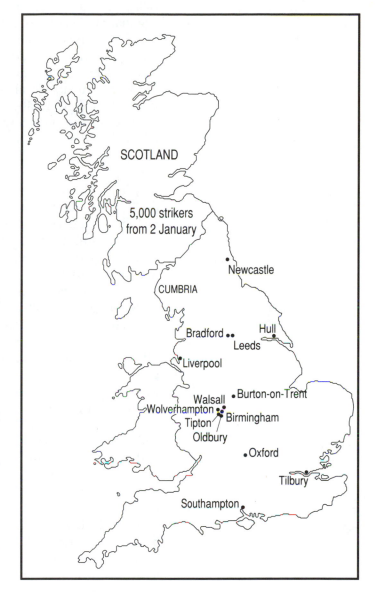

is part of a fraternity' (*Daily Telegraph*, 8 January 1979). In many areas local strike committees issued permits for the movement of goods. This was a matter that especially incensed Margaret Thatcher, who complained vehemently in the Commons that 'the place is practically being run by the strikers' committees' (*Financial Times*, 17 January 1979) who had no right to allow or deny the free movement of lorries.

One reason that the strike was made official was to allow the unions to try to regain control of their members. Moss Evans, when announcing on 11 January that the strike was official other than in the Birmingham area (where it was made official on 18 January after local negotiations failed), stressed that the strike only involved the 58,000 drivers covered by agreements with the RHA. Hence picketing should only affect the RHA, not the National Freight Corporation or firms outside of the RHA agreement. He also appealed to pickets to give sympathetic consideration to the transportation of animal foodstuffs. The next day the United Road Transport Union, based in Manchester, made the strike official for its 35,000 members. Thereafter the TGWU leadership made efforts to curb secondary pickets. On 12 January they sent telegrams to regional officials in which they listed priority supplies which should be allowed through, including animal foodstuffs, fuel for heating schools and other institutions and pharmaceutical products. This was later followed by a call to permit perishable food to be transported.

In some areas secondary picketing was lessened in response to the TGWU leadership's efforts. Elsewhere the union's advice was ignored. In many areas, including the North, the North-west, Wales, Scotland, the West Midlands and at Southampton and several other ports, picketing was stepped up. As a result the TGWU leadership tried again on 18 January, issuing a detailed code of practice to all its senior regional officials, clarifying with more details which goods should be allowed through and emphasising again that picketing should be restricted to the hire and reward sector of road haulage.

The government seriously considered declaring a state of emergency. That it did not do so was partly political and partly practical. Having narrowly avoided doing so during the petrol tanker dispute, it would have been a clear admittance that Labour in office could not deal with the unions by better means than those resorted to by Edward Heath's government. It would also have divided the Labour Party and the Labour movement. In practical terms it was less easy to use the army than in the petrol tanker dispute. According to Tony Benn, Fred Mulley, the Secretary of State for Defence, told the Cabinet on 18 January:

> . . . there are half a million vehicles normally operating in Britain, and I could lay on only 10,000 army drivers. We'd get a good press for a day, and then we'd be proved to be impotent (Benn, 1990, p. 441).

Moreover, the use of the army might inflame the situation, leading to more picketing and more sympathy strikes.

On 19 January Roy Hattersley, the Secretary of State for Prices, announced that the government would not make a prices order to restrain increases in haulage rates. In the context of the strike, this was a signal to the RHA to make a speedy settlement. In fact the RHA's unity crumbled and the various areas made settlements of £64 or £65 between 28 January and 6 February. Tony Benn wrote in his diary of the Cabinet meeting on 30 January: 'Jim began by saying that the road haulage drivers' settlement of between 15 and 20 per cent reminded him of Munich, that's to say he felt relief and disquiet in equal proportions' (Benn, 1990, p. 446).

The road haulier strike had considerable political implications. It was this strike which resurrected secondary picketing as a major issue. This was taken up by the Confederation of British Industries, the press and Margaret Thatcher. The press also unleashed attacks on James Callaghan, who was much more highly rated in the opinion polls than Margaret Thatcher. The *Sun* came up with its infamous 'Crisis, What Crisis?' headline, purporting to be Callaghan's words on returning from a summit conference in Guadeloupe. The *Daily Express* printed across its front page a rear view of Callaghan in a creased suit, with a banner at the top reading 'The man in the crumpled suit who turned his back on crisis-ridden Britain' and in large letters below the large picture 'Inaction man: Premier — suit crumpled — comes home to No. 10 yesterday' (11 January 1979). Even the *Financial Times* printed above a major feature on the strikes a picture of pickets side by side with a picture of a sunny beach, captioned 'Away from it all . . . Mr and Mrs Callaghan in Guadeloupe' (13 January 1979). Even more damaging were the alarmist reports in the press of likely lay-offs arising from the lorry drivers' strike and the secondary picketing. These proved generally to be exaggerated. Industry provided the press and the Department of Industry with estimates of one to two million people being laid off by 19 January whereas by that date the total proved to be about 150,000. Both the director general of the CBI and Denis Healey gave the one million forecasts, to their later embarrassment. The prediction of the President of the Food Manufacturers' Federation, that 'If the picketing goes on, I believe that some old people could be in danger of starvation' (*Financial Times*, 18 January 1979), also proved to be alarmist.

The petrol tanker and then the road hauliers' disputes transformed government–trade union relations from an area in which the Conservatives needed to tread warily into their strongest card. This was especially the case when the local authority workers' and other strikes were added to the impact of the lorry drivers' actions. Earlier, given the events during Edward Heath's term of office, the Labour Party appeared the party best able to deal with the unions and Margaret Thatcher took pains not to suggest she would wish to confront the unions. However, with substantial disruption arising from secondary picketing, Margaret Thatcher was quick to respond to changes in public opinion. On 7 January she declared, 'People have been afraid for the past four years to talk about trade unions but everyone has to grasp the nettle' (*Financial Times*, 8 January 1979). She promised that the Conservatives would introduce laws to curb the trade unions, suggesting that these might subject strikers' social security benefits to taxation and allow the state to pay for secret strike postal ballots, and would review the right to strike in essential industries and also the unions' current legal immunities. She went on to boost her standing as Leader of the Opposition by giving an effective performance in the House of Commons debate of 16 January on the industrial unrest in which she called on the government to take action to control picketing and to curb 'the excessive power of the trade unions' (*Financial Times*, 17 January 1979). The Conservative Party also took delight in highlighting the ill-timing of Labour's poster campaign 'Keep Britain Labour And It Will Keep Getting Better', with the Conservative Director of Publicity even offering Labour a number of Tory poster sites to put up more of these posters.

Sources and further reading

For the road hauliers' dispute and the service's past industrial relations see Paul Smith's 'The Road Haulage Industry: from statutory regulation to contested terrain' in C. Wrigley (ed.), *A History of British Industrial Relations 1939–1979* (Aldershot, 1995). For the Cabinet, see Tony Benn, *Conflicts of Interest: Diaries 1977–80* (London, 1990), James Callaghan, *Time and Chance* (London, 1987) and Denis Healey, *The Time Of My Life* (London, 1989). More generally on the 'winter of discontent' see R. Taylor, *The Trade Union Question in British Politics: Government and Unions Since 1945* (Oxford, 1993) and M. Holmes, *The Labour Government 1974–79: Political Aims and Economic Reality* (London, 1985). This case study also draws on reports in the *Financial Times*, *Guardian*, *Daily Telegraph*, *Birmingham Post*, *Observer* and *Daily Express*.

28. The 1984–5 miners' strike

Few strikes can have had a more powerful sense of history than the 1984–5 miners' strike. It was seen on all sides as a further instalment of the disputes of 1972 and 1974 which had rectified very real grievances over pay but in so doing had humbled Edward Heath's Conservative government. In a longer perspective, the dispute was part of a tradition of national struggles, stretching back through the Second World War to the General Strike, 1919–21, 1912 and to 1893. On the government side, the miners represented 'the enemy within' (as Margaret Thatcher put it), the industrial group which since 1912 had often been the most militant and one which had embarrassed not only Heath but also Stanley Baldwin in 1925–6 and Winston Churchill in 1943–4.

The 1984–5 dispute was strong in other symbolism. The miners could be depicted as Real Men fighting for Real Jobs. Indeed most of the active pickets were young men who were well aware that in many of their communities unemployment was already high, as in the North East where in some places it stood at 25 per cent and over. Yet the strike was also marked by the courage and determination of women's support groups. These were not as novel as some thought, having been very important in sustaining the miners' ability to continue in dispute in the 1970s, 1920s and earlier. However, in 1984/5 in some *areas* the women were not so confined to traditional secondary roles as earlier. The 1984–5 strike also heard echoes of the 'Direct Action' calls of 1910–26, both in Arthur Scargill's and other leaders' rhetoric and in the slogans of socialist splinter groups that claimed that the workers united could never be defeated. Perhaps above all the strike projected — in spite of the savage divisions within the NUM — the values of community against market forces.

As in the period from 1921, the application of market forces to the coal industry led to a bitter industrial struggle in 1984–5 and then to further vigorous campaigning in 1992–3. In 1984 the dispute centred on the government's plans to cut back the coal industry, involving the initial closure of 20 pits and the loss of some 200,000 jobs. While the NUM had accepted the closure of old, high-cost mines in recent decades, the big difference in the early 1980s was that now closures were part of a programme to cut overall capacity. Moreover, the 'market forces' were heavily rigged against coal, as was brought out clearly by several witnesses before a House of Commons Select Committee in November 1992.

As in the 1920s, ministers saw the miners as the body of organised labour likely to be most obstructive to reductions in the labour force and to the acceptance of downward flexibility in labour market rewards. In short, the government was ready and willing for a show-down with the NUM, and the depressed demand for coal and the landslide victory of the Conservatives in the 1983 general election gave the government considerable advantages. The government indicated its resolve by appointing Ian MacGregor head of the National Coal Board with effect from 1 September 1983. MacGregor was a tough Reaganite Republican who had no time for trade unions and who had dealt major blows to the United Mineworkers of America in 1975 and to the British steel unions in the early 1980s. Before his appointment, the terrain had already been partially prepared for battle by the steady boosting of alternative fuels and alternative sources of coal (including sizeable NCB investment in Australian coal) as well as by encouraging major stockpiling of coal.

The dispute began sooner than expected, sparked off by the local announcement of the closure of the Cortonwood pit (located between Barnsley and Doncaster). While Cortonwood was an expensive pit which did not have great reserves and local demand for its coal had fallen with the decline of the steel industry, the announcement of its closure angered the miners. The NCB had recently invested over £1 million in the pit to prolong its working life by five years and the manner of the announcement constituted a technical breach of the agreed closure procedure. This action in South Yorkshire sparked off a strike over pit closures and job losses, with men walking out of Cortonwood on 4 March and from many other pits from 5 March 1984. The strike ended a year later, with a return to work without an agreed settlement on 5 March 1985.

The NUM was defeated for several major reasons. One was the determination of Ian MacGregor and the government, with the latter being ready to deploy the financial and law-and-order resources of the State to defeat the miners. This was shown in advance by the government's willingness to subsidise nuclear power, stockpiles of coal and also facilities for the importation of overseas coal. It was also shown in the apparently unlimited resources available during the strike, illustrations being the huge police presence over two months to get a solitary working miner in and out of a pit at Easington, the three thousand police mustered one day at Harworth Colliery to control 30 pickets and the NCB's expenditure of £4,566,000 on press advertising. Another reason was the usual weakness of a union facing poor market conditions for its product. Demand was not only low but the government showed its ability to move domestic stockpiles and foreign coal by road to the power stations. Government policy and depressed demand for coal also made many miners pessimistic about the future. Many older men were attracted by the £1 thousand per year of service redundancy terms on offer and those in the more profitable pits in traditionally moderate areas were less willing to take strike action on behalf of those in other areas. The pressures of 1984–5 brought vividly into view what David Howell has rightly described as 'the industry's endemic sectionalism' (Howell, 1989, p. 213). As he has observed, the NUM has 'never been the solidaristic strong organisation feared by opponents and feted by members and would-be allies...Areas jealously guarded their autonomy and maintained clear and usually stable political identities.'

The divisions between areas and within areas of the NUM were crucial in the defeat of the NUM. The miners were not united in anger in 1984 as they had been in early 1974 at the erosion of their real wages in the period following the 1972 strike. Then all areas had polled well over the 55 per cent required for a national strike. In the four ballots of November 1979, January 1982, October 1982 and March 1983 none of the areas other than Yorkshire, Scotland, South Wales and Kent had ever polled higher than 50 per cent in favour of strike action. Indeed, South Wales and Kent had only cleared the 55 per cent hurdle twice, with Yorkshire and Scotland both passing it on three occasions.

The areas' voting records in these national ballots clearly reveal the divided attitudes within the NUM (see figure 28.1). Over these years the Nottingham, Midlands, Leicestershire and South Derbyshire areas polled more than 10 per cent below the NUM average in strike votes, whereas Yorkshire, Scotland, South Wales and Kent polled more than 10 per cent above (with only Derbyshire, a little above, and Durham, slightly below, near to the

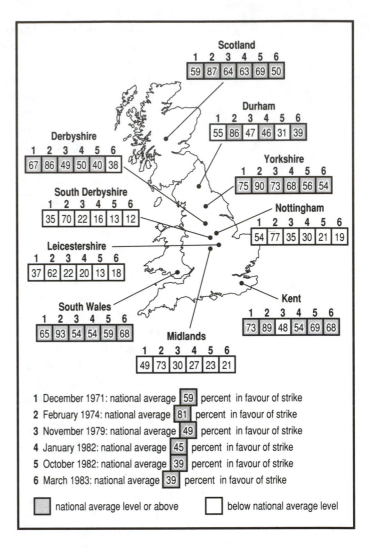

Figure 28.1
Area strike ballots 1971–83.
Source: Data in C. Griffin, *The Leicestershire Miners Vol. 3: 1945–88* (Coalville, 1989). (The 1974 South Wales figure has been corrected.)

average). The former group was radicalised in 1972–4 by the inflationary pressures on their standards of living. Thereafter many miners in these areas were dissatisfied with the NUM's resistance to incentive schemes (which could be especially attractive in these areas) and were reluctant to take strike action again (though many were willing to support the overtime ban which preceded the 1984 dispute). Also, a higher proportion voted Conservative in the 1979 and 1983 general elections. The latter group was notable for the increasing relative militancy of the Kent, Scotland and South Wales areas. In these more miners were anxious about pit closures and about local levels of unemployment, more supported Labour, fewer were attracted by productivity deals or were critical of national NUM policies.

Such area strike ballots as took place in early 1984 fit in well with this pattern of voting (see table 28.1). However, the Derbyshire and Northumberland figures suggest that the more militant areas might well have passed the 55 per cent level; but, even so, the overall national vote on a strike against pit closures might well then have been under 50 per cent (a rule change on 19 April removing the 55 figure to a simple majority being required for strike action). One of the great 'what might have beens' of modern history is to guess what would have happened if Arthur Scargill and the NUM executive had called a strike ballot in mid April 1984, when it is likely that support for a strike was at its greatest. Had he done so, and achieved a majority in support of strike action, it is highly likely that the numbers of working miners would have fallen substantially. Another 'might have been' was the possibility in October 1984 that the colliery supervisors would close down the coal industry. However, though National Association of Colliery Overmen, Deputies and Shotsfirers (NACODS) members voted 82.5 per cent in favour of strike action, the union's leadership reached agreement with the NCB on 24 October.

Table 28.1 Area strike ballot results by late March 1984.

	Percentage for Strike
Cumberland	8
Derbyshire	50
Leicestershire	13
Midlands	28
Northumberland	52
North Wales	32
Nottinghamshire	27
Lancashire	41
South Derbyshire	17

The most militant areas — Scotland, South Wales, Yorkshire and Kent — did not hold ballots.

Source: C. Griffin, *The Leicestershire Miners*, Vol. 3 (Coalville, 1989), p. 222 (drawing on NCB *Statement on Area Ballot Results*, 30 March 1984).

The NUM areas which did not support the strike followed the earlier patterns (see figure 28.1). Some 50,000 miners remained at work. In the Nottingham area

Table 28.2 NCB's regional assessment of pits on 2 November 1984.

	working normally	some coal produced	some working: no coal	on strike
Scotland	–	1	5	6
North Yorkshire	–	–	2	10
Doncaster	–	–	4	6
South Yorkshire	–	–	4	11
North Derbyshire	–	3	5	1
North Nottinghamshire	14	–	–	–
South Nottinghamshire	11	–	–	–
Western	9	5	2	1
South Wales	–	–	–	28
North East	–	–	1	14
South Midlands	11	1	2	1
Overall	**45**	**10**	**26**	**93**

Source: Daily Telegraph, 3 November 1984.

some 24,000 worked, while at least 2,300 went on strike. In Leicestershire all but 39 worked — 'the Dirty Thirty' (a name from 30 who insisted on striking at Bagworth). The South Derbyshire miners also overwhelmingly continued to work. Elsewhere there were minorities working, as in North Staffordshire, North Wales and Cumberland. In North Wales Point of Ayr and in Lancashire Agecroft were notable throughout in this respect, with returns to work in August 1984 at Bersham in the former area and Parkside in the latter. Table 28.2 provides an indication of the spread of working miners (both those who had never gone on strike plus those who had returned to work) by early November 1984.

The figures for returning miners are more contentious, as each side exercised its presentational skills on them (for example, the NCB gave percentages of those working on one shift, ignoring the cancellation of other shifts, to suggest a sizeable drift back to work at some pits). The NCB claimed on 2 November that in Scotland 366 miners were working, 201 of whom were at Bilston Glen, whereas the NUM claimed that there were only 121 miners working in Scotland, of whom 114 were at Bilston Glen. The NCB figures for 1 November included 8,859 men working (5,421 on the day shift) in the Western area (Lancashire, Staffordshire, Cumbria and North Wales) and 1,187 of 10,100 in North Derbyshire. As for individual

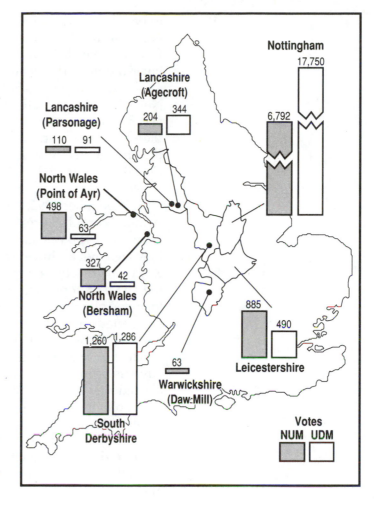

Figure 28.2
NUM–UDM Divisions.
Sources: P. Wilsher, D. McIntyre and M. Jones, *Strike* (London, 1985), D. Howell, *The Politics of the NUM* (Manchester, 1989) and C. Griffin, *The Leicestershire Miners*, Vol. 3 (Coalville, 1989) as well as the national press.

pits the NCB stated on 4 November that about 400 of 600 miners at the Point of Ayr colliery, North Wales, were working and 325 of 1,800 at Shirebrook, North Derbyshire (which was used by management as the first centre of its back-to-work campaign).

After the strike was over, the Union of Democratic Mineworkers failed to secure as much support as expected above and beyond the backing of the predictable Nottingham and South Derbyshire areas and the 1,300 strong Colliery Workers and Allied Trades Association (which had broken away from the Durham Mechanics) (see figure 28.2). In Leicestershire, Jack Jones, the area general secretary, avoided his area being stampeded into an early decision on whether to join the UDM. When a ballot was held, Jones campaigned vigorously to stay in the NUM and by 885 to 490 (on an 86 per cent poll) his members voted to do so. However the Ellistown pit was to be a UDM stronghold, with some 140 UDM and 35 NUM in mid 1988. In Lancashire there were votes in favour of the UDM at the Agecroft and Parsonage pits but in the end no branches seceded. Eventually, less than 400 Lancashire miners individually joined the UDM. In North Wales, two potential UDM pits — Point of Ayr and Bersham — voted overwhelmingly to stay within the NUM. However, by initially offering UDM members preferential treatment in pay and, implicitly, in jobs, the Coal Board helped the UDM establish itself and remain viable.

In September 1992, John Major's government made Arthur Scargill's direst warnings come true when it announced 31 pit closures. Many in the UDM found that they were not excluded from dramatic cuts in capacity. Roy Lynk, shortly before being defeated as President of the UDM, complained on 14 October that these cuts 'demonstrate to trade unionists that if you are moderate the Tories see you as "an easy touch"' (Ceefax news service). British Coal, while planning the closure of much of its operation, tried to market its new expertise, advertising in *Personnel Today* (October 1992) its services as an adviser 'to any company which is about to reorganise its employment profile' and also its euphemistically entitled 'Outplacement Information Pack'. By late January 1993, in the face of hostile public opinion, the government was forced to reconsider its package of closures. However, when the uproar died down most of the closures went ahead.

Sources and further reading
The literature on the strike is huge. Useful national surveys include P. Wilsher, D. Macintyre and M. Jones (with the *Sunday Times* Insight Team), *Strike: Thatcher, Scargill and the Miners* (London, 1985), G. Goodman, *The Miners' Strike* (London, 1985) and M. Adeney and J. Lloyd, *The Miners' Strike 1984–5: Loss Without Limit* (London, 1986) while H. Beynon (ed.) *Digging Deeper: Issues in the Miners' Strike* (London, 1985) is a wide-ranging set of essays. There is a brief analysis in S. Meredeen, *Managing Industrial Conflict: Seven Major Disputes* (London, 1988). Interesting oral records are contained in The People of Thurcroft, *Thurcroft: A Village in the Miners' Strike* (Nottingham, 1986) and R. Samuel, B. Bloomfield and G. Boanas (eds), *The Enemy Within: Pit Villages and the Miners' Strike of 1984–5* (London, 1986). D. Howell, *The Politics of the NUM: A Lancashire View*

(Manchester, 1989), C. Griffin, *The Leicestershire Miners Vol. 3: 1945–88* (Coalville, 1989) J. Winterton and R. Winterton, *Coal, Crisis and Conflict: The 1984–85 Miners' Strike in Yorkshire* (Manchester, 1989) and W. J. Morgan and K. Coates, *The Nottinghamshire Coalfield and the British Miners' Strike 1984–85* (Nottingham, n.d.) are all very good area studies. Ian MacGregor provided his account in *The Enemies Within: The Story of the Miners' Strike 1984–5* (London, 1986). The Campaign for Press and Broadcasting Freedom published *Media Hits The Pits: The Media and the Coal Dispute* (London, 1985); see also N. Jones, *Strikes and the Media* (Oxford, 1986). This case study also drew on reports in the *Daily Telegraph, Financial Times, Guardian* and *The Times*.